New Norms and Knowledge in World Politics

This book examines the process of norm development and knowledge creation in international politics, and assesses these processes in case studies on protection from torture, intellectual property rights and climate change.

Drawing on the theories of constructivism and the sociology of scientific knowledge, author Preslava Stoeva demonstrates that international norms are a product of a sequence of closures and consensus reached at different social levels. She contends that it is this process which makes norms permeate the social and political fabric of international relations even before they become official principles of state behaviour. Proposing a theoretical model which indicates the stages of the development of norms, she studies the roles that various actors play in that process, together with the interplay of various types of power. Through this endeavour, this book succeeds in providing the reader with a better understanding of the social processes that lead to normative change in international relations.

New Norms and Knowledge in World Politics will be of interest to students, scholars and practitioners of international relations, comparative politics, globalisation, sociology and anthropology.

Preslava Stoeva is an Assistant Professor of International Relations at Hult International Business School in London, teaching a range of courses on Global Governance and International Law, Human Rights and Environmental Governance.

Routledge advances in international relations and global politics

New Norms and Knowledge in World Politics

Protecting people, intellectual property and the environment

Preslava Stoeva

Routledge
Taylor & Francis Group

LONDON AND NEW YORK

First published 2010
by Routledge
2 Park Square, Milton Park, Abingdon, Oxon OX14 4RN

Simultaneously published in the USA and Canada
by Routledge
711 Third Avenue, New York, NY 10017

Routledge is an imprint of the Taylor & Francis Group, an informa business

© 2010 Preslava Stoeva

Typeset in Times by Wearset Ltd, Boldon, Tyne and Wear

British Library Cataloguing in Publication Data
A catalogue record for this book is available from the British Library

Library of Congress Cataloging in Publication Data
Stoeva, Preslava.
New norms and knowledge in world politics: protecting people, intellectual property and the environment/Preslava Stoeva.
p. cm.
Includes bibliographical references and index.

1. International law. 2. Human rights. 3. Intellectual property. 4. Environmental law, International. I. Title.
KZ3410.S76 2009
341–dc22

2009012201

First issued in paperback 2013

ISBN13: 978-0-415-84905-0 (pbk)
ISBN13: 978-0-415-54737-6 (hbk)
ISBN13: 978-0-203-86983-3 (ebk)

To my parents Iliya and Pavlina for their unconditional love and unreserved support.
With love and gratitude

Contents

Illustrations

Figures

Table

Boxes

Acronyms and abbreviations

ACAT	Action by Christians against Torture
ACTPN	Advisory Committee on Trade Policy and Negotiation
AGBM	Ad-hoc Group on the Berlin Mandate (relating to the Convention on Climate Change)
AI	Amnesty International
AOSIS	Alliance of Small Island States
APPEN	Asia-Pacific Peoples' Environment Network
APT	Association for the Prevention of Torture
ASEP	Asian Society for Environmental Protection
BIPs	Bilateral Intellectual Property Agreements
BIRPI	United International Bureaux for the Protection of Intellectual Property
BITs	Bilateral Investment Treaties
BMA	British Medical Association
CAT	Convention against Torture
CHR	Commission on Human Rights
CINAT	The Coalition of International NGOs against Torture
CIOMS	Council for International Organisations of Medical Sciences
CO_2	carbon dioxide
CoP	Conference of the Parties taking place under the Framework Convention on Climate Change
CPT	Consumer Project on Technology
CSCT	Swiss Committee against Torture
ECOSOC	Economic and Social Committee of the United Nations
EEC	European Economic Community
EU	European Union
FCCC	Framework Convention on Climate Change
FIELD	Foundation for International Environmental Law and Development
FTA	Free Trade Agreement

GATT	General Agreement on Tariffs and Trade
GCC	Global Climate Coalition
GCMs	General Circulation Models
GEF	Global Environmental Facility
GHGs	Greenhouse Gases
HAI	Health Action International
Health GAP	Global Access Project Coalition
IAPL	International Association of Penal Law
ICCPR	International Covenant on Civil and Political Rights
ICJ	International Commission of Jurists
ICRC	International Committee of the Red Cross
ICSU	International Council of Scientific Unions
ICTSD	International Centre for Trade and Sustainable Development
IGO	International governmental organisation
IIPA	International Intellectual Property Alliance
ILO	International Labour Organisation
INC	Intergovernmental Negotiating Committee to Negotiate a Framework Convention on Climate Change
IP	Intellectual Property
IPC	Intellectual Property Committee
IPCC	Intergovernmental Panel on Climate Change
IPRs	Intellectual Property Rights
IR	international relations
IRCT	International Rehabilitation Council for Torture Victims
LDC	Least Developed Country
MIT	Massachusetts Institute of Technology
MSF	Médecins Sans Frontièrers (Doctors Without Borders)
NASA	National Aeronautics and Space Administration
NGO	Non-governmental organisation
NIEO	New International Economic Order
OECD	Organisation for Economic Cooperation and Development
OMCT	World Organisation Against Torture
OPCAT	Optional Protocol to the Convention against Torture
OPEC	Organisation of Petroleum Exporting Countries
PhRMA	Pharmaceutical Research and Manufacturers of America
PR	Public Relations
R&D	research and development
RCT	Rehabilitation and Research Centre for Torture Victims
SCEP	Study of Critical Environmental Problems
SCOT	social construction of technology
SEI	Stockholm Environmental Institute

SMIC	Study of Man's Impact on Climate
SSK	sociology of scientific knowledge
TB	tuberculosis
TNC	transnational corporation
TRIPs	trade-related aspects of intellectual property rights
UDHR	Universal Declaration of Human Rights
UNAIDS	United Nations Programme on HIV/AIDS
UNCED	United Nations Conference on Environment and Development (1992)
UNCHE	United Nations Conference on the Human Environment (1972)
UNCTAD	United Nations Conference on Trade and Development
UNDP	United Nations Development Programme
UNEP	United Nations Environment Programme
UNESCO	United Nations Educational, Scientific and Cultural Organisation
UNFPA	United Nations Population Fund
UNGA	United Nations General Assembly
UNHCHR	United Nations Office of the High Commissioner for Human Rights
UNICE	Union of Industrial and Employers' Confederations of Europe
UNICEF	United Nations International Children's Emergency Fund
USITC	United States International Trade Commission
USTR	United States Trade Representative
VSO	Voluntary Service Overseas
WB	World Bank
WCED	World Commission on Environment and Development
WCP	World Climate Program
WHA	World Health Assembly
WHO	World Health Organisation
WIPO	World Intellectual Property Organisation
WMA	World Medical Association
WMO	World Meteorological Organisation
WPA	World Psychiatric Association
WTO	World Trade Organisation

Acknowledgements

This research would not have been possible without the financial support of the Department of Politics at the University of Exeter. I would like to extend my gratitude to Prof. David Armstrong for giving me the chance to explore the realm of international norms, knowledge and global governance in greater depth, and to his wife Maggie Armstrong for her encouragement and kindness. I am grateful to Prof. Theo Farrell for his enthusiasm and dedication, for his invaluable advice and support in difficult moments. Thank you for seeing this project through with me and for your tireless efforts. Your encouragement and guidance were indispensable along the way to making this book a reality. I owe special thanks to Prof. Bruce Stanley, who inspired me, guided me, and never stopped believing in me. Prof. Stanley is a mentor, a colleague and a dear friend, with a contagious passion for world politics.

Comments, constructive criticism and advice were generously provided by Dr Bice Maiguashca, Dr Jutta Weldes and the three anonymous reviewers, and this book is better for that.

I am grateful to my parents for their loving care and quiet sacrifices, to my wonderful friends for their patience and support, and to Julian, who brings love, inspiration and infinite happiness every day.

1 Introduction

International norms are at the core of discussions on international order and justice, law, power and the power of law, which have taken centre stage in debates among scholars and practitioners of both international law and international relations. Norms have received much public and research interest in the dynamic context of the post-Cold War years. International norms are neither an end in themselves, nor a beginning of norm compliance, they are an integral part of the flow of politics, aimed at meeting instrumental needs and addressing normative concerns. It is thus essential to develop a better understanding of the nature and evolution of this key element of global policy-making. Analysts have been trying to make sense of the development, presence, relevance and power of norms, because they do not fit comfortably within existing perceptions of the global system. Theorists have approached the question of norms from many angles and as a result, explanations and descriptions abound. There has been little agreement, however, on an analytical framework to address the question of the origin of norms and the source of their power to shape state behaviour.

Researchers have not yet agreed on a way to conceptualise international norms. This study seeks a more structured understanding of the process of norm building and of the participating actors, which would provide the basis for an improved insight into norm compliance. What forces help individual ideas develop into international legal rules or non-legal norms that bind states across the world? What are the necessary conditions that turn a normative campaign into an integral part of our constructions of appropriate behaviour? Who determines which moral principles will grow to become a behavioural norm and which ones will be discarded? Why are some norms questioned and challenged while others are not? The answers to these questions provide the basis for understanding norm development in a broader context.

Building a better understanding of norm development requires the combination of insights from the fields of international law and international relations, from the sociology of scientific knowledge, and social constructivism. Each of these fields has explored normative processes from different viewpoints, generating an abundance of material that needs to be incorporated into a more comprehensive study of norm formation. The existing research on international norms has tended to be confined to separate fields and, even though much effort has been put into framing norm building processes, evaluating compliance, and the role of non-state actors, these insights have not been framed in a way that can be used more broadly. Taking advantage of the findings of theoretical discussions and empirical analysis, this study proposes to address these weaknesses by adjusting some of the underlying assumptions and to consolidate a theoretical model of normative development, which is valid for a wider range of norms.

For the purposes of studying norm evolution, norms are divided into two categories – security norms and non-security norms. Security norms are narrowly defined and refer to issues directly affecting national security – such as arms control, access to strategic resources, conflict and security. These norms need to be studied separately, because negotiations of security norms are distorted by power relations between states, by considerations of sovereignty and national security. Normative concerns do not necessarily affect this field and technical knowledge is selectively favoured.

The field of non-security norms is broad, including issues of human rights, trade, development, environmental protection, governance of resources, etc. Developments in these fields may be seen as affecting national security indirectly, but as the case studies further demonstrate, international agreements on non-security concerns are not concluded for strategic security reasons. The main concern of this nature continues to be the threat and use of military force. The development and spread of non-security norms is counterintuitive to the notion of states as rational, unitary actors, preoccupied with security and the maximisation of national interests. It is in these fields that traditional theories of international relations have found it hardest to explain cooperative state action, as it falls outside the immediate realm of national security. These norms emerge despite state politics, and not because of them, reflecting cooperation patterns that are more difficult to explain and justify in national security terms. This study focuses on the patterns of development of non-security norms and argues that these norms evolve in a similar fashion.

Most models of norm evolution have described norm building, but have not sought to understand and theorise the factors influencing state behaviour in the process, nor indeed have they hypothesised how and why states agree to construct new behavioural norms. Two main questions arise as a result. What are the key shortcomings of current approaches to the study of norm building? How can these be overcome? The next two sections deal with these questions in turn. I argue that current knowledge of norm development suffers from three main shortcomings and they relate to our conceptualisation of the *process* of norm development, to our assumptions about the nature of norms, and to the disconnectedness of existing knowledge of norm creation. I propose to address these shortcomings by bringing together insights from two literatures – social constructivism and the sociology of knowledge. Three key concerns need to be revisited for an improved theoretical model of norm construction to be devised. First, theoretical insights and empirical research from both fields will be engaged to provide the basis to re-construct social processes as dynamic and open-ended. Second, special attention will be paid to the concept of 'closure', which has remained understudied in the field of international politics. Closures are important social moments indicating that consensus has been reached on a given issue. They propel normative ideas forward in the process of norm building. The third concern that this study addresses is the conceptualisation of actors in the global system. Previous studies have defined actors too narrowly and have put them in categories that have restricted our understanding of the role that they play in normative development. These assumptions have also limited the scope of studies into the types of power that they use and the logic of their behaviour.

Rethinking the nature of norm evolution

The way in which norm evolution is conceptualised would be profoundly affected by key assumptions that are made concerning the nature of norms and the character of the process culminating in norm creation. Efforts to gain a better understanding of norm evolution have been sketchy and disjointed. A structured critique of existing assumptions would allow for the consolidation of a more inclusive theoretical model with broader validity.

What is wrong with our understanding of norm building?

Studies of the evolution of norms have assessed a variety of stages of norm building, but have failed to construct the latter as a *dynamic process*. One of the leading studies of norm dynamics and political change, conducted by Finnemore and Sikkink, is a prime example of this shortcoming.[1] While the article is groundbreaking and insightful, it fails to evaluate the forces and dynamics that push normative ideas along a continuum of development. The interests of actors participating in normative negotiations often clash and competing demands must be reconciled, creating a dynamic of fact-finding, bargaining, persuasion, sometimes even coercion. This process may have differing components, but ultimately, it is centred on negotiations and closures. The dynamics of norm development, however, encapsulate not only the communications between actors and the closures reached along the way, but also the sum of the changes in the emerging norm, and the resulting alterations in the identities and interests of the actors involved in negotiating it. These are different layers of the same process, but if we collapse them into static development stages, we would have a qualitatively different system and actors at the end of the process, in comparison with its beginning. Our theories would then be unable to explain the resulting shift. This study argues that norms and normative prescriptions permeate the social and political fabric of international relations even before they become established principles of state behaviour, which could then account for state-compliant behaviour in relation to norms not explicitly linked to the national interests of these states.

The nature of norms – fusing scientific knowledge and normative beliefs

Non-security norms comprise technical knowledge and normative beliefs. Authors have previously argued that some norms are strictly based on principled beliefs, others on scientific knowledge. This assumption does not hold true, as will be demonstrated by the empirical research of this study. Conceptualising technical knowledge and normative beliefs as essential parts of international norms is central to building an improved understanding of the nature and character of the latter, as well as for constructing a more versatile theoretical model to reflect patterns of evolution. The technical element of norms determines causal relationships leading to a problem, and provides practical solutions to address it, while the ethical part of norms assigns moral values and provides justifications for the need of action. Norms should not be considered as only ethical or only technical because that undermines our understanding of their very nature and hinders our perspective on their development and role. What are the ways in which technical knowledge and normative beliefs interact in the different stages of the process of norm development? What is the character of this interplay? In what ways do different actors make use of them in their campaign for new norms? The theoretical discussion in this research seeks to supply answers to these substantive questions.

Revisiting theoretical versatility

Theoretical models are built to be applied to a broad spectrum of situations. Models of norm development have tended to be specifically formulated to reflect governance dynamics and norm building in given issue areas. Limiting model validity takes away from its reliability. The principal hypothesis of this research is that it is possible to propose a theoretical model that would apply to all non-security norms. Normative ideas have similar and logically ordered paths of evolution, where the actors involved aim to generate scientific knowledge and formulate normative beliefs in a way that will secure support for a new behavioural norm. Consolidating a synthetic model on the basis of previous studies and new empirical research requires closer attention to be paid to the causal relationships between the different stages of norm development, the types of power involved in the process and the role of normative persuasion and knowledge in the process.

Building on theoretical insights

The interplay between the normative and the rational has been underemphasised in the current literature, as social scientists have failed to reach agreement on the nature of this relationship.[2] This relationship can best be conceptualised by bringing together two sets of literature – the conventional constructivism in international relations and the sociology of scientific knowledge – as they provide the most useful tools to address the substantive questions raised. These two approaches provide the theoretical framework within which norm construction will be reexamined. They need to be engaged in conjunction with each other because of their expertise in analysing dynamic social relations and questioning what already exists as 'hard fact'. While 'conventional constructivism [aims] to "denaturalise" the social world, that is, to empirically discover and reveal how the institutions and practices and identities that people take as natural and given, are, in fact, the product of human agency, of social construction',[3] the sociology of scientific knowledge is concerned with 'what comes to count as a scientific fact and how it comes so to count'.[4] The need to bridge these two literatures has been recognised by other authors in the past, who have acknowledged that the expansion of scientific knowledge is a political process,[5] as well as that social interactions produce not only ideas, understandings and identities, but also facts and artefacts.[6] A closer examination of the interplay between science, politics and social forces enables this study to add new dimensions to the understanding of norm development.

Constructing dynamic process

Understanding norm evolution will require breaking down the process of norm development into distinct stages that lead to normative change, studying the channels through which ideas travel to become legal rules or non-legal norms, and examining the changing patterns of interactions between scientific knowledge and normative beliefs. This analysis is best conducted through the historical reconstruction of the events leading up to the creation of a given norm. In this way, we can also begin to appreciate the influence of the wider political and normative concept on the construction of international norms. It is argued here that similar factors influence ideas to evolve into successful norms. Solid scientific knowledge and strong normative arguments help a normative campaign pick up speed and support, and draw the attention of policy-makers. Historically reconstructing this process will supply valuable insight not only into the mechanisms of international policy-making, but also into the power relationships among states, between states and non-state actors, and among non-state actors. The methodology of process tracing in recreating the evolution of norms points to conventional constructivism as the appropriate theoretical approach.[7] The sociologists of scientific knowledge draw attention to the fact that any change in science and technologies 'cannot be explained in isolation from the economic, political and other social circumstances of that change'.[8] An improved conceptualisation of international negotiations, of causes and effects, and of successful negotiating tactics can provide insight into when and how this process can be influenced or changed, as well as a more profound understanding of who the movers and shakers of the international system are.

Closure

There is another reason why the social constructivists in international relations and the sociologists of knowledge need to communicate and that is their shared interest in the social moment of closure or tipping in the process of development of norms/scientific facts. Closure, according to the sociologists of scientific knowledge, signifies the end of a scientific debate and the transition of a newly established scientific fact into the larger body of knowledge.[9] Tipping has been defined by constructivists as the moment at which a new norm is agreed upon and processes for its institutionalisation begin.[10] Obtaining a clearer understanding of the dynamics of closure, its importance in the continuum of norm development and the processes that lead to it, is essential for this study, as this social moment has been understudied with regards to international behavioural norms.

Actors

Non-state actors have emerged as new nodes of power in the global political system, most notably over the past 40 years. The current research draws attention to their role in world politics, and to the types of power that they engage in normative campaigning. Non-state actors form diverse networks, which may sometimes wield more power than nation-states, command more public support than politicians and pool more finance than national governments. This certainly complicates our concept of the way in which world politics operates, but it represents the only way we can gain a clearer and more pragmatic idea of what drives international relations and with what effect. Reconceptualising the nature and role of non-state actors in the norm development process brings in a broader spectrum of relations that may not have been considered by other contemporary approaches.

Tools for re-constructing normative developments

The empirical part of this research is based on theoretically informed historical reconstruction of the sequence of events leading to norm formation.[11] This approach will help uncover the relationship between the product – a new behavioural norm, and the complex process of conflict and collaboration between a range of social actors leading up to norm creation, and the patterns of interplay between scientific knowledge and normative beliefs.[12] The historical reconstruction of negotiations allows a reevaluation of actors' positions, the changes in these positions, the argument and persuasion techniques employed, as well as the techniques that were successful, as these reveal information about actors, power and process in international relations.

One aspect of this study focuses on the closure of scientific, normative and political debates, and how we can show that closure has taken place. An important controversy surrounding normative research is related to the issue of proving that a norm exists. Some authors have claimed that we can infer the existence of a norm from state practice;[13] others argue that state action alone does not signal the existence of a norm;[14] yet others point out that it is the justifications that states give for their actions that indicate the existence of a norm.[15] Norms are 'shared and social'[16] prescriptions of behaviour; they are 'intersubjective in that they are beliefs rooted in, and reproduced through, social practice'.[17] Intersubjectivity infers more than a subjective existence – beliefs need to be expressed, if not codified and recorded, in order to be shared. In this way beliefs leave physical residues. Further proof for the existence of norms can be found in the justifications that states use for their actions when in breach of a written or customary norm. Disapproval and justification are both based on the acceptance of a behavioural norm, as a prescription for appropriate behaviour.

There is a quantitative element involved in judging whether a norm has been accepted by enough states. Norms that are in the process of becoming legalised need a minimum number of states to accept them, but what is also important is that they are underpinned by the 'concurrence of the major powers in the particular field'.[18] It is clear that the participation and the willing cooperation of the powerful states in the system can speed up a process of norm evolution; however, this in itself is not a sufficient condition to establish a new norm and make it work, as normative agendas and national priorities change. Finnemore argues that 'rules backed only by force, without any legitimacy or normative authority, are difficult to sustain and tend not to last long'.[19] This is demonstrated by the empirical studies presented in this book.

Historical reconstruction of the events leading up to the creation of a new norm will show the role and influence of non-state actors in the evolution of a norm. Evidence of the evolution of normative ideas can be found in historical records, memoirs, journal articles, newspapers. The processes of network configuration and of specifying the parameters of an issue are normally marked by conferences and meetings, which means records of such meetings and conferences can be a valuable source of information. Qualitative content analysis of the speeches of delegates and transcripts of debates will reveal the dynamics of network formation, issue specification and processes of bargaining and persuasion. Speeches and debates will hold clues as to which arguments tend to prevail in these initial meetings and whether it is moral ideas or technical knowledge that sets the agenda. Some political speeches and government positions are determined in advance and this means that they carry less personal bias and more organisational bias, which could help engender a better understanding of the standpoint and interests of groups and organisations involved in these meetings. Interviews with participants in such conferences also represent a valuable and helpful source in reconstructing historical events. The dialogue with the conservative actors may be a challenging process to follow, since the records of some interstate negotiations are not made public and one has to rely on the recollection of participants and other secondary sources. When normative ideas previously publicised by civil society or scientific research become the subject of international negotiations, one can begin to find more in-depth analysis of the surrounding controversies and debates in academic journals and books. Conferences are also being held more regularly among states and there are usually parallel civil society conferences, which also supply abundant research materials.

The sources analysed in this research are largely primary, where available, such as historical documents, legal documents, memoirs, personal accounts, speeches, debates, newspaper articles, statements of state officials; some secondary sources have been considered such as books, articles from academic journals and conferences. Interviews have been conducted where possible with individuals who were close to the real negotiations – representatives of nongovernmental organisations (NGOs) and inter governmental organisations (IGOs), technical experts and state officials.

Scope of research

The empirical scope of this book encompasses contemporary non-security norms. All have been created within the past 30 years, so that the controversies surrounding them have still not had a chance to settle completely. The analysis of the historical development of the norm outlawing the use of torture, the norm protecting intellectual property in the pharmaceutical industry, and the norm for the protection of the atmosphere and the control of climate change, aims to provide a varied context within which the interplay between scientific knowledge and normative beliefs is studied in more detail, and a synthetic theoretical model is tested. There is no relationship between the case studies, apart from the growing concern for the protection of the individual, evident from the changing behaviour of states under pressure from civil society and other actors in global politics. The combination of case studies coming from different social fields indicates similar trends in the process of policy-making at the international level, and reinforces the claim that international norms emerge in a similar fashion.

The three case studies have purposefully been chosen as ones not directly threatening state security or determining security objectives. This, in my view, softens the impact of strategic national interest as the reason for states to negotiate and act, and makes the question of why states get engaged in norm development in the first place even more relevant. Some may claim that issues not directly related to national security interests make negotiations more likely because states feel less threatened by the outcomes of such negotiations. I argue that when national security interests are not directly at stake, negotiations are not more likely per se; instead, they are more likely to be successful. This, however, still does not explain why states choose to get involved in the development of new behavioural norms that could affect the scope of policy choices and acceptable behaviour in the future.

In Chapter 2 I outline the theoretical framework of this study by spelling out the contributions of the literature of social constructivism of international relations (IR) and the sociology of knowledge. These are then critically evaluated and incorporated in the synthetic model of norm development, which is presented in some detail.

Chapter 3 studies in detail the historical development of the first empirical case study – the norm prohibiting the use of torture, which has been institutionalised by the Convention against Torture (CAT) and its Optional

Protocol (OPCAT). This is a norm protecting individuals and stemming from the more general context of human rights and concerns for individual welfare. CAT may appear to be a logical continuation of human rights legislation, supported by the 'civilised world', but, despite its seemingly natural evolution, severe problems of implementation and compliance have emerged in various states. This signals a fault in the normative determinist's reasoning because if the norm's development was as logical as portrayed, states would have automatically taken it on board. The norm evolution process in this chapter reveals how scientific knowledge and normative ideas merged into one powerful normative campaign to persuade states to create a new behavioural norm.

Chapter 4 is an inquiry into the development of intellectual property rights in the pharmaceutical industry. This international norm evolved in a manner that few could have predicted. It started as a strong case in favour of increased worldwide protection of intellectual property, based on the science put forward by some of the largest corporations in the world, but was later defeated by global civil society working together with the global South, using a strong normative campaign and technical knowledge to attack the claims made by corporate experts. The industries interested in intellectual property protection are some of the most powerful industries in the business world. They had the governments of most of the economically developed countries on board for the creation of a blanket norm to protect all intellectual property with the strongest possible norm. With time and with the increased interest of NGOs, social movements, nongovernmental professional organisations and advocacy networks, the normative belief in the rights of human beings to life and health prevailed over corporate interests and nation-states agreed to concessions towards those most needy in the international system. This is an interesting case study with an unexpected end, which shows most clearly that conventional wisdom and generalisations with regards to actors, power and process in international relations, need to be reexamined and redefined.

The third case study presented in Chapter 5 concerns the creation of a norm for the protection of the atmosphere and the reversal of climate change. The reasons for choosing this study are multiple. Negotiations on the issue of climate change have been long and difficult, riddled with claims of scientific uncertainty, political opposition, normative issues of responsibility, equity and justice, as well as by controversies among industries. A real blow to the implementation of the norm to reverse climate change was dealt by the US President George W. Bush's coming into power, when he rejected the scientific agreement that the earth's climate was changing with long-term effects on human activity. This norm is very rich in material for analysis – there is the disagreement among experts worldwide regarding the causal relationship between carbon dioxide (CO_2) and anomalies in the environment and world climate; negotiations are difficult among states who are unwilling to give up what they call their chance for economic development; one of the most powerful countries and one of the largest polluters – the United States – refuses to sign one of the major documents for the implementation of the UN Framework Convention on Climate Change (FCCC), i.e., the Kyoto Protocol; while the biggest problem is that there is no reliable prediction of how bad the effects of climate change are going to be. The development of the Kyoto Protocol is the most contemporary of the case studies.

2   Theorising norm development

In this chapter I develop a theoretical framework for conceptualising norm development and generating a more systematic understanding of the interplay of scientific knowledge and normative beliefs in the process of norm evolution. This framework is based on the research and findings of two fields of social research – social constructivism in international relations and the sociology of scientific knowledge. After examining these paradigms and outlining some of their limitations, I propose a synthetic model, which reflects the main stages in the evolution of international norms. There are a few key questions that this chapter seeks to address, namely, how international norms evolve, what roles different actors play, how the interplay between knowledge and norms changes during the different stages of the process, and how closures on new norms are reached. The emphasis on theoretically informed process tracing throughout this study makes it crucial that the studies of conventional constructivism are engaged.[1] The analysis of the types of actors involved in the process of norm development is one of the meeting points of social constructivists of IR and the sociologists of knowledge. Both of these theories examine a larger spectrum of internationally active social groups and engage in analysing the varying degrees of persuasion, argumentation and coercion that they use. The moment of closure, which has been studied in more depth by the sociologists of knowledge and to a lesser degree by social constructivists, is considered in this research to have three vital components – social, scientific and political.

My discussion, however, will begin with the definition of the concept and form of international behavioural norms, which are then distinguished from other ideational phenomena that affect actors' behaviour and decision-making patterns. Norms are often defined as shared expectations about or standards of appropriate behaviour for actors with a given identity.[2] These definitions, however, are not precise, because 'shared expectations of appropriate behaviour' do not constitute norms – they result from already existing norms or a given normative context. Furthermore, the concept of shared expectations does not indicate with enough authority the level of agreement and support needed to create a norm. The term 'standard of appropriate behaviour' should not be perceived as a synonym for the term norm either, because standards presuppose a high degree of specificity and not all norms are always stipulated in precise terms. Moreover, within a context which has not been precisely regulated, states can still project would-be standards of appropriate behaviour within the context of existing normative principles, but that would not constitute a norm. In other words, while 'shared expectations' is a term that is too loose to be synonymous to a norm, 'standards of appropriate behaviour' is a term too strict to convey the same meaning as 'norm', since 'standards of behaviour [are] defined in terms of rights and obligations',[3] while that is not always true for norms.

The term 'norm' will be used here to mean prescriptions for appropriate and acceptable behaviour,[4] from which the standards of behaviour are further negotiated and institutionalised. Farrell argues that norms 'regulate action by defining what is appropriate (given social rules) and what is effective (given laws of science)'.[5] However, the internal division of a norm into a technical and normative part is artificial and only helpful for the study of the interplay between technical knowledge and normative beliefs in the process of constructing norms. Norms are a product of both social rules and laws of science and they carry forward elements of both. Norms are guiding posts for state behaviour; they become embedded in the belief systems of policy-makers, thus influencing state behaviour. Norms can remain tacit prescriptions for appropriate behaviour but they can also develop into legal principles – either customary or codified. Legal rules institutionalise norms by stating them in technical terms – asserting the parameters of a norm, its definition, its subjects, what constitutes a breach of it, often including specific consequences of non-compliance.

In this research 'norms' and 'behavioural norms' will be used interchangeably. Neta Crawford draws attention to the need to differentiate between behavioural norms and normative beliefs.[6] Normative beliefs are thus similar to the conventional understanding of moral principles and/or ethical principles. They are held by individuals and result from the overall social constructions of good and bad, appropriate and inappropriate, right and wrong. Breaking these principles does not result in an institutionalised punishment, but is condemned and ostracised within the social group. 'Idea' is another term that is used in this research and it indicates individual perceptions. They result from the interaction between the individual and the social, and political environment, as well as from the interactions among individuals. Ideas can be beliefs held by individuals, normative judgements and proposals for normative change that are not necessarily shared by others.

Scientific knowledge has come to occupy an important place in normative research. Drori *et al.* argue that the role of science is expanding, and so is its authority, and that globalisation is both demanding and assisting the spread of scientific knowledge in all parts of the world.[7] Researchers of epistemic communities also indicate the prominent place of scientific knowledge in the policy-making process, while the sociologists of knowledge assert the social nature of science. Constructivists in international relations agree that science plays an important role in certain areas of policy-making – economic policy, environmental politics, military policy.[8] The current research argues that rationality, precision, understanding of causal relationships, and possessing the professional authority to produce scientific knowledge play a vital role in the development of norms in all spheres of political activity. Furthermore, knowledge is one of the indispensable components of a normative campaign. The terms technical and scientific knowledge will be used interchangeably in this research, because both these terms indicate knowledge that is accumulated in a systematic manner, and that complies with the basic laws of scientific research – involving method, testing, interpretation, peer review, authority.

Theoretical approaches

Social constructivism in IR

In general,

> constructivists hold the view that the building blocks of international reality are ideational as well as material; that ideational factors have normative as well as instrumental dimensions; that they express not only individual but also collective intentionality; and that the meaning and significance of ideational factors are not independent of time and place.[9]

Research has been conducted into how material and ideational factors influence actors' behaviour and identities, and into the driving forces and principles that guide social action. This helps our understanding of how ideas get established – whether by means of coercion, persuasion or argumentation.

Constructivists adopt a unitary stance on the question of ontology. They share the understanding that there is a 'constructed social reality'[10] within which the material environment gains meaning and value, and where day-to-day activities make sense and have a purpose. Alexander Wendt argues that the 'fundamental structures of international politics are social rather than strictly material and these structures shape actors' identities and interests, rather than just their behaviour'.[11] What still divides constructivism are the debates over the nature of interaction between agents and structures, as well as questions of epistemology – whether there really exists a common intersubjective ideational reality, outside of individuals' heads, which can be studied with the tools of the social sciences.

The main assumptions of constructivism have attracted some criticism. Some IR theorists envisage constructivism not as a theory, but as a framework of analysis,[12] a method,[13] which relies on assumptions and variables that are difficult to measure and quantify. In response, constructivists have outlined the importance of intersubjectivity and the existence of collective knowledge, shared by the relevant actors.[14] Finnemore argues that 'norms make similar behavioural claims on dissimilar actors, [thus creating] coordinated patterns of behaviour, which we can study and about which we can theorise'.[15] Evidence of coordinated patterns of behaviour can be found, and the causal link between given norms and state behaviour can be established, meaning that constructivist research can provide verifiable theoretical claims.

Another criticism of constructivist work is that it has tended to study concepts/issues that are comparatively stable over time – identities, interests, culture, norm-consistent state behaviour, but change in world politics, as Hopf argues 'is both possible and difficult'.[16] In the past decade of dynamic international relations constructivists have acknowledged the need to adapt their methods to the study of change.[17] This is where the methods of the sociologists of scientific knowledge could contribute to improving IR theorising, with their deeper understanding of dynamism and change in the social context.

Moving from the more general debates of constructivism to the specific topic of norm evolution, I outline some of the key findings of constructivist analysis, relevant to the problematique of the current research. My inquiry into the constructivist understanding of norm evolution is concerned with several questions – what *types of actors* initiate and promote new norms in the international system? What are the *means* that they employ in negotiations? Is there a recurring *process* of norm development and is that consistent across various fields of social research? The following overview further gives me an opportunity to search for the patterns of interaction of scientific knowledge and normative beliefs.

Typology of actors

Social constructivism in international relations became more widespread following the end of the Cold War when non-state actors were gaining wider recognition as being relevant to IR analysis. These two developments are often perceived as one, resulting in constructivism being associated primarily with the study of non-state actors in the international system. Not all constructivists, however, believe in the importance and influence of these actors – some have tended to focus their analysis on states,[18] while others would add IGOs as relevant too.[19] The largest and growing segment of constructivist thought acknowledges the role and influence of non-state actors in the making of international norms.[20]

Keck and Sikkink categorise the non-state actors in their study of transnational advocacy networks as actors with instrumental goals (transnational corporations (TNCs) and banks), actors who share causal beliefs (scientific groups or epistemic communities) and actors who share principled beliefs or values, namely transnational advocacy networks.[21] Audie Klotz adds that scientists are often part of the bureaucracy and that advocacy networks are more concerned with social issues[22] thus excluding the role of scientific knowledge in her analysis of the anti-apartheid and anti-slavery movements. The studies of epistemic communities also distance themselves from the work of NGOs and advocacy networks. The term epistemic community is used here as defined by Peter Haas – a 'network of professionals with recognised expertise and competence in a particular domain and an authoritative claim to policy-relevant knowledge or issue-area'.[23] The assistance of epistemic communities is most frequently *requested* by governments in situations of uncertainty, following shock or crisis.[24] According to Haas the expertise of epistemic communities is sought primarily in extreme cases, but other authors propose that the latter are more active agents in the international system who can create an intellectual climate favourable to starting up a particular debate.[25]

The above typology of actors emphasises on the one hand, a 'three-fold bias against the state and state decision-makers',[26] while drawing a clear dividing line between the good and the bad actors – where states/policy-making elites are inevitably bad and non-state actors unquestionably good. Very few studies of the work of non-state actors discuss NGO biases, the influence that those who fund scientific research have on scientific findings, the selectivity of the cases that advocacy networks take on, etc. Although authors have acknowledged that such perceptions are naive, the IR literature continues to largely operate on the basis of these assumptions.

The typology of actors as discussed by the social constructivists involves a process of grouping actors according to the social role of their participants, e.g., scientists work in epistemic communities, individuals get involved in different types of non-state civil society organisations, lawyers and advocates form advocacy networks, and so on. Previous research has also tended to link the type of the actors partaking in norm development to the character of the resulting norm.[27] This view tends to exclude the role of scientific knowledge in fields that are not conventionally perceived of as scientific (e.g., human rights), which in turn limits the possibility of an in-depth understanding of international norms. I propose that we examine the networks in which actors choose to participate instead, with no prejudice to the type of these actors and their perceived policy goals. The empirical evidence from the case studies of this research demonstrates that coalitions of actors work on a variety of norms, and that actors come together to seek strength in numbers and to take advantage of each other's strengths and expertise.

The empirical case studies of this research demonstrate that actors who come together to form networks for persuasion follow the same logic of action. The term logic of action indicates the type of considerations that actors take into account or act upon, whether consciously or subconsciously, in the process of making decisions. According to March and Olsen, actors are guided either by calculations of consequences (logic of consequences) or by careful consideration of identities, obligations and rules (logic of appropriateness).[28] The logic of consequences drives behaviour when actors 'choose among alternatives by evaluating their likely consequences ... conscious that other actors are doing likewise';[29] the logic of appropriateness is at play when 'action involves evoking an identity or role and matching the obligations of that identity or role to a specific situation'.[30] Thomas Risse adds a third logic of action and that is the logic of truth seeking and argumentation according to which 'actors try to challenge the validity claims inherent in any causal or normative statement'.[31] The logic of argumentation is particularly relevant to this research, because where normative change is occurring or norms are developing in areas where no norms previously existed, actors cannot rely on the logic of appropriateness, since there are no standards to prescribe action and the conception of identities and interests has no ready answers. Considering the logics that drive the behaviour of actors thus helps us understand how and why actors with technical expertise team up with actors advocating normative ideas, for example, which is an aspect of norm building that constructivists have largely omitted.

Constructing a process

Constructivists conceptualise the *process* of norm development around certain types of actors as central figures in norm building. Thus, one can recognise at least three distinct propositions about the structure of the *process* of norm development, based on the category of the norm entrepreneur. These have only slight differences, supporting my thesis that there is a common logical sequence, according to which norms develop, which does not depend on the field of norm evolution.

Constructivists who focus their research on the behaviour of nation-states and IGOs tend to explain normative change in terms of the strategic interests and identities of these actors.[32] The norm entrepreneur state is usually one of the powerful of the day, at least in the area of the norm in question, and perceives itself as needing to take action to avoid damage to its reputation both at home and internationally. The entrepreneur state further tries to persuade other states to join a new practice by means of both argument and power.

There has been considerably more research on the scenario in which NGOs and other advocacy networks play the leading role in norm development. Finnemore and Sikkink (1998) present a theoretical model of the process of norm evolution and most of the other authors who have conducted empirical research in this sub-field seem to fit in that framework. The norm life-cycle presented by Finnemore and Sikkink has three main phases – norm emergence, norm cascade and internationalisation.[33] The emergence of norms is itself characterised by a process, comprising of three levels – norm initiation, organisational level and institutionalisation or tipping point. Risse and Sikkink also propose a causal model of formulating human rights norms, which is based on five stages – repression and activation of network, denial, tactical concessions, governments accepting the prescriptive status of a new human rights norm, and rule-consistent behaviour.[34]

The third view on *process* is compiled by the authors who focus attention on the activities and influence of epistemic communities. Case studies reflect work in a number of different fields, ranging from the Mediterranean Pollution Control Plan,[35] the reform of the International Food Aid Regime,[36] the research on the construction of a regime for trade in services,[37] the evolution of the idea of nuclear arms control,[38] Long-Range Transboundary Air Pollution[39] and many more. The formation of a regime is based on a complex process of negotiation between technical experts (ecologists, marine scientists, development-oriented food aid specialists, etc.), economic actors in some cases, and nation-states. The first crucial stage of norm development is that of *issue formation*, as it defines the interests of the actors involved, and opens a niche for development of regulations and standards.[40] Stage two of the process is the formulation of *collective knowledge and meaning* – this is the stage where different epistemic communities form a common 'core set of beliefs about cause–effect relationships'[41] and 'create collective understandings'.[42] Collective knowledge and meaning is further translated into the *definition of state interests* and the *framing of the political controversy*.[43] Apart from changing the domestic agenda epistemic communities are engaged in *policy diffusion*.[44] Epistemic communities play an active role in the process of finalisation of a new norm as well,[45] but as Haas observes, technical knowledge and expertise might be compelling, but the exercise of political power is crucial as well.[46]

The studies of the *process* of norm development, as presented by authors with different views on the leading actors in the system, exhibit a number of similarities. This research argues that the process of norm development is the same regardless of who the leading actors are envisaged to be. Epistemic communities, advocacy networks and NGOs, economic actors and states, all take part at one stage or another in a process of developing international norms, which influence human well-being. In other words, the various cases presented above are only different viewpoints on the same process.

Theories of the sociology of scientific knowledge (SSK) and the social construction of technology (SCOT)

The sociology of knowledge began evolving as a discipline in the 1970s and the 1980s.[47] The theories of the social construction of scientific knowledge focus attention on the study of the relationship between the material and ideational world by revealing the social beginning of scientific facts. One of the main contentions of SSK theorists is that there isn't a single true, material world waiting 'out there' to be discovered; rather, human knowledge and search for facts is socially conditioned and socially constructed. The main concern of the sociology of scientific knowledge is the character of 'what comes to count as scientific knowledge' and the mechanism that makes facts count as scientific knowledge.[48] Researchers of SSK and SCOT have repeatedly reported the relevance of power and research experience in the process of constructing knowledge and technologies. They have also commented on the influence of the context within which these developments take place. In this sense, the sociology of scientific knowledge comes very close to the research on social norms, which is influenced by similar factors. Apart from these similarities, the contributions of the sociologists of scientific knowledge to this research project are twofold. First, SSK theorists have expertise in process tracing and conceptualising complex power relations, as well as in-depth experience in analysing the social moment of *closure* of scientific debates, which as they have demonstrated shapes the nature and potency of newly created knowledge. Second, SSK studies one of the main components of behavioural norms – namely, scientific knowledge – which makes it vital that we consider how knowledge comes into existence, under what circumstances, and how this relates to other social processes. Below, I will draw attention to the findings of SSK and SCOT regarding the *process* of the construction of scientific knowledge and the *closure* of scientific debates.

The search for consistency of perceptions and convention is a central notion to understanding the way in which facts are established. As Fleck stresses 'whatever is known has always seemed systematic, proven, applicable, and evident to the knower. Every alien system of knowledge has likewise seemed contradictory, unproven, inapplicable, fanciful, or mystical.'[49] The studies of the creation of scientific knowledge thus focus on the process of transition from the contradictory, unproven, fanciful to the systematic, logical, evident. This process of fact construction and fact recognition has been studied in different environments and with regards to diverse issues[50] and one general conclusion has emerged – scientific knowledge and technologies are 'limited by cultural constraints and the distribution of power, rather than internal technical knowledge or logical possibility'.[51] Sociologists of scientific knowledge thus argue that 'there is nothing epistemologically special about the nature of scientific knowledge: it is merely one in a whole series of knowledge cultures'.[52] The change in the perception of natural sciences means that scientific knowledge does not necessarily uncover a non-controversial, systemic and logical environment, neither is science impartial in its depiction of the material world. This in turn indicates that we can use similar tools to study the development of social and scientific facts, which broadens the knowledge base of the current research.

The change of attitude towards scientific knowledge is reflected in the working assumptions widely accepted by SSK theorists. These include the relativity of knowledge; the requirement for symmetrical and impartial inquiry regarding scientific theories; the role of the human element in scientific knowledge and the resulting biases and misperceptions. The significance of relativism in scientific knowledge is that 'it assumes neither fixed points in the physical world, nor a fixed realm of logic'.[53] The denial of fixed truths and facts in the material world in essence denies the perceived objective material foundation of natural sciences, revealing their social roots. The necessity of symmetrical and impartial inquiry into scientific knowledge was formulated and highlighted by David Bloor. He argues that 'in investigating the causes of beliefs, sociologists should be impartial to the truth or falsity of the beliefs, and that such beliefs should be explained symmetrically'.[54] The importance of this relativism is most clearly seen in the examination of the relationships between 'science' and 'pseudoscience', between 'hard' and 'soft' scientific facts, which can only be comprehended if the nature of the definitions of both antipodes is objectively examined.[55] Equal treatment of both scientific truth and falsity is crucial in social relations that are constantly in flux, because the history of humanity is a history 'complete with all [our] errors'.[56] Human agency in itself presupposes that imperfections will be passed on to anything that individuals do; which brings me to the third contribution of SSK – the influence of the human element. In the words of Barnes and Edge and in the context of SSK,

> in controversial situations, the value premises of the disputants colour their findings. The boundaries of the problems to be studied, the alternatives weighed, and the issues regarded as appropriate – all tend to determine which data are selected as important, which facts emerge.[57]

Individual expectations of what there is to be discovered may also determine what is actually discovered.[58]

SSK thus emerges as an important tool in understanding authoritative social processes that produce knowledge, which is then incorporated in the fabric of society. The approach is holistic, looking both at what is perceived as truth and falsity, and challenging conventional assumptions of knowledge as in-built rationality. These theorists problematise scientific knowledge, exposing its social beginnings, as well as its imperfections and shortcomings. The current research is going to take advantage of two aspects of SSK work – of their research tools and concepts in studying dynamic social processes and of their understanding of how knowledge is constructed.

Understanding process

The studies of SSK and SCOT have engaged heavily with empirical research and have focused primarily on demonstrating and pinpointing the influence and bias of the social world and political power on the construction of knowledge and technology rather than on creating a theoretical model of the process of knowledge construction.[59] Some inferences can be made, however, and one can begin to deduce a theoretical model from these works. The process of fact and technology construction can roughly be taken to consist of two parts – first, there are experiments and debates among experts, which are supplemented by debates between experts, policy-makers and industry; and second, there is closure – this is where scientific facts get established and technologies get accepted. The point of closure means that 'a fact ... loses all temporal qualifications and becomes incorporated into a large body of knowledge drawn upon by others'.[60]

The process of fact formation begins with research and findings. Findings need to come in the format and with the precision accepted throughout the field of research[61] if they are to be recognised as worthy of attention. Format and precision is supplemented by the identity of those who present them – the reputation of scientists in the laboratory, their rank and experience all influence the extent to which their claims to knowledge are taken seriously. An observation of laboratory discussions concludes that '*who* had made a claim was as important as the claim itself'.[62] Scientists in laboratories as well as groups working on the construction of new technologies all tend to work in networks and these networks in turn confront each other, as well as communicate with government officials and industry representatives. The process of the construction of facts is one of lengthy discussions and reference to previous research and to the rules of reasoning available in the respective field, but clearly the focus of the findings of Latour and Woolgar remains on the fact that 'the epistemological qualities of validity and wrongness cannot be separated from sociological notions of decision-making'.[63] In other words, experiments and testing are not the sole determinants of resulting knowledge and/or technologies. This discussion of how the course of science and technology changes under the influence of both scientific and social factors takes me to the second stage of the formation of scientific knowledge – the closure of scientific debates.

Closure

The concept of closure as presented by Engelhardt and Caplan (1987) is very similar if not identical to the concept of 'stabilisation' of a scientific fact, as discussed by Latour and Woolgar (1979) and both of them resemble the 'tipping point' of a moral norm as discussed by Finnemore and Sikkink (1998). The common feature of the three terms is that they signify a moment in which actors with conflicting views and differing roles and positions in the social system agree on a fact or a norm and accept it as an integral part of their understanding of the material environment (in the case of scientific facts) and their own identities (in the case of normative change). I will come back to this discussion in my theoretical model of norm development. The term *closure* 'indicates the conclusion, ending or resolution of a controversy',[64] which according to the authors inevitably involves ethical and political layers, if not directly then implicitly as a part of the 'scientist's cultural milieu'.[65] The point of stabilisation 'entails the escape of a statement from all reference to the process of construction.... Up to a certain point ... the inclusion of reference to the conditions of construction is necessary for purposes of persuasion'; after that a fact becomes established and the former is no longer required.[66] In other words, achieving closure or stabilisation is indicative that a controversy has been resolved and a fact accepted, which is in turn evidence that interests, power, science, ethics have reached a common ground and formulated new knowledge.

Studies of closure have come up with a classification of the types of ending that scientific debates can have. 'Scientific controversies are usually seen to be the sort of disputes that are to be resolved by appeal to facts and to rigorous reasoning concerning facts.'[67] The appeal of facts is that they are perceived as objective, material and can be reported repeatedly by more than one observer. This view, however, is in complete opposition to the findings of SSK research. Engelhardt and Caplan conclude that when a debate has different layers to it, e.g., political, scientific, social, ethical – the political interests prevail and the political rules of closure apply.[68] The types of closure are broadly summarised in five categories – closure through loss of interest, closure through force, closure through consensus, closure through sound argument, and closure through negotiation.[69] Having looked at empirical studies of social constructivism in IR, one can easily recognise patterns of closure similar to the ones listed above; the only difference is that the studies of social constructivism have not paid nearly enough attention to that particular part of the norm evolution process. Before proceeding with a discussion of the synthetic model of norm evolution, and the interplay between norms and knowledge, a brief review of the types of closure proposed by Engelhardt and Caplan is in order, so that further reference to them will be possible.

Closure through loss of interest, also called 'natural death closure' or 'abandonment',[70] indicates an end to a debate due to loss of its relevance or due to actors losing interest in it. This type of closure is not based on logic or material evidence. Closure through force is the termination of debates on 'the basis of non-epistemic factors, such as the authority of the state, or the withdrawal of publication facilities'.[71] This type of closure indicates a situation where governments are, for whatever reason, no longer interested in supporting a debate or financing further research in a controversial field. Closure is again not achieved on the basis of objective knowledge and scientific research and the hunt for answers is suppressed by political influence. Closure through consensus is reached when 'the participants embrace a particular viewpoint, not through general rational arguments, negotiation or established procedures but through non-epistemic influences that lead to a community of belief'.[72] Closure through sound argument is based on rational argument, which follows the laws of scientific inference. In controversies with heavy political content, however, it is highly unlikely that argumentation will be completed by resort to sound argument. Closure through negotiation indicates the reaching of an agreement between the parties involved in a controversy. '[N]egotiation closure creates (as opposed to discovers or discloses) a solution.'[73] The study of closure and fact stabilisation affords useful insights, which are not confined to the sphere of scientific knowledge and will be further applied to the study of norm development.

The synthetic theoretical model of norm evolution

Combining the findings of social constructivists in IR and the theorists of SSK and SCOT, this research proposes a model of norm evolution, which can be applied to the study of a greater variety of behavioural norms. This synthetic model is an attempt to fine-tune already existing knowledge of norm building, to reflect more fully the complexity of norm construction, and to understand the social processes involved in creating norms across different fields of international politics. The process of establishing new behavioural norms consists of a complex web of relationships of power, influence, knowledge, morality, justice. Examining the various stages of this process in greater detail will help give answers to important questions. Why do some norms develop while others do not? How does the interplay between normative beliefs and scientific knowledge shape norm building? Why do states agree to amend the standards of appropriateness to higher and more demanding levels? Understanding the way in which norms are negotiated will also help explain norm-compliant state behaviour within an anarchical international society – an issue that is often at the heart of IR debates. In tune with constructivist research, I argue that state interests and identities are shaped throughout the process of norm development and some normative ideals are internalised before norms are legalised and institutionalised.

The empirical case studies in this research are chosen from different issue areas of global politics to demonstrate that the interplay between scientific knowledge and normative beliefs is a central dynamic that moves norm development forward. This is the case even in areas of policy-making not usually perceived of as scientific. The historic reconstruction of events leading to successful norm creation seeks to study and map the patterns of norm-knowledge interaction in each of the stages of the norm development process, and to reaffirm the relevance of the theoretical model proposed below.

Reconceptualising patterns of cooperation among different types of actors is another one of the central proposals of this research. Constructivists have been grouping actors according to the methods that they are *per-*

ceived to employ in the process of norm construction.[74] Actors should not be classified according to these criteria, as outlined in the review of constructivist literature, because the proposed categories do not match the networks that actors create, but instead overlap in places or draw dividing lines where none exist. It will be much more productive and informative to study how different actors form negotiating coalitions, what the power dynamics in these coalitions are, what roles different types of actors assume and how the negotiating coalitions influence the policy-making process. Actors form coalitions on the basis of their vested interests and the members of coalitions often follow the same logic of action. The demands of the different logic of action and the aim of the actors involved often pull in opposite directions. When the different logics of action can be reconciled and when actors manage to find common interests, the negotiating coalitions are at their strongest.

The proposed theoretical model also aims to provide a more exhaustive list of the stages of norm development, which, I argue, are relevant to a wider range of issue areas. The binding force of these stages is a sequence of closures and these are traced throughout the empirical case studies. The closures cause normative campaigns to progress. They indicate that key agreements on scientific and normative issues are reached and persuasion and bargaining can take the normative campaign forward.

The theoretical model of norm development that I propose has seven stages – formation of the initial idea, network configuration, issue formation, dialogue between proactive and conservative states, reaching political closure, institutionalisation/operationalisation and legalisation (see Figure 2.1). Normative ideas do not always become legal norms that are effective in governing state behaviour; the process of development can come to an end at any stage and normative ideas may remain undeveloped; some norms can even be discarded and attention to those may wane over time, which makes this model dynamic and open.

Stage one – initial idea

Various factors can generate the need for a new norm – a disaster, a crisis, the anticipation of a disaster,[75] shocking revelations of information about large-scale human suffering,[76] a need for international regulation where there is none.[77] The initial idea can be formulated by an individual – a norm entrepreneur[78] – or by a group of individuals – communities of experts[79] – by an organisation – a state[80] or an economic actor.[81] The identity of the norm entrepreneur, his/her social position and power status, will inevitably influence the process of the development of an idea, its chances for success, the time that it takes for the idea to become a norm. There are

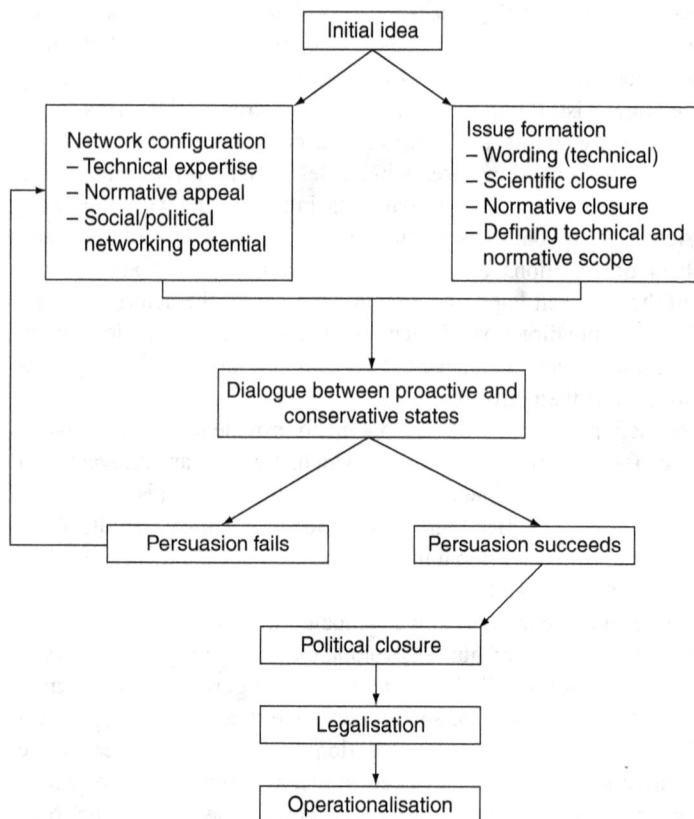

Figure 2.1 Synthetic theoretical model.

different theories as to which actors make the most successful norm entrepreneurs – some argue that actors close to the policy-making elites have
the best chance of realising their normative beliefs;[82] others argue that only
individuals or organisations who come from the periphery of the political
system and have not been corrupted by bureaucratic power, have undam-
aged and worthy normative ideas that can become useful norms.[83] Theo
Farrell summarises the constructivist position that proximity to authority
'can aid norm entrepreneurs' but is not a 'condition of success'.[84] Taking
into account Checkel's critique of the constructivists for portraying states
as negative characters, this research is based on the assumption that all
actors are capable of initiating normative ideas, which are not necessarily
either good or bad. The closer an actor is to the policy-making circles,

however, the easier it is likely to be for an idea to become established, but contacts with politicians are not a sufficient condition for a norm to be created. Although causal relationships will be sought throughout the case studies to which this model is applied, the research hypothesis is that it is not so much the social position of the norm entrepreneur as it is the ability to form an effective normative network that influences the successful norm development process.

The circumstances in which an initial idea has been formulated also influence the following stages of norm development. If an idea is formulated amidst a humanitarian crisis or a disaster, there are chances that this idea will evolve faster and will aim to make a practical difference to those suffering. Instances of human suffering have indeed drawn public attention and increased pressure on politicians to take action.[85] The lack of an immediate crisis, normative interest from strong states or public pressure, on the other hand, can protract negotiations or lead to the overall dismissal of the need to develop a particular norm.[86] In other words, the political and normative context within which an initial idea is formulated is quite important for its further development and should be studied where such evidence can be obtained.

Stage two – network configuration

The norm entrepreneur, whether an individual, a group or a state, needs to form a network of supporters in order to begin gaining critical mass and voice to initiate change in world politics. I am using the term 'network configuration' because networks need not be created from scratch in each instance of norm creation – actors may benefit from existing networks, or look to combine new activists with existing networks. The configuration of an influential network of supporters is one of the decisive moments of a successful campaign for the creation of a new behavioural norm in international relations. The support of a network of actors helps an idea to gain credibility and authority, which adds momentum to the process of lobbying national governments. Network configuration is understudied and the existence of proactive networks of support is often viewed as a given. If we choose to ignore this process, however, we are missing out on important instances of bargaining and persuasion as well as a careful division of responsibilities among actors who may be very different in terms of their nature and power capabilities. The success/failure of this stage determines whether an idea will take off or not. In other words, the stronger, more convincing and more authoritative the network is, the greater its chances for successful normative persuasion.

Stage two is one of information gathering by the norm entrepreneur (individual or group) in which the latter has to convince others to join in a coalition for the creation of a particular norm. In cases where transnational civil society actors have come up with the initial idea, they often look for the support of scientists and technical experts who can help establish in technical, rather than emotional terms, the realm of the problem, its implications, the best way to deal with it, etc.[87] Clearly, technical knowledge does not always have to agree with normative ideas, as the case study of intellectual property rights in the pharmaceutical industry illustrates. The only way out of such a deadlock is negotiation – between the experts and the normative proponents, where both sides search for alternatives that would meet their requirements. Scientists and experts look to expand the existing body of knowledge so that solutions can be found, while social movements assess the implications for those who can potentially suffer. Where states are norm entrepreneurs, one can discern similar processes of negotiations, coalition building[88] and knowledge sharing, which have an impact on the bargaining power of the group.

Networks are often consolidated at conferences and workshops where normative and scientific issues are raised and groups sympathetic to the cause begin communicating. Social movements and NGOs seek out scientists – both within the organisations and outside of them – as scientific knowledge is an important factor for network consolidation and for the formulation of the normative issue.

Stage three – issue formation

The process of issue formation often takes place at the same time as the configuration of the supportive network. Networks are formed as actors meet to discuss issues that they consider problematic. Work to construct the causal relationships that help problematise certain concerns over others is conducted in official and unofficial meetings and conferences. In this process the parameters of the issue at stake are specified and the actors need to reach agreement on the technical and moral scope of the problem that they wish to present policy-makers with. The stage of issue formation comprises a process of information sharing and negotiation. NGOs, charities, advocacy networks, corporations, scientists, professional analysts, intergovernmental organisations, etc., from different fields and with different expertise, participate in conferences and workshops where they communicate their concerns and findings in an attempt to find the common ground between normative issues, technical concerns and the actors' own interests[89] (which may clash at times).[90] At this stage, normative issues are clad in scientific terms – as causes and effects, as dependent and independent variables, and as a set of actions needed to remedy human suffering or an injustice. Scientific findings are in turn evaluated in a normative context where causes and consequences are examined for their fairness and compliance with collective morality.

In the process of issue formation, actors work towards establishing the technical and moral scope of the future norm. The technical scope includes reaching agreement on cause-and-effect relationships, as well as identifying the problem resulting from these causal relationships and in some cases defining a technical solution to that problem. As discussed previously, however, science is not always unequivocal and when complex issues are at stake, scientists may disagree on different aspects of the technical scope of the new norm. Scientific knowledge is often produced in response to demands for further clarity. I argue that in the process of formulating the problematic issue, it is crucial that experts reach *scientific closure* on its technical scope, just as it is crucial for civil society actors to reach *normative closure*, that is, to reach agreement on the moral scope of the proposed norm. The lack of closure in the scientific or normative realm does not mean that the norm will not progress further; rather, it means that the political negotiations that are to follow will be more difficult with actors continually referring to scientific or normative uncertainties.

Scientific knowledge can help to persuade actors of the need to act on a given issue. Scientific closure enhances actors' faith in the success of a developing norm and creates conditions for the realisation of the need for a particular norm. Science, however, is a product of public, political or economic demand and may be tainted to reflect the interests of those who fund scientific research. '[I]n the international arena, neither the processes whereby knowledge becomes more extensive nor the means whereby reflection on knowledge deepens are passive or automatic. They are intensely political.'[91] In other words, scientific knowledge is created within a specific social, cultural and political context, which is bound to affect the questions that scientists ask and the answers that they find.

Civil society may also bring in biases towards the interests of the groups that are most actively involved in the creation and definition of a particular norm. These interests may not always be benign and social groups are not always concerned with the greater good of the greater number of people.

Issue formation also relates to constructing a problematic issue within a particular context and choosing an institutional forum best able to address this problem. When the problem of landmines was constructed against the background of conventional weapons disarmament treaties, it was not successful in attracting enough political attention; however, once it was presented as a humanitarian problem with a very high human cost, policymakers created the Convention Banning the Use of Landmines.[92] In another example, which will be discussed in more detail in Chapter 4, the protection of intellectual property rights in the pharmaceutical industry was initially part of a one-size-fits-all approach to intellectual property, looking after the interests of innovators, constructed in a context of fair trade practices. When public pressure started to mount and the issue was constructed as one reflecting on the developed world's morality, depriving those in the developing world from access to basic medicines, the norm was reshaped and redefined to cater for those who could not afford expensive patented medicines. Wording and contextualising an issue in the most effective and attention-grabbing way brings norm entrepreneurs a step closer to successful norm creation.

Stage four – dialogue with the conservative actors

Some states take an active interest in the processes of network configuration and issue formation alongside civil society and epistemic communities. Those governments who are convinced of the need for the creation of a new norm become part of the activist network and help raise concerns at the intergovernmental level. The states which support the normative status quo, together with other actors who are opposed to the proposed changes, constitute the group of conservative actors. The dialogue stage is in essence another stage of negotiations, but this time mainly among states that have the material capabilities, the bargaining power and the administrative authority to effect change in international norms and regulations. This phase is critical because convincing states and other actors of the need for urgent action on a question not on their agenda is no easy task, and if these negotiations fail, a normative idea goes off the international agenda and back to the preparation stages.

The dialogue between proactive and conservative states is a complex process of balancing of interests, negotiating trade-offs, calculating costs and benefits, threats and opportunities. What makes this process of negotiations even more challenging is the existence of large disparities between the participants in intergovernmental negotiations, as they have different political agendas, strategic positioning within the global system, and perceptions of risk, uncertainty, economic development, etc.

Power dialogues take place between state experts and independent experts who are part of the norm-promoting network; experts working for industries that are directly affected may also join in the discussions.[93] In essence, these dialogues revolve not only around interests and power; they weigh up the normative and technical side of the issue, which make the intergovernmental agenda. The dialogue with states can lead to their agreement on the need for the creation/change of a norm in the international system or to their declining to deal with the proposed issue. If states are not interested or strongly disagree on the need or feasibility of the creation/change of a norm, this could either end the life of the normative idea or take it back a stage or two in its evolution for the idea to be modified and made more attractive or at least less threatening for states' interests. Once states have agreed in principle to the need of creating a new norm-regulating behaviour, we can say that they have reached the point of political closure on the normative issue.

The dialogue between proactive and conservative states usually takes place over protracted periods of time. It may take years for states to agree even in principle that there is a need for a new norm to further regulate their behaviour. Non-state actors take an active part in these negotiations by providing information and expertise, by lobbying national governments, by mobilising public opinion, etc. States, however, are better equipped to complete these negotiations, as they often have leverage against each other in the world system. Government officials can bargain their way through normative negotiations by means of offering and accepting trade-offs, as well as by means of threats and coercion; persuasion is not always based on the merits of the problem at hand.

Stage five – reaching political closure

The concepts of stabilisation, closure and tipping all denote a social moment in which a scientific fact or a norm becomes accepted as default and as a part of the operational environment of actors. As discussed earlier, the specificity of this point stems from the fact that in one way or another, the differences between scientists, civil society, political actors, industry representatives, which are seemingly irreconcilable, are resolved and they reach an agreement to establish a behavioural norm. This social moment is extremely important even though it remains understudied. Political closure, I argue, similarly to scientific closure, as discussed by Engelhardt and Caplan, may come in different forms. Political closure may be a result of genuine consensus; it may be reached by coercion and threat; closure may be a product of political bargaining and trade-offs. The manner in which closure is arrived at affects the creation of more or less effective behavioural norms. When closure is forced, for example, the created norm is likely to be contested in the future and controversies are likely to re-open closures. Political closure, it must be kept in mind, however, is different from normative and scientific closures in that the former are horizontal closures, reached among like-minded actors, who are willing to find a point of consensus. Political closure, on the other hand, is vertical, involving both states and non-state actors. It is often based on the smallest common denominator among actors' interests, and even on coercion or political pressure by the more powerful. Political closure needs to be studied separately from the other two types because of the dynamics of power, which are completely different among states and between states and other actors. Political closure is based on normative and scientific closures and in cases where the latter are solid, emerging from genuine consensus, political closure is more likely to be more stable, resulting in more effective norms.

State negotiations draw together activists from transnational civil society, independent experts and other organisations interested in the development of the normative idea. Since most negotiations are conducted at the United Nations or one of its agencies, procedures have been put in place, over the years, to involve non-state actors in the processes of norm negotiations.[94] When states discuss changes to the international normative environment the debates attract the attention of economic actors as well. International businesses, TNCs and industry organisations often choose to set their agendas at the national level where they have better access to policy-makers through established channels of lobbying. Depending on the normative issue, economic actors may choose to build coalitions at the international level, and these often command impressive material resources. Economic power tends to always be represented at international negotiations. Despite the fact that states are willing to cooperate with other actors, one needs to keep in mind that they still have the power to choose not to do that (as sovereigns).

The point of closure is reached when the majority of states involved in these political negotiations agree on the need to create a new norm. This crucial moment needs to be examined in more depth. According to the sociologists of knowledge, the point of stabilisation is a social moment when the new norm loses its reference to the process of negotiation and the actors involved in its formation, and becomes part of the recognised moral context of international relations.[95] Similarly, constructivists in IR define the tipping point as the point when 'the old norms [begin to] produce social disapproval'.[96] Therefore, this is also the moment when the need to regulate behaviour with a clear normative prescription is accepted by states. Those states who are normative entrepreneurs tend to internalise the new behavioural norm early during the negotiations. Their governments often create domestic legal norms on the new normative issue to reflect on their conviction on the new normative principles. The states who oppose the need for a new norm may be lured into agreeing by means of persuasion, coercion or bargaining. But these states are also the ones who avoid compliance where possible.

Proof that political closure has taken place can be found in intergovernmental debates, where discussions move on from the normative negotiations on the need for a new norm to more practical negotiations of how best to achieve the objective of the new norm. Further proof that political closure has taken place is the changing nature of political debates – from normative and scientific (truth seeking) to more technical, concerned with spelling out clear normative principles. Political closure signifies the beginning of a process of internalisation of a normative prescription. Evidence that closure has taken place can be found in the negotiating records, in political speeches and reviews of governmental conferences.

The concepts of closure of a debate, a resolution of a scientific dispute, a norm cascade, have been studied only in so far as to identify them as a part of the scientific, historic, political and social processes of truth seeking. The 'closure project'[97] has focused attention primarily on the classification of the existing types of closure and on the historical study of the types of closure applied to issues with different composition of social, political and scientific elements.[98] More research, however, is needed to assist in devising clearer mechanisms of detecting and measuring political closure, as it is a complex and multilayered social event.

Stage six – legalisation

Not all behavioural norms reach the stage of legalisation, as some remain customary practices and tacit understandings. Legalisation is a complex process because states primarily, but also other non-state actors involved in the discussions of legal texts, are particularly meticulous about the use of language and even punctuation. Legalisation can take years to complete and sometimes norms lose the momentum of the negotiations leading up to the decision to legalise and may become meaningless in technical and political terms by the time they are legalised. The process of legalisation can be sped up by demands of industries for efficiency, by strong political personalities, by awareness of large-scale human suffering, by pressure from the public, etc. What is important, however, is that legalisation is effective and not purely fictitious. States are careful when they spell out obligations that will be binding them in the future and are likely to affect national interests, domestic agendas and strategic calculations. States which have been conservative in the previous stages often see in the process of legalisation a chance to avoid being bound and responsible for their actions in a particular normative area, or a chance to bargain on other normative issues, making their acceptance of one document contingent upon benefits in another sphere of international politics. There has been a growing interest among IR scholars in studying the processes of legalising new and existing standards of behaviour,[99] as the process involves not only political negotiations, but also technical legal knowledge and expertise and reflects a side of international relations that has been largely ignored by the traditional theories.

Stage seven – insitutionalisation/operationalisation

There has been an increasing tendency to legalise international norms and to spell out clear rules, parameters to state obligations, and timelines for adopting specified policies. However, the process of legalisation has often not succeeded in producing strong enough mechanisms and clear prescriptions that are sufficient to induce norm-compliant state behaviour. Further legal documents – like specific agreements and protocols – are then negotiated when the initial pressure from public opinion, normative, scientific and business networks has died away. Secondary agreements and protocols provide an opportunity to fine-tune international norms, to improve their effectiveness and further clarify, if needed, their meaning and scope. The process of institutionalisation may take place both in stage six and stage seven, and relates to the creation of institutions to oversee the functioning of and compliance with the new norm. Institutionalisation is a vital part of norm development but is a purely administrative process.

This research argues that in its evolution every norm passes through the above stages at least once. The process of norm development does not guarantee that ideas and normative beliefs will always evolve into an institutionalised, operational international norm. However, this theoretical model seeks to be more relevant to a greater number of issue areas, to provide more clarity on the roles of the different actors involved, on the importance of the interplay between scientific knowledge and normative beliefs, and on the way in which these shape a new norm. It also leads to an inquiry into the link between norm compliance and the process of negotiating new norms. The research tools of the social constructivists and the sociologists of knowledge will be valuable in enabling a more holistic and in-depth understanding of the processes leading up to the creation of new norms, as they are sensitive to the influence of such factors as social dynamics, power relationships and shared understandings.

3 Protecting individuals from torture

After centuries of practising torture in different forms, for various purposes and under the veil of diverse justifications, humankind, indirectly represented by the UN General Assembly, finally decided to draw up a prohibition of the practice of torture in a dedicated legal document – the Convention against Torture (CAT), which was followed by an Optional Protocol (2002) to ensure implementation. Why did this process of outlawing the use of torture work in 1984 and not earlier or indeed later? What were the factors that fostered agreement among states to outline a stricter ban on the use of torture? What role did scientific knowledge and normative beliefs play in the process of norm building? And what was the nature of the coalitions that actors formed?

Some suggest that humanity matures, evolves, becomes civilised and this evolution explains the creation of new norms of state behaviour.[1] Studies of torture in medical journals, social and historical accounts, reveal that humanity (or at least some authoritative parts of it) indeed evolves, if only to invent newer and more ingenious ways to break down the human body and spirit without physically killing an individual.[2] Sparing the reader gruesome tales of death, survival and the continuation of life in trauma and pain, I present a review of processes and campaigns by means of which I aim to reconstruct the historical development of the norm postulating a complete ban on the use of physical and psychological torture. In the context of this process, I search for patterns of interactions between scientific knowledge and normative beliefs, as well as for an improved understanding of the ways in which different actors make use of the latter in their campaign for new norms.

My account of the processes leading up to the creation of the behavioural norm that prohibits torture will begin with a brief examination of the failed attempts to ban the practice. The latter holds clues and recurring themes that are of great importance to our understanding of the underlying nature of torture as well as the type of prohibition needed to make torture as morally unjustifiable as slavery or genocide, for example. The failures of previous campaigns to outlaw torture can indicate what makes some campaigns successful while others remain insufficient to make the needed difference.

I will track the changing purpose and justification for the use of torture from early human societies, through the times of Ancient Greece and Rome and the European Enlightenment. I will then draw attention to a period of European history (nineteenth century) when according to historical accounts, judicial torture came to be outlawed in Europe,[3] before it was brought back to life during the two World Wars, and the Cold War. The end of the Second World War, infamous for its atrocities, marked the beginning of a new normative era where human dignity and integrity acquired a prominent place and an ever-increasing importance in international politics. Medical and psychological research conducted with concentration camp survivors of the Second World War, in seeking appropriate methods of rehabilitation and compensation, began to show the width and depth of problems experienced by survivors of torture and other cruel, inhuman, degrading treatment and punishment.[4] A number of authoritarian regimes came to power in Central and South America in the 1970s, during the peak of the Cold War when the Soviets were determined to withstand any political opposition at home, and torture was one way of achieving this political agenda. In this hostile and violent political climate Amnesty International (AI) embarked on a worldwide campaign against torture, which eventually led to the creation of CAT.

The driving force behind this normative campaign was the consistent effort of Amnesty International to concentrate political attention on the problem of torture, starting in the early 1970s. The work of this normative movement was supplemented by other more technical campaigns concerned with the consequences of torture, with the involvement of medical professionals in this inhumane practice, with the definition of torture in unequivocal technical terms. The interplay of normative ideas and scientific knowledge, in this case study, created a solid foundation for a successful normative campaign, one which left very little room for manoeuvre to states who were unwilling to bind their behaviour with a new norm. The overview of the history of torture reveals the dynamic of its use and the failures of previous campaigns to outlaw it, which can afford valuable insights as to what went wrong and why. Thus, by the end of this chapter, there will be not one but two types of proof of what circumstances aid and hinder the evolution of behavioural norms.

One of the central debates in this campaign has focused on constructing a comprehensive definition of torture. Since part of this chapter, however, is dedicated to the study of how the legal definition of torture was arrived at, adopting the current legal definition might result in circular reasoning. Accordingly, a working definition of torture will be employed up until the moment when I consider the construction of the current legal definition of this practice. In its first report on torture published in 1973, Amnesty International cited the following explanation of what its campaign considered torture to be: 'Torture is the systematic and deliberate infliction of acute pain in any form by one person on another, or on a third person, in order to accomplish the purpose of the former against the will of the latter.'[5] Although the above definition is a clear depiction of the contemporary practice of torture, it by no means represents the limits of the use to which torture has been put through the ages.

History of the use of torture

From the tribal world to the eighteenth century

Most historical accounts of the use of torture refer us to the time of Ancient Greece and Rome.[6] But George Riley Scott argues that there is hardly 'a savage or primitive race which does not employ torture either in its religious rites or its code of punishment'.[7] Scott continues by pointing out that

> torture is rarely absent from the theosophic, initiatory and other rites adopted by the savage tribes. The callous attitude of primitive man towards bloodshed, the lack of sympathy for suffering, and the phlegmatic reaction to death itself, are all in accord with the exhibition of stoicism in circumstances of danger or suffering.[8]

In other words, 'the systematic and deliberate infliction of acute pain' to fellow individuals has been an inseparable part of the social life of humans from the early centuries of human existence.

Ancient Greece and later the Roman Empire saw the institutionalisation of justice dispensation and the centralisation of this power in the hands of a chosen few[9] (eighth–fifth century BC). Torture, some historians say, was a procedure applied only to slaves and only when they had been convicted of a crime, while 'torture of the citizen was forbidden'.[10] The free citizen could also be tortured, but only in cases of accusations for treason. According to historians, this was not the case in practice. Gibbons indicates that

> the extension of legal torture to cases of treason virtually annulled the principle by which the free-man was supposed to be exempt from the *quaestio* except in these supposedly rare cases of treason, because it

was a comparatively easy matter to bring a variety of offences into this somewhat elusive category.[11]

Peters notes a similar trend, dated to the period between the second and fourth centuries:

> [it was] indicated by a rescript of the Emperor Valentinian in 369 ... that although torture could be routinely applied in the case of treason, and exceptionally by personal command by the emperor, it was, nevertheless, widely and indiscriminately applied to freemen for far less offences.[12]

These historical accounts indicate that torture once authorised was hard to control even when the perimeters of its use were strictly limited.

The following centuries saw the continued application of torture – 'the Christian Church adopted the Roman law of torture in regard to treason, applying it to heresy, which they construed to be "treason against God"'.[13] Torture became the natural punishment for anyone accused of heresy. The spread of torture as punishment for heresy was a bottom-up development, if we are to classify these social dynamics in contemporary terms. The lack of condemnation from the larger public removed any incentive for the rulers to limit the use of torture. While the practice was justified by the Church and in the eyes of the broader public, the use of torture for judicial purposes was denounced at a very high level.[14] These double standards on the permissibility of the use of torture indicate that from the early days of the exercise of judicial torture, the practice had its opponents mainly due to the chance that innocent persons could be punished. Historical sources show, however, that regardless of objections by the Church and by philosophers, both religious prosecution and the judicial system in Europe continued to apply the methods of torture carried on from Roman times.[15]

The Holy Inquisition represented the peak of the use of torture as a punishment for heresy – historically spreading from the twelfth to eighteenth century, geographically encompassing almost all of today's Western Europe – Germany, Holland, Spain, Portugal and France.[16] The Catholic Church ruled by means of terrorising the populace and wielding its unrestrained power over everyone *irrespective* of political, economic or social status. Apart from the Holy Inquisition, the secular judicial system became quite fond of torture itself. Torture has been documented as an 'irregular police procedure' in the twelfth century.[17] The practice quickly evolved within the legal system that was emerging under the political order of the Catholic Church, to become the 'queen of proofs'.[18] Torture was not only established as a legitimate part of the legal proceedings in criminal cases, but also as an official instrument for extracting confessions. It was initially quite crude – if a confession under torture was confirmed by a confession away from the torture chambers, this amounted to enough evidence for a judge to pass a guilty verdict. The use of torture as part of the law of proof was refined by the German law on criminal procedures – *Constitutio Criminalis Carolina* of 1532.[19] Some limitations were introduced – for example, a person who is tortured cannot be subjected to 'suggestive questioning', he/she is not expected to merely confess guilt but to relate details of the crime, which need to be verified in turn,[20] etc. All these rules were 'designed to enhance the reliability of the confession of guilt'[21] and limit false confessions under torture. At this point in the sixteenth century torture could not have been abolished because no other mechanism of judicial proof existed to replace it, so moral arguments, no matter how strong, stood no chance in producing any practical difference. To sum up, in the period between the twelfth and eighteenth centuries, torture was an integral part of the criminal branch of the legal system; it was practised openly and supposedly served a clear purpose – to provide sufficient evidence for indictments.

Torture was practised openly in many other parts of the world – China, Japan, India, America, Africa, the West Indies and Mauritius were all involved in the slave trade, and slavery was intricately related to torture as the latter was one of the methods of ensuring obedience and control.[22] What all these early accounts of torture have in common is that the practice was engaged from a position of power to suppress dissent and to secure obedience and unconditional submission to a certain authority – be it the Church, the slave master, or the social order. And although the Catholic Church publicly denounced judicial torture in the fourth century, this moral condemnation alone did not suffice to discontinue the practice.

Torture in the eighteenth and nineteenth century: movements to discontinue the use of judicial torture

In the eighteenth century judicial torture was first outlawed by European rulers – judicial torture was discontinued in England in 1640; in 1740 Frederick the Great abolished torture in Prussia; in 1786 the practice was abolished in Italy; in 1789 France followed suit; then came Russia in 1801, Spain in 1812, Japan in 1873.[23] The abolition of judicial torture, however, was insufficient to rule out torture altogether, since the practice remained an acceptable punishment.

The abolition of judicial torture marked an important normative turning point in the history of outlawing the use of torture. There are two rivalling explanations for the discontinued use of judicial torture. The first one is that the humanitarian spirit of the Enlightenment, along with the powerful rhetoric of respected philosophers, influenced the rulers, who in turn changed the laws.[24] The argument against the application of torture in the judicial process dates back to the fourth century and the writings of St Augustine. The context of the eighteenth century, according to Scott, when famous names such as Cesare Beccaria in Italy and Voltaire in France published their strong views and justifications against the use of judicial torture culminated in its prohibition. The work of Beccaria is considered particularly influential:

> No man can be judged a criminal until he be found guilty; nor can society take from him the public protection, until it has been proved that he has violated the conditions on which it was granted.... If guilty, he should only endure the punishment ordained by the laws, and torture becomes useless, as his confession is unnecessary. If he be not guilty, you torture the innocent; Besides, it is confounding all relations, to expect that ... pain should be the test of truth, as if truth resided in the muscles and fibres of a wretch in torture. By this method, the robust will escape, and the feeble be condemned.[25]

The discussion is in tune with the values of the Enlightenment era and provides solid advocacy for the rights of individuals. But the inevitable question arises – whether rhetoric alone is capable of influencing policy-makers, and if not what other factors had been at play to foster changes.

Arguments against the use of torture, however, were not new at this time and there is no evidence of an explicit causal relationship between these arguments and its abolition. The second explanation for the historic abolition of judicial torture was that a revolution in the law of proof had taken place, because neither the political authority, nor the judiciary, had any further interest in preserving the practice.[26] Langbein argues that philosophers alone could not change the policies that monarchs chose. 'The critique of judicial torture ... did little to demonstrate the workability of a criminal justice system shorn of the power to investigate under torture.'[27] It was thus the lack of a mechanism to replace judicial torture that had prevented the philosophers from making an impact in the past and there was no reason to believe that this should change in the eighteenth century.

Langbein provides a considerably stronger argument for the abolition of judicial torture in eighteenth-century Europe. According to his research, what made torture obsolete[28] was an evolution in the methods of punishment, which spared many from death (often preceded by torture).[29] The sixteenth and seventeenth centuries were the time when judges gradually obtained the power to make decisions on the basis of 'circumstantial evidence', namely evidence different from a confession or the accounts of two witnesses. This radical move away from the old type of proof was due, in the words of Langbein, to a gradual change in the method of governance, where

> judicial discretion could be tolerated because it could be controlled. The centralisation and professionalisation of the judiciary that occurred in the absolutist states of the 16th and 17th centuries was an essential prerequisite for a system of free judicial evaluation of the evidence.[30]

The need to secure obedience for the relatively weak governments emerging in the Middle Ages was no longer so pressing.

Torture during the First and Second World Wars

The First and Second World Wars saw the resurrection of unchecked human cruelty – millions died on the battlefields in the First World War, while the Second World War was marked by the number of civilian deaths, the gruesome cruelty of concentration camps and the conduct of scientific research on humans. The end of the Second World War brought about a new era – one in which individual human rights were spelled out and in which gross violations of human rights would incur personal accountability.[31] The institutional, legal and social studies of human rights violations were accompanied by medical and psychological studies of concentration camp survivors.[32] This is the first instance in human history when scientific knowledge about the consequences of torture, cruel, inhuman and degrading treatment began to evolve. The scientific findings took time to gain recognition and to surface in the medical literature. The peak of publications on this issue was not reached until the 1970s.[33] One should not, however, give these developments more credit than they are worth. Much of the medical research of the period following the end of the Second World War was not so much philanthropic as practical in character. Medical research on concentration camp and labour camp survivors was meant to yield information on the basis of which governments and local authorities could calculate and give out compensation and social benefits.[34] This early research laid the foundations for further studies into the effects of extreme mental and physical suffering, which helped the campaign for the abolition of torture secure solid scientific evidence.

In the late 1940s, for the first time, the Medico-Legal Council of Denmark drew an important conclusion that 'there cannot ... be any doubt that the distress described here (namely nervous illness and mental suffering) must be regarded as illness in the normal medical meaning of the word'.[35] The psychological symptoms and suffering of torture survivors were recognised for the first time as a sufficient basis of monetary compensation,[36] as well as a medical condition in contemporary medicine. These first steps of evolving scientific knowledge supplemented much larger social and political processes in the years leading up to 1984.

Reviewing the fluctuating traditions of the use of torture in varying aspects of social activity indicates that part of the reason why torture had not been outlawed through the centuries was that its definition was leaving room for interpretation of the scope of the prohibition. Interpretation, in turn, allowed for the practice to be repeatedly reintroduced in social relations. Another important conclusion is that the context of other social forces, practices and traditions played a significant role in outlawing torture. Thus, norm development should always be studied in relation to the contemporary normative, social and political context, which some authors have called 'world time'.[37] There is no single formula that can help us determine the influence of context and it needs to be examined on a case-by-case basis.

Normative and political context of the postwar world

A number of fundamental political changes took place after the end of the Second World War. The Cold War began, constructing a bipolar international context, with each superpower (the US and the USSR) forming its own set of allies, supporters and spheres of influence. The superpower rivalry had indirect implications for the revival of the practice of torture because strategic security (or rather insecurity) issues were prevailing over issues of human justice. We can clearly read this in Hedley Bull's account of the international society of states of 1979, who is convinced that 'international order comes prior to human justice' and that the current 'international order does not provide any general protection of human rights, only a selective protection that is determined not by the merits of the case but by the vagaries of international politics'.[38]

While the use of torture was not limited on either side of the Cold War, Amnesty International observed that 'the developing system of the protection of human rights was centred in Western Europe'.[39] The rest of the world was relatively unconcerned about human rights, or the containment and control of the use of torture, which made the normative campaign to outlaw this practice rather challenging. The support of Western European nations, however, became the political foundation for this normative campaign.

In addition to the bipolarity of the Cold War, there were other powerful political processes taking place outside of Western Europe and North America. The 1960s saw the crumbling of colonial empires. The process of decolonisation went peacefully in some parts of the world but not in others – the examples of Algeria as one of the bloodiest self-determination campaigns, which became infamous for its violence and cruelty;[40] and the politics of apartheid in South Africa[41] – illustrate this.

Violence and terror were brewing in South America as well, where authoritarian regimes came to power in the 1960s and 1970s – Brazil (1964), Chile and Uruguay (1973), Argentina (1976).[42] Following the Cuban Revolution and the Cuban Missile Crisis (1962), the United States was growing fearful that Soviet Communist influence might be spreading on their very doorstep,[43] and much effort was put into covert CIA operations to destabilise democratically elected socialist governments across Central and South America. The most notable case, which also became one of the catalysts of Amnesty International's campaign to outlaw torture, was the military dictatorship of General Augusto Pinochet of Chile, who 'instituted a pitiless campaign of repression against leftist groups in the country.... Military governments in Argentina and Brazil also clamped down hard on domestic dissidents during the 1970s, striking out at communist, socialist, and liberal democratic elements alike.'[44] Some parts of Europe also witnessed the hard hand of political violence under oppressive regimes – most notable examples are Spain and Greece.[45] Reports were leaking out of the USSR as well where, following the cruelties of the Stalinist regime, Brezhnev was reconstructing his methods of suppressing opposition by enlisting psychiatry to redefine and 'treat' dissidence as a form of mental illness.[46] Torture, violence and disappearances were the only way for all these regimes to hold on to power and to terrify their population into obedience. It thus becomes clear that 'torture was to be part of political struggle [in the period 1945–1970s] used either by the colonial power as a weapon against national liberation forces, or by local governments against domestic opposition'.[47] The common denominators of torture in this period was that it was government-sponsored violence, it was often covert, and governments were reluctant to submit to demands for openness and the protection of human rights.

The normative context of the times was complex, due to the clash between the newly established principles for the protection of human rights and the Cold War normative reality where the principle of sovereignty was still overwhelmingly powerful. The principles of human rights protection were hard to ignore not least because of the precedents that had been set. The principle of individual accountability for participation in gross violations of human rights was established. The War Crime Tribunals of Nuremberg and Tokyo postulated that 'a state's treatment of its citizens in peacetime was appropriate for general international regulation';[48] and also that [there is] a system of international law under which individuals are responsible to the community of nations for violations of rules of international criminal law, and according to which attacks on the fundamental liberties and constitutional rights of peoples and individuals … constitute international crimes not only in time of war, but also in time of peace.[49]

The legal language of the proceedings set important standards, but these were not necessarily at the top of the agenda of all states. The newly formed postcolonial states sought a different international agenda from the traditional 'high politics' of the security and geo-strategic considerations of the Cold War. They needed an agenda concerned with development, human rights and cooperation. The United Nations was trying to balance the conflicting demands of state sovereignty, economic development and individual human rights, while ensuring that the Cold War did not turn hot.

Amidst this very unsettled climate of the early 1970s Amnesty International undertook a campaign to draw attention to the problem of torture. Before the theoretical model of norm creation is compared to the findings of this research, a timeline of the international and regional developments prohibiting the use of torture is presented in Box 3.1. This timeline encompasses the processes, actors and dynamics that shaped and formed the idea to ban the use of torture and led unequivocally to the Convention against Torture.

Constructing the prohibition against torture

Formulating the idea

With the advance of the Cold War – the nuclear stand-off between the superpowers, the dividing of the world into spheres of influence, the demands for self-determination and self-governance in the newly independent countries – the political will to make the protection of human rights a top priority faded away. The international political context of the 1970s was one of turbulent change, 'industrial militancy, student revolts, neo-nationalist terrorism and shadow armies of the right'.[50] This political turmoil and instability not only generated the initial impetus for the campaign to abolish torture but also helped to sustain the determination of its supporters all the way through to 1984.

By the early 1970s it seemed as though the 25 years that had passed since the end of the Second World War had managed not only to dilute the resolve of nations to cater for individual human rights, but also to

Box 3.1 Timeline for the creation of international and regional instruments prohibiting torture

1946	The Economic and Social Committee of the UN (ECOSOC) sets up the Commission on Human Rights, whose first task is to draw up the International Bill of Rights.
10 December 1948	Universal Declaration of Human Rights – Article 5 reads 'No one shall be subjected to torture or to cruel, inhuman or degrading treatment or punishment.'
1949	Geneva Conventions – Article 3 – forbids 'cruel treatment and torture of persons taking no active part in the hostilities' and also proscribes 'outrages upon personal dignity, in particular, humiliating and degrading treatment'.
1949/1950	European Convention for the Protection of Human Rights and Fundamental Freedoms (signed in Rome) – Article 3 – 'No one should be subjected to torture or to inhuman or degrading treatment or punishment.'
1957	Standard Minimum Rules for the Treatment of Prisoners – adopted by the UN Congress on the Prevention of Crime and the Treatment of Offenders – 'Corporal punishment, punishment by placing in a dark cell, and all cruel, inhuman or degrading punishments shall be completely prohibited as punishments for disciplinary offences.'
16 December 1966	International Covenant on Civil and Political Rights – Article 7: 'No one should be subjected to torture or to cruel, inhuman or degrading treatment or punishment. In particular, no one should be subjected without his free consent to medical or scientific experimentation.'
1969	The American Convention on Human Rights – signed in San Jose, Costa Rica, under the auspices of the Organization of American States, Article 5, paragraph 2 reads 'No one shall be subjected to torture or to cruel, inhuman, or degrading punishment or treatment. All persons deprived of their liberty shall be treated with respect for the inherent dignity of the human person.'
1973	The delegations of Sweden, Austria, Costa Rica, the Netherlands and Trinidad and Tobago – submitted a draft resolution according to which the General Assembly would decide to examine the question of torture.
1973	Amnesty International's *Report on Torture* published.
1973	Conference for the Abolition of Torture held in Paris.

November 1974	UNGA Resolution 3218 – *Torture and Other Cruel, Inhuman or Degrading Treatment or Punishment in Relation to Detention and Imprisonment* – adopted with 125 votes in favour, 1 abstention and 0 votes against – envisages the development of an international code of ethics for police and the drafting of principles of medical ethics.
November 1974	Resolution 3219 – *Protection and Human Rights in Chile*.
June 1975	AI organised a seminar on an international code of police ethics in the Hague – participants included police authorities and members of police forces and of national and international police organisations from eight European countries.
August 1975	Conference on Security and Cooperation in Europe produced the Helsinki Agreement.
August 1975	A Resolution on the Role of the Nurse in the Care of Detainees and Prisoners adopted by the International Council of Nurses in Singapore
October 1975	The World Medical Association adopted the *Tokyo Declaration* – containing Guidelines for Medical Doctors concerning Torture and Other Cruel, Inhuman or Degrading Treatment of Punishment in relation to Detention or Imprisonment.
December 1975	UNGA Resolution 3452 – *Declaration on the Protection of All Persons from Being Subjected to Torture and Other Cruel, Inhuman or Degrading Treatment or Punishment* – Article 3 – 'No state may permit or tolerate torture or other cruel, inhuman or degrading treatment or punishment. Exceptional circumstances such as a state of war or a threat of war, internal political instability or any other public emergency may not be invoked as a justification of torture or other cruel, inhuman or degrading treatment or punishment.'
December 1975	UNGA Resolution 3453 – to consider issues of torture, cruel, inhuman and degrading treatment or punishment in relation to detention and imprisonment.
1977	Jean-Jacques Gautier founded the Swiss Committee against Torture (CSCT).
1977	World Psychiatric Association – adopted the *Declaration of Hawaii* – 'the psychiatrist must never use his professional possibilities to violate the dignity or human rights of any individual or group.... The psychiatrist must on no account utilize the tools of his profession, once the absence of psychiatric illness has been

	established. If a patient or some third party demands actions contrary to scientific knowledge or ethical principles the psychiatrist must refuse to cooperate.'
1978	Three separate versions of the Convention against Torture were drafted – 1) CSCT – Gautier along with the Henry Dunant Institute; 2) Government of Sweden; 3) International Association of Penal Law.
December 1979	UNGA Resolution 34/169 contained an Annex, which spelled out the Code of Conduct for Law Enforcement Officials.
1981	African Charter on Human and People's Rights – signed in Nairobi under the auspices of the Organisation of African Unity – Article 5 – 'All forms of exploitation and degradation of man, particularly ... torture, cruel, inhuman or degrading punishment and treatment shall be prohibited.'
1981	Universal Islamic Declaration of Human Rights – Article 7 – 'No person shall be subjected to torture in mind or body, or degraded, or threatened with injury either to himself or to anyone related to or held dear by him.'
1981	The International Conference on Islamic Medicine adopted the *Declaration of Kuwait.*
1982	UN Principles of Medical Ethics relevant to the Role of Health Personnel, particularly Physicians, in the Protection of Prisoners and Detainees against Torture and Other Cruel, Inhuman or Degrading Treatment or Punishment – Principle 2 – 'It is a gross contravention of medical ethics, as well as an offence under applicable international instruments, for health personnel, particularly physicians, to engage, actively or passively in acts which constitute participation in, complicity in, incitement to or attempts to commit torture or other cruel, inhuman or degrading treatment or punishment.'
1984	Amnesty published its report *Torture in the Eighties.*
December 1984	UNGA adopted the Convention against Torture and other Cruel, Inhuman and Degrading Treatment or Punishment.
1985	The UN Centre for Human Rights established the post – Special Rapporteur on Torture – Peter Kooijmans.
December 1985	Inter-American Convention to Prevent and Punish Torture.
1987	ACAT and other national groups formed an International Federation.
November 1987	European Convention for the Prevention of Torture and Inhuman or Degrading Treatment or Punishment.

1988	European Principles of Medical Ethics – adopted by the European medical regulatory associations.
December 1988	Body of Principles for the Protection of All Persons under Any Form of Detention or Imprisonment.
December 2002	Optional Protocol to the Convention against Torture is adopted by UN Resolution A/RES/57/199.
June 2006	The Optional Protocol to the UNCAT enters into force after 20 states ratify it.

obliterate the public memory and revulsion at the large-scale atrocities of torture, dictatorship and inhumanity. Dictatorial regimes were employing all possible means to eradicate opposition and political dissent (Algeria, Southeast Asia, Chile, Argentina, USSR). The United States was more interested in not allowing the spread of Communism than in alleviating the suffering of individuals under authoritarian rulers in its sphere of influence. The US foreign policy was one of appeasement of political leaders in the name of attracting their allegiance to the cause of anti-Communism and capitalism.[51] Atrocities as gruesome and widespread as those committed by the Nazis in the Second World War were taking place unchecked. Western Europe remained the stronghold of human rights protection. Although political violence was not an alien concept (Greece, Spain and Portugal all experienced periods of dictatorial regimes) and the Communist bloc was the nextdoor neighbour, the Western Europeans represented the driving force behind the campaign against torture.[52]

It was in this unstable and often hostile political climate that Amnesty International highlighted for the first time the magnitude of the problem of the spreading use of torture, declaring in its 1973 Annual Report that the practice had taken on 'epidemic proportions'.[53] Amnesty International was not alone in sounding the alarm – the International Commission of Jurists (ICJ) was conducting independent inquiries into the legal practices of various countries in the world, acknowledging in its reports that there were breaches of human rights and that torture was being used on prisoners who were often held without trial.[54] The United Nations were also concerned about the use of political coercion and discrimination, reported from Chile, South Africa, Argentina and Algiers, to name but a few.[55]

The ICJ formulated this continued recourse to torture as a problem of political will, because the existing legal provisions already contained a prohibition on the practice. Amnesty International observed the problem of torture in its entirety – as a breakdown of legal procedure, as a political method of coercion and intimidation of the opposition, as a social problem of the morals and ethics of those who participated in torture and other inhuman treatment of fellow individuals.[56] Amnesty emerged as the moral entrepreneur of the campaign to establish a new behavioural norm and to effect a comprehensive prohibition on the practice of torture. The organisation produced a number of country reports aimed at raising awareness of what went on under some military dictatorships.[57] It participated in and organised a number of conferences discussing the use of torture and the possible avenues for its effective prohibition. Amnesty's *Report on Torture* of 1973 highlighted that:

> The widespread use of torture is alarming in itself, but what is especially alarming is that the consensus against torture is being weakened not only by its constant violation but by the attitude of people in general. Many people are indifferent and some appear ready to accept the practice, and to say so in public.[58]

The organisation identified a trend towards allowing torture to trickle back into society, as had been the case following previous prohibitions on its use. AI was determined to take a prominent stance on the issue, because a great number of the people affected were prisoners of conscience and they were the focus of Amnesty's work.

Amnesty began a campaign to render the practice of torture inexcusable under any circumstances. Torture had to be perceived, in the words of Amnesty's Chairman Sean MacBride, 'as unthinkable as slavery'.[59] The historical overview of the use of torture confirmed that what all previous campaigns to prohibit the use of torture had in common was that they had not aimed for a complete ban on the practice.[60] This makes the focus on an unconditional consensus against torture, as discussed in Amnesty's *Report on Torture*, one of the most important characteristics of the campaign of 1972.

Amnesty International, working closely with the International Commission of Jurists and other regional and local human rights NGOs, accumulated information about the atrocities and human rights violations that political regimes were committing worldwide. These reports exposed the scale of the problem, indicating that torture was widespread in more than 60 countries around the world.[61] The original focus of Amnesty's work in support of prisoners of conscience explains the interest of Amnesty in matters concerning the rights of prisoners, their well-being in custody, along with issues of freedom of political opinion, affirming the status of AI as one of the major norm entrepreneurs in this campaign. The political climate in which state interests came prior to individual rights combined with the growing awareness of the widespread use of torture by governments, to open a caveat for normative debate. The campaign against torture began with a petition to the UN General Assembly, which had more than one million individual signatures from all over the world and requested the UN 'to outlaw immediately the torture of prisoners around the world'.[62]

The identity and specific characteristics of the actors who initiated this normative campaign influenced the seriousness with which their claim was received by the society of states. Amnesty International is an influential NGO, and a trusted network partner with consultative status in ECOSOC, the International Labour Organisation (ILO), the United Nations Educational, Scientific and Cultural Organisation (UNESCO); the International Commission of Jurists is made up of highly qualified professionals, closely networked with government circles and awarded consultative status by ECOSOC and other UN agencies; the interest of UN agencies provided a vital normative and institutional impetus too. Amnesty's appeal for a total ban on the use of torture became, as we will see, a significant characteristic of this campaign.

Network configuration

Network configuration and issue formation in the case of the Convention against Torture took place simultaneously at a number of conferences that brought together a broad spectrum of actors. The two processes are examined separately because they have distinct dynamics. Whereas network configuration involved a process of finding the commonalities between the actors from the different fields drawn in the campaign, the process of issue formation focused on the definition of the nature and scope of the problem.

The network of support for the outlawing of torture began to materialise out of a much larger network of actors working to strengthen the human rights regime. Non-state actors who seemed to have a direct impact on the development of the new behavioural norm included professional organisations from the legal and medical fields whose efforts were linked by Amnesty International and the International Committee of the Red Cross (ICRC) to form a strong coalition (Figure 3.1). Smaller social groups such as the Swiss Committee against Torture, the World Council of Churches, the International Association of Penal Law (IAPL) and other grassroots and professional organisations also played a role by adding their voice to the campaign. As we shall see, however, the most pressure was exerted by a handful of powerful non-state organisations and communities of experts – such as the British Medical Association (BMA),[63] the International Commission of Jurists,[64] the Council for International Organisations of Medical Sciences (CIOMS),[65] Amnesty International and its branches.

At the time when Amnesty International began its campaign, scientific knowledge about the effects of torture, and other cruel, inhuman and degrading treatment was limited and scattered;[66] the ethical segment of the

Medical professionals working on the creation of scientific knowledge (Danish Medical Group)

Medical professionals working on the creation of codes of medical ethics (World Medical Association)

Legal professionals concerned with the creation of effective protection (IAPL)

Legal professionals concerned with the generation of political will (ICJ)

ICRC

| Medical aspect | Moral aspect | Legal aspect |

Volunteers and professionals working on the creation of knowledge for purposes of rehabilitation of torture survivors (British section of AI)

Volunteers from non-governmental organisations working for the protection of medical personnel under threat of torture (AI)

Amnesty International

Volunteers concerned with the creation of institutional procedures to ensure compliance with the norm (Swiss Committee Against Torture)

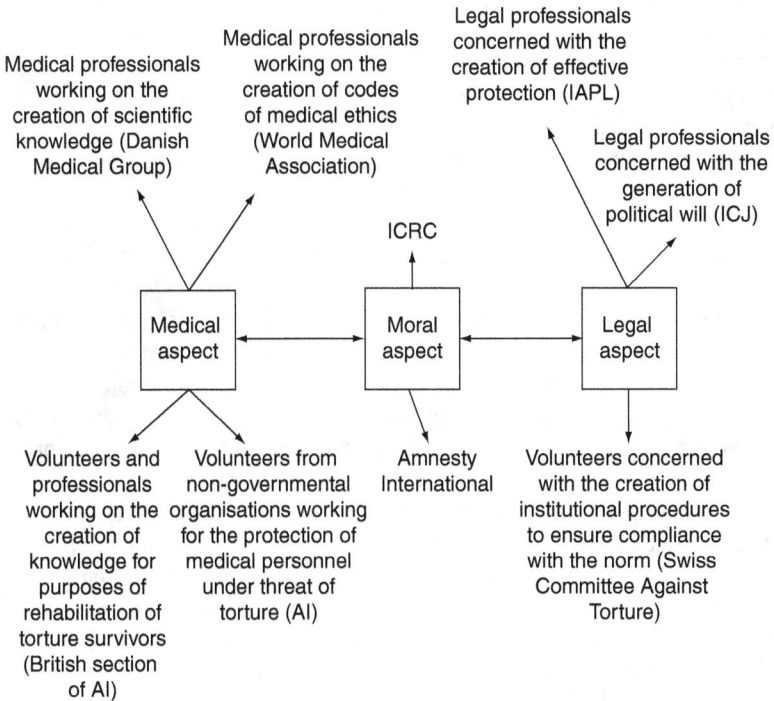

Figure 3.1 Network configuration.

campaign had the broad support of public opinion but that was not enough to impress policy-makers; and the legal campaign, while well supported by international human rights legislation (see the timeline in Box 3.1), had yet to yield practical results. The network of support emerged with the task of consolidating knowledge, expertise and ethics in order to communicate persuasively the need for action against torture.

The medical and legal segments of this complex network of support were the two major providers of scientific and technical knowledge in the normative campaign. Over time, they were drawn closer together by other professional organisations and normative networks committed to the protection of human rights and dignity. It is important to note here that some states were very supportive of the campaign for the prohibition of torture and were to a large degree responsible for the discussions and work done at the United Nations General Assembly (UNGA). The role of these states will be discussed in more detail in the following stages of the campaign, as at this stage most of the work was done by non-state actors.

The medical professionals and other members of scientific associations approached the issue of torture from a variety of angles. The medical segment of the normative network requires attention not only to understand its configuration but also because it was the context of the interplay between the forces of demand and supply of technical knowledge, which had an enormous impact on the creation of the actual Convention against Torture. Four distinct areas of interest for scientific communities developed over time – one group of medical professionals focused attention on the acquisition of medical knowledge of the sequelae (both physical and psychological) of torture and ill treatment for the purposes of rehabilitation and medical treatment of torture survivors. These medical professionals will be designated as Medical Theme 1 (MT1). A second cluster of experts were concerned with studying the sequelae of torture and ill treatment as a source of scientific proof for purposes of obtaining compensation and social benefits for torture survivors, and for participation in judicial proceedings of those who suffered ill treatment – Medical Theme 2 (MT2). A third grouping of both doctors and nurses were concerned with the issue of medical ethics in general and the participation of doctors, both directly and indirectly, in torture and ill treatment, which includes resuscitation of patients for more torture, medical exams declaring patients fit for torture, the provision of false information on patients' records that conceals or undermines the torture applied, the participation of doctors in the invention of new methods of torture, experimentation on humans – Medical Theme 3 (MT3). Medical Theme 4 (MT4) – was the concern of doctors and nurses for colleagues who may be under threat of being tortured themselves. The scientific knowledge produced by these various networks became instrumental in outlawing the use of torture.

MT1 is most clearly reflected in the work of the British and Danish medical sections of Amnesty International. Observations of the work under MT1 are based on two major sources – the biography of Helen Bamber and publications of Amnesty's medical groups in medical journals. In the early years of the campaign against torture, Bamber became a member of Amnesty International and soon came to assume an executive position. She worked directly with torture survivors and in the mid-1980s felt that the urgent actions of Amnesty did not fulfil the needs for rehabilitation, care and socialisation of those who were rescued from the torture chambers.[67] This led in 1985 to the creation of the Medical Foundation for the Care of Victims of Torture.[68] The work of Helen Bamber shows the connections that are built between issues, organisations and individuals in the process of network configuration. Individuals are the building blocks of these social networks, and the moral standards of these individuals are the glue that holds the networks together.

The focus of Medical Theme 1 is intricately related to that of Medical Theme 2. Nowhere was this more obvious than in the work of the Danish medical group of Amnesty International. It was formed in 1974 by Dr Inge Kemp Genefke, shortly after Amnesty began its worldwide campaign against torture.[69] The medical group was engaged with active scientific research into the sequelae of torture and ill treatment. Its primary goal was the accumulation of knowledge of the after-effects of torture, which would then allow medical professionals to treat survivors, and legal professionals to use medical evidence in a court of law. The Danish medical group participated in and organised professional seminars specifically focused on torture. Attention was drawn to the study of Greek torture victims in 1975 and 1976,[70] exiled Chileans in Denmark, exiled Uruguayans in France, Argentinians in Italy, with missions sent to Northern Ireland and Spain, all in the period between 1975 and 1982.[71] The majority of publications revealing the findings of the Danish medical group were in the *Danish Medical Bulletin*. The Danish Medical Group worked actively to both produce and diffuse scientific knowledge. There were difficulties and limitations in the process of research, because so little was known about the psychological after-effects of physical abuse and not many people were willing to come forward as subjects of such research.

In 1982 the Amnesty International Danish medical group extended its activities and reached ordinary doctors and nurses who worked in hospitals. Dr Genefke initiated the creation of the Rehabilitation and Research Centre for Torture Victims (RCT), which was housed at the National Hospital of Denmark.[72] Alongside the medical examinations, which were leading to the construction of knowledge on physical and psychological sequelae of torture and ill treatment, patients were given highly skilled professional care aimed at their rehabilitation and the handling of any emergency situations. The RCT marked a moment when more marginal, unconventional research was accepted by the conventional medical profession, which gave more weight and authority to the knowledge produced.

Concerns over medical ethics (MT3) were not new but had been subdued for a considerable amount of time before being brought to the attention of the medical profession in the 1970s. One of the first works to stir discussions was Maurice Pappworth's book *Human Guinea Pigs*, which came out in 1967. Pappworth, a British doctor, described in detail 205 experiments with British patients under the National Health Service, naming the doctors who conducted the experiments. Bamber, who was his assistant at the time, recalled that the reaction to the book in public and professional circles was one of criticism and denial.[73] This illustrated that unwritten codes of medical ethics had not sufficed to protect patients at the time. The theme was picked up by the *British Medical Journal* and distinguished professors began to side with Pappworth.[74] This move amongst the British medical circles laid the foundations for the creation of codes of professional ethics.[75]

The World Medical Association (WMA) became the focal point for international discussion of medical ethics, which was one of the first concerns of the organisation in the immediate aftermath of the Second World War. The practices in concentration camps, the medical experimentation that turned into torture and the use of medical expertise to exterminate people, outraged the world and raised questions about the moral norms that bound doctors and other medical personnel. The WMA denounced 'the violations of medical ethics and the crimes committed by doctors in times of war ... [and recognised the] need to implement safeguards in human experimentation'.[76] These concerns were reinforced by the practices of dictatorships and military regimes around the world which made use of doctors and medical knowledge in appalling ways. In 1952 the WMA created a permanent Committee on Medical Ethics. A request for help was taken to the Committee by the British Medical Association in 1974 with regards to the growing crisis in Northern Ireland and the mounting concern of the doctors of the armed forces involved.[77] With the help of the BMA and other national medical organisations and the Committee on Medical Ethics, in 1975 the WMA drew up the ethical guidelines for medical practices concerning torture and other cruel, inhuman or degrading treatment or punishment in relation to detention and imprisonment. These were incorporated in the *Declaration of Tokyo*,[78] which inspired the United Nations to request the World Health Organisation to compile a code of professional ethics for medical staff as early as 1975.[79] The final version of the Draft Code of Medical Ethics was approved by the UN General Assembly in 1979.[80] These developments reveal the complex interactions between various actors on a number of different aspects of the norm outlawing the use of torture. The cooperation among them ensured that the medical community presented a thorough evaluation of the problem of torture, which was evidence that could not be ignored.

Medical Theme 4 incorporates the protection of and assistance to doctors who have become victims of torture themselves. Amnesty has reported that in some instances health professionals may be subjected to human rights violations and has furnished details of individual cases of doctors who have been under threat of imprisonment or torture and have had to flee their countries.[81] MT4 has thus become part of the larger concern for individuals under threat of torture.

The medical segment of the normative network against the use of torture has spread to incorporate a number of important issues stemming from this particular type of human rights abuse. Medical professionals responded to the normative and practical demand for accumulating scientific knowledge, which in turn helped other actors to formulate the use of torture as an issue of concern that states need to address. The organisations (medical groups and foundations) and the emerging codes of medical ethics further demonstrate the importance of 'world time' and normative context. These can be considered separately as normative achievements, but can also be perceived as an intricate part of the process of norm building.

The legal aspect of the network of supporters was represented principally by the International Commission of Jurists – an organisation of professionals which remained involved throughout the campaign for the creation of a norm prohibiting the use of torture and during the construction of the subsequent instrument for safeguarding it – the Optional Protocol of the Convention against Torture. The ICJ comprises both individual jurists and national organisations[82] and cooperates closely with a range of NGOs and IGOs.[83] According to the historian of the ICJ, during the seven years between 1963 and 1970, when Sean MacBride[84] was elected Secretary General, the commission acquired an interest in international legal reform and standards setting.[85] Since the ICJ was primarily concerned with the creation and the improvement of legal instruments for the protection of human rights, MacBride's relations with Amnesty International meant that the two organisations could combine their efforts and expertise.[86] MacBride became another link between the moral campaign and the expert campaign for the creation of an effective ban on torture.

In the international campaign against torture, the ICJ 'used their technical expertise and elite contacts to lobby public officials for limits on state power'.[87] The organisation took an active part in the creation and adoption of various standards of professional ethics and the Standard Minimum Rules for the Treatment of Prisoners and Offenders. The ICJ was also an important participant in the discussions of the Draft Convention Against Torture and took part in the drafting of other regional documents dealing with the issue. The ICJ cooperated with a couple of other organisations that contributed greatly to the campaign with their enthusiasm, expertise and practical ideas. One of these was the Swiss Committee against Torture, founded by Jean-Jacques Gautier in 1975.[88] The CSCT was very active in drawing attention and support for the campaign against torture. Gautier began his work with a very specific idea – to produce an effective legal norm against torture, which will have provisions to avoid impunity.[89] It was only due to the close cooperation between Gautier, De Vargas and Niall MacDermot (the Secretary General of the ICJ at the time) that this idea materialised and later became the foundation of the Optional Protocol to the CAT.[90]

Another organisation that deserves attention is the World Council of Churches in International Affairs. The actions of churches against torture has been documented by the Catholic Institute for International Relations, which, for example, published a report on torture in Southwest Africa, which was banned prior to publication by the South African authorities. The report included a number of letters from priests to the authorities expressing concerns about the use of torture by police and the negligence of medical staff towards torture victims; it further demanded that torture be condemned 'without any qualifications or relativization'.[91] US church-men who visited Uruguay in 1972 reported the widespread use of physical and psychological torture on political prisoners in the country.[92] The CSCT reported on its joint activities with the World Council of Churches in the campaign against torture[93] and the ICJ published a report from the 30th Meeting of the World Council of Churches' Central Committee, which discussed the need to celebrate the 30th Anniversary of the Universal Declaration of Human Rights by taking special actions to eliminate torture.[94]

The International Association of Penal Law was an integral part of the campaign against torture, as it submitted a Draft Convention against Torture to the UN General Assembly. The IAPL had been working closely with the ICJ, Amnesty International, the CSCT and the ICRC to prepare the draft, which, as became known later, was very close in substance to the proposal submitted by the government of Sweden.[95] The activities of the organisation, however, have not been expressly focused on the fight against torture and this is why IAPL is only considered here as a marginal actor.

The medical and the legal aspects of the campaign against torture were drawn together by two powerful moral entrepreneurs – Amnesty International and the International Committee of the Red Cross. These two organisations worked to enhance the cohesion needed for a better chance for the campaigners to lobby nation-states. AI and the ICRC fused the ethical, medical and legal aspects of torture to form an authoritative network for the protection of individuals against the excesses of secret state activities or anyone else.

For its part, Amnesty International organised a number of conferences bringing together the representatives of the legal and medical professions. The Conference for the Abolition of Torture in Paris in 1973 ended with a list of recommendations for action by the legal profession, the medical experts, trade unions, business enterprises, educational and religious organisations, etc. Another seminar, organised by Amnesty International in Strasbourg, emphasised the need for the creation of codes of professional conduct, especially in spheres that are prone to abuse, such as medical ethics, police ethics, military ethics and legal ethics. This seminar was attended by more than 90 participants, representing nation-states and organisations such as the WMA, the World Psychological Association, the International Commission of Jurists, the ICRC and the International Association of Lawyers.[96]

The International Committee of the Red Cross played an important role as well, acting as a bridge between the medical and the legal aspects of the issue of torture. On the one hand, the organisation had extensive first-hand experience with torture victims, as the ICRC is the only organisation which can visit prisoners both in peacetime and war, even behind enemy lines.[97] On the other hand, the ICRC has the trust of and some influence over national governments due to its high professionalism and continued political neutrality. The ICRC has played an important role in constructing the principles of the Geneva Conventions and consequently in successfully lobbying states to accept them, making it an organisation with ample experience of norm creation and persuasion.

Normative closure was reached in the campaign against torture, as is illustrated by the widespread consensus that this practice should be made illegal. Since there was little disagreement that torture is wrong, most of the negotiations among non-state actors were centred on discussions of how best to formulate the issue so that policy-makers have limited room to wriggle out of their responsibilities to uphold human rights.

Several important conclusions stem from this discussion of network configuration. First, normative networks can be in a perpetual state of flux. They may be unstable as the configuration of the participating actors changes with the progress of norm evolution. Some actors leave the campaign – like Helen Bamber, who after years of working with Amnesty International became the founder of the Medical Foundation for the Care of Torture Victims and shifted her humanitarian efforts to the field of care and rehabilitation of survivors. The World Medical Association and other regional or national medical associations also left the overall campaign against torture after the codes of medical ethics were agreed upon by the UN General Assembly. There were also actors who became active partners in the campaign at a later stage. In the case of CAT, these actors were national governments (such as those of Sweden, the Netherlands, Austria, Costa Rica and Paraguay) in favour of the normative idea to prohibit the use of torture.

The second concluding point is that the various themes advanced by the network of supporters are interdependent. The medical and ethical aspects of the campaign, for example, are so closely interrelated that their separation is artificial. Medical knowledge influenced moral norms and vice versa to the extent that it is hard to say which influence is stronger and which influence came first. Legality and morality too are inseparable as legal norms are not merely technical scripts – they reflect the morality and sense of justice of the society that they govern.

The normative network against the use of torture became very strong and influential. Medical research of the sequelae of torture furnished solid scientific proof that torture is a very cruel practice that leaves behind physically and psychologically broken individuals. The information gathering by doctors and legal professionals that took place independently in the 1960s and 1970s helped the issue of torture surface on the international agenda. In this case, scientific knowledge not only sided with the normative idea but also supplied a strong impetus for its evolution. Global civil society represented by Amnesty, the World Council of Churches, the Swiss Committee against Torture and other NGOs, supported by the accumulated knowledge and expertise, became a normative network that was hard to ignore even in the climate of the Cold War. The social demand for the development of medical knowledge soon became political (when nation-states got involved in the campaign) and the issue began to gather vital momentum.

Issue formation

Setting the limits of what exactly constitutes torture, cruel, inhuman and degrading treatment or punishment was central to outlawing these practices. Issue formation is the stage at which the network of support for the new norm determines the substance and limits to the new norm. Issue formation is most influential when based on scientific closure and consensus, and this campaign was successful in reaching consensus and gaining overwhelming support. This stage includes not only the formulation of a norm in technical and normative terms but also an agreement on its parameters and normative scope, i.e., whether the norm applies in all circumstances or only in some, whether there are exceptions to it or not, and so on. Defining torture is no easy task as the experience of physical or psychological ill treatment is different for every individual. Amnesty International discussed the problem of definition in its first comprehensive *Report on Torture* (1973). The authors commented on the shortcomings of some of the already existing legal texts. The Geneva Conventions, for example, take torture to mean: 'suffering inflicted on a person to obtain from him or a third person confessions or information'.[98] Here Amnesty emphasised the lack of reference to degree, which is covered by the term 'suffering' and the definition was considered insufficient to safeguard individuals. As earlier noted in Gardiner's Report on interrogation methods for detainees in Northern Ireland, however, 'what people can stand in relation to both physical exhaustion and mental disorientation [varies greatly] ... [and] no precise limits for interrogators ... can safely be specified'.[99] This observation made the task of coming up with wording that would neither compromise the individual's well-being or allow perpetrators to avoid justice by denying they had caused suffering, all the more difficult.

Amnesty also expressed disapproval at the wording of the European Commission on Human Rights, which said that 'torture is ... generally an aggravated form of inhuman treatment ... [where] the notion of inhuman treatment covers at least such treatment as deliberately causes severe suffering, mental or physical, which in the particular situation is unjustifiable'.[100] The issue of justifiability was one to which Amnesty drew special attention as a possible slippery slope. Justifiability often rests on the concept of effectiveness, which means that if torture is found to be effective, then it could be recognised as justifiable. Regardless of whether torture was used for extracting information, or for political repression, whether the practice was effective or not: 'no act is more a contradiction of our humanity than the deliberate infliction of pain by one human being on another, the deliberate attempt over a period of time to kill a man without his dying ... it is the ultimate human corruption'.[101] The definition arrived at by Amnesty International in its first comprehensive report on torture is the following: 'Torture is the systematic and deliberate infliction of acute pain in any form by one person on another, or on a third person, in order to accomplish the purpose of the former against the will of the latter.'[102]

Scientific understanding of the after-effects of torture began to evolve tentatively after the end of the Second World War when concentration camp and labour camp survivors were in need of both medical and psychological treatment and care.[103] What began as a scientific study to establish a medical basis for disability compensation, extended to the comparison of the sequelae exhibited by concentration camp and torture survivors and thus the basis of medical knowledge in this sphere.[104] In-depth scientific knowledge took time to evolve – it was not until the late 1960s and the 1970s that relevant medical discussions emerged on the pages of medical journals and other specialised publications. The publications of Amnesty International and medical journals allow us to begin to examine and understand this complex process of knowledge development.[105]

A number of important conclusions were reached by medical professionals, which helped define the technical and moral scope of this problem. These conclusions were supplemented by the independent findings of other non-state actors, which pointed towards closing the scientific debate on the need to regulate behaviour in such a way as to make torture unjustifiable. First, it was established that the effects of torture constitute 'a disease of a traumatic nature.... This means that torture should be studied in regard to symptoms and diagnosis to gain insight into etiology, treatment and profylaxis.'[106] Second, medical research over the years had shown that there were sequelae that were explicitly related to particular kinds of torture (allowing this type of structured knowledge to be used in the legal system) but also that humans reacted differently to the type of extreme stress that torture and ill treatment cause.[107] The continued scientific research into the after-effects of torture echoed a statement made by Amnesty International experts in 1971 – interrogation procedures aimed at 'causing malfunction or breakdown of a man's mental processes ... constitute as great an assault on the inherent dignity of the human person as more traditional techniques of physical torture'.[108] It is widely accepted in medical circles today that when people are subjected to imprisonment and continuous extreme stress related to the anticipation of or indeed to suffering physical or mental damage, they develop long-lasting physical and mental sequelae.

The growing understanding of the after-effects of torture and the outrage at human experimentation necessitated the creation of unified principles of medical ethics. At its very first conference on the abolition of torture, Amnesty International made recommendations to the medical profession to safeguard their research against the possibility of it being used for torture or other forms of ill treatment, and to refuse participation in torture and in training others for the use of medical knowledge to harm individual humans.[109] The principal efforts towards the creation of ethical codes were expounded by the members of the WMA in the *Declaration of Tokyo*,

> The doctor shall not countenance, condone or participate in the practice of torture or other forms of cruel, inhuman or degrading procedures, whatever the offence of which the victim of such procedures is suspected, accused or guilty, and whatever the victim's beliefs or motives, and in all situations, including armed conflict and civil strife.[110]

This declaration, along with the *Resolution on the Role of the Nurse in the Care of Detainees and Prisoners* (1975) and the *Declaration of Hawaii* (1977) illustrated the resolve of medical professionals to uphold their moral principles in their work and to protect colleagues under abusive regimes. The declaration of the WMA and WPA inspired the UN General Assembly to further institutionalise such normative principles as another safeguard against the sovereign powers of oppressive governments. These ethical guidelines helped construct the use of torture as unethical and unacceptable, and thus promoted scientific closure on the political plane, planting the above principles into the general social normative context.

Although the acceptance of the principles of medical ethics go some way towards defining the scope of torture and creating some individual safeguards, effective change in the attitudes and actions of states can better be achieved by establishing firmer international legal standards. There are two major avenues to establishing and defining principles of law – the legal professionals, who construct new principles which are then proposed to policy-makers; and courts of law, which in the process of interpreting the law and making decisions lay the foundations of new principles.

The efforts of the legal profession were reflected most clearly in the work of the ICJ. The organisation was liaising with other nongovernmental organisations, as well as with international governmental organisations, including UN agencies, to support the principles of upholding the rule of law, protecting human rights and individuals. The ICJ employed various tactics to influence nation-states, such as sending trial observers, producing country reports, organising public protests and committees of inquiry, applying diplomacy or outright negative publicity. Pressure on nation-states was seen as one of the ways to change the attitudes of governments towards the issue of torture. A report of the Secretary General of the ICJ confirmed that the practice of torture was not only contrary to the laws of almost any nation but also that explicit prohibitions of torture existed in a number of regional and international legal instruments.[111] Hence, the problem as formulated by the ICJ was the lack of political will to implement and abide by these regulations. The solution was to generate the necessary political will by constructing firmer legal rules that would be more effective in directing states to avoid the use of torture, cruel, inhuman or degrading treatment or punishment.

Various courts of law adjudicated issues relating to victims of torture and other ill treatment. As early as 1969, the European Court of Human Rights examined the issue of torture in the *Greek Case*, finding for the first time that particular methods of extracting information constituted torture.[112] The report of the European Commission on Human Rights in these proceedings addressed two important aspects of torture – its definition and its justifiability. Since Article 3 of the European Convention on Human Rights prohibits the use of torture, and other inhuman or degrading treatment or punishment in similar words as the Universal Declaration of Human Rights (UNDHR) (Article 5),[113] the discussion of the meaning of these terms was guaranteed to have implications that reached far beyond the borders of the European Union. The European Commission on Human Rights stated:

> All torture must be inhuman and degrading treatment, and inhuman treatment also degrading.

Inhuman treatment covers at least such treatment as deliberately causes severe suffering, mental or physical, which in the particular situation is unjustifiable.

Torture connotes inhuman treatment which has a purpose, such as the obtaining of information or confessions, or the infliction of punishment and it is generally an aggravated form of inhuman treatment.[114]

This elaboration of the European Commission on Human Rights served as another confirmation both of the importance of the issue of torture, and the definition of the actions that constituted torture. There were to be further discussions of actions that constituted torture, inhuman and cruel treatment, which further contributed to solidifying consensus, in technical and normative terms, on the need to outlaw the practice.

The minority report of Lord Gardiner on 'the five techniques' of in-depth interrogation (keeping detainees hooded, depriving them of sleep, food and water, subjecting them to continuous monotonous noise, keeping them standing against the wall in a required posture) that were deployed by the British Government in Northern Ireland, clearly placed these techniques in the realm of cruel, inhuman and degrading treatment.[115] Although Lord Gardiner commented that these proceedings were strictly within the domain of domestic jurisdiction and hence *sub judice* before the European Court on Human Rights, the impact of this report was significant in that it clearly distinguished between acceptable and unacceptable, moral and immoral treatment of prisoners. The report also declared that emergency conditions did not constitute a sufficient reason to justify the use of secret and illegal interrogation methods,[116] further outlining the limits of its justifiability. This issue became one of the key aspects of the Convention against Torture. The question of whether the use of torture, cruel, inhuman and degrading treatment could be justified by emergency situations was also discussed by the European Court in the *Greek Case*, where some believe that the court left the question open to interpretation.[117] In the case of *Ireland* v. *United Kingdom* (1976) the European Commission on Human Rights corrected this misunderstanding by concluding that 'The Convention prohibits in absolute terms torture and inhuman or degrading treatment or punishment, irrespective of the victim's conduct. Article 3 makes no provision for exceptions and ... there can be no derogation there from even in the event of a public emergency threatening the life of the nation'.[118]

The process of legally formulating the problem of torture benefited greatly from the growing medical understanding of the consequences that torture survivors experience. Although it is very rarely that a direct link is drawn between the advancement of medical knowledge and the development of the law, the link exists and legal professionals have made good use of it. The findings of medical experiments on the effects of solitary confinement, the exposure to noise and the anticipation of ill treatment have provided the basis for lawyers to claim that the use of such techniques amounts to ill treatment. Hence, the findings of Lord Gardiner's report and the conclusions of the court in the *Irish Case* have not been reached independently of the development of scientific knowledge. The existence of the network of supporters who have concentrated their efforts on accumulating evidence that torture should be prohibited has thus made it easier for actors from different fields to work in unison and in the name of the same cause.

Closure on the technical parameters of the proposed norm to outlaw torture was reached gradually, not so much as a result of debates among actors with conflicting views, but due to the complexity and multilayered character of the norm. Technical knowledge and standards were created in more than one professional field in a sustained effort to prevent torture perpetrators from avoiding justice. Evidence of technical closure can be found in the unified position of non-state actors in their attempt to persuade states to adopt a new norm, and also in the lack of debate over the technical parameters of the norm. Professional ethical principles emerged and were agreed on at the international level; legal decisions at the national and regional levels signalled the acceptance of the prohibition on torture; medical professionals agreed that the consequences of torture were of a traumatic nature and rendered the practice unacceptable in the 'civilised world'. All of these developments indicated an expanding agreement, which was becoming so solid, as not to allow states much room for political manoeuvre.

Dialogue with the conservative actors

Studies of network configuration and issue formation have been drawing attention mainly to the work of non-state actors – NGOs, epistemic communities, professional organisations. But since it is ultimately down to states to create international norms that can effectively guide and regulate behaviour, we need to evaluate their normative positions too. The existing research on the Campaign against Torture has tended to consider separately the work done by non-state actors and the activities of states who supported the need for a prohibition on torture.[119] Reports from various conferences organised by Amnesty International show, however, that delegations from some states had participated in the discussions along with non-state actors.[120] The distinction between non-state and state actors in this case is not sufficient to classify the position of the actors in favour or against the development of this norm.

When reports of non-state conferences and workshops on the issue of torture and other forms of ill treatment are examined in conjunction with the records of the discussions that have taken place at the UN General Assembly and its Third Committee, it becomes obvious that the governments whose representatives had taken part in the conferences were also those which had initiated and played a leading role in UN discussions of state attitudes and actions concerning the problem of torture.[121] These states, which linked the activities and efforts of non-state actors to the influence of the UN, played the role of moral leaders. The states which attempted to downplay the problem of torture or in any way deny the need for an effective international instrument to ban its use, will be considered here as the conservative actors. In this campaign there were no states that explicitly defended the use of torture, even though, as reports published by Amnesty International and the International Commission of Jurists indicate, there was ample evidence that many governments had authorised its practice. Open support for torture as state policy was made unthinkable by the Universal Declaration of Human Rights, in which states had agreed in principle on the individual's right to be free from torture and other cruel, inhuman or degrading treatment or punishment. The normative context of the 1970s had fundamentally changed with the coming into force of the International Covenant of Civil and Political Rights (ICPR) (1966). The task of the moral leaders in the beginning of the campaign against torture was thus to generate consensus for the creation of an *effective* instrument banning torture and other forms of ill treatment. The records of the discussions on this issue can be found in the meetings of the Third Committee of the UNGA.

The problem of torture was raised at the United Nations by Amnesty's petition carrying more than one million signatures.[122] In November 1973, the delegations of Sweden, the Netherlands, Austria, Costa Rica and Trinidad and Tobago prepared a draft resolution, which stated that the General Assembly would examine the issue of 'torture, and other inhuman, cruel and degrading treatment or punishment in relation to detention and imprisonment in a future session'.[123] The influence of the work of Amnesty, ICJ, IAPL has been acknowledged by nation-states at the UNGA meetings,[124] as well as by authors who have related detailed accounts of the historical development of the Convention against Torture.[125] The basis of the relationship between states and the non-state actors had been the provision of information. Securing a constant flow of professional advice and information regarding atrocities, as well as possessing a fast-flowing channel for disseminating this information, made these non-state actors valuable allies in a coalition to create a new behavioural norm. Although much of the background work on the new norm was done primarily by these non-state actors, the political effort committed to the cause by the supportive states was undoubtedly critical.

The norm prohibiting torture and other ill treatment was elaborated in direct response to a humanitarian disaster. This context of an increased sense of urgency speeded up negotiations and decision-making at the international level. The deliberations at the Third Committee of the UNGA in 1973 and 1974, following Resolution 3059, which outlined the concerns of the UN General Assembly about the question of torture, and the resolve of the organisation to examine this issue further,[126] were entirely engaged with the situation in Chile – representatives of states from different parts of the world expressed their concerns about the scale of the practice of torture.[127] The representative of Chile used three lines of defence – that torture was not a governmental practice, although there might have been isolated incidents; that other states, in particular the USSR, were using torture against their own citizens; and that, in any case, the concern with the domestic affairs of Chile ran counter to the principle of sovereignty laid out in Article 2(7) of the UN Charter.[128] Although the coalition against the practice of torture seemed quite strong, the growing cohesion of the non-aligned movement and the increasing concern to uphold the principle of sovereignty against attempts to meddle with the domestic policies of states stood in its way.[129] The conservative actors attempted to change the agenda by downplaying the problem of torture and by emphasising the importance and precedence of the principles of sovereignty, non-intervention and self-determination. The normative leaders, however, were not prepared to let the discussion of torture slip away. Delegates from Sweden, the Netherlands, the UK, France, Norway, Austria and the Federal Republic of Germany focused on persuading the other delegations of the need to establish an international norm that effectively outlawed the use of torture, cruel, inhuman and degrading treatment. The proactive delegations not only vigorously advocated policy creation, they were engaged in constructing and supporting the texts of various resolutions for action, codes of professional ethics and the very drafts of the Convention against Torture.[130] Discussions were not merely political, they were normative and grounded in the emerging knowledge about torture and related practices. Some of the supporting states were regulars at nongovernmental forums, so they were in a position to take full advantage of the emerging normative-technical consensus.

The dialogues at the Third Committee of the UNGA were making slow progress but through extensive discussions the list of supporters for the new norm was growing (for the dynamics of the international negotiations, see Table 3.1). Poland declared its full support for all draft resolutions condemning torture,[131] as did Denmark,[132] Romania,[133] Pakistan[134] and Yugoslavia.[135] The campaign against torture continued with small, tentative steps, which did not counter to the concerns of Chile and the other non-aligned states (including African and Middle Eastern states who disagreed with the development of the new norm).

In November 1974 the UNGA adopted Resolution 3218, which stressed the need to develop codes of professional ethics for police and other law

Table 3.1 Dialogue with the conservative actors

	States not in opposition to the creation of the new norm	States openly expressing support for current status quo	States that do not participate actively in the creation of the new norm	States expressing open opposition
1973	Sweden, the Netherlands, Austria, Trinidad and Tobago (normative entrepreneurs)	Chile, USSR, South Africa, Yugoslavia	Poland, Romania, Denmark, Pakistan	None
1974	Sweden, the Netherlands, UK, France, Norway, Austria, the Federal Republic of Germany, USA, Poland, Romania, Denmark, Pakistan,	Chile, South Africa, USSR	Portugal, Mexico, Greece, Australia, Belgium, Saudi Arabia, Syrian Arab emirates, Costa Rica, Lesotho, Spain, Ireland	None
1976–1977	Same as above, Portugal, Mexico, Greece, Australia, Belgium, Saudi Arabia, Syrian Arab emirates, Costa Rica, Lesotho, Spain, Ireland			None
1978	All of the above, Chile, South Africa, USSR			None

Note
The information included in the above table is based on the discussions and the opinions voiced at the Third Committee of the UN General Assembly.

enforcement officials, requested the World Health Organisation (WHO) to take into account the work of the WMA and draft an outline of the principles of medical ethics, and decided that the General Assembly would deal with the issue of torture and other inhuman, cruel, degrading treatment or punishment in its next session.[136] In 1975, the 5th UN Congress on the Prevention of Crime and the Treatment of Offenders took place and gave further impetus to the campaign. The Congress was attended by 'representatives from 101 states, [many of whom] were at the highest level of influence and competence'.[137] The Congress's General Rapporteur noted that the heated discussions reflected 'passionate concern over the use of torture'.[138] The adoption of Resolutions 3452 and 3453 in December 1975 is evidence of the building up of normative momentum. Resolution 3452 contained the Declaration on the Protection of All Persons from Being Subjected to Torture and Other Cruel, Inhuman or Degrading Treatment or Punishment. This declaration was an important stepping stone in the evolution of the norm outlawing the use of torture. Marc Schreiber, who was at the time the Director of the Division of Human Rights, commented that the ease and swiftness with which this declaration was adopted was indicative of the importance that the organisation attached to the problem of torture and other forms of ill treatment.[139] The American representative found the voting unanimity suspicious in that governments seemed to adopt the resolution too easily, while the problem of torture persisted around the world. Indeed, some conservative actors might have acted in the hope of adopting a weak document, while wishing to continue their unrestrained domestic powers. Another possible explanation is that some states might have hoped that a speedy adoption of a resolution would sideline the discussions of torture and the issue could then be quickly forgotten. This might account for the rigorous discussions that followed in 1977 when Sweden advocated the need for the creation of a binding convention against torture, to which I will return in the next stage.

Resolution 3453 of 1975 requested the Commission on Human Rights to 'study the question of torture and any necessary steps for: ensuring effective observance of the Declaration ... and the formulation of a body of principles for the protection of all persons under any form of detention or imprisonment'.[140] Discussions at the Third Committee continued throughout 1976 with no practical outcome. Many states continued to express their support for the evolving new norm.[141] Delegates often turned their attention to the situation in Chile, which made the Chilean representatives uneasy and defensive, and they resorted to previous defensive tactics.[142] The impasse had to be overcome for the norm to continue to evolve.

In this stage of norm development the logic of persuasion and argumentation can play a more effective role than the logic of consequences. Since the issue of torture had no direct strategic consequences for the national security of states, governments could not turn to the logic of consequences as a reason to discontinue or hinder negotiations in this particular issue area.[143] Without the hidden breaks that states take advantage of to exit discussions, and within a context of appropriateness created by the Universal Declaration of Human Rights, conservative actors had little space to manoeuvre, not least because they did not wish to stand out from the community of 'civilised nations'.

The stage of bargaining and persuasion in the evolution of this particular norm did not draw too much public attention (outside the work of the non-state actors who were directly involved). The pressure on the conservative states was mounting, as there seemed to be no good reason to back out of negotiations (or in this case the process of persuasion). It was also difficult to find a sufficient reason to oppose the development of the new norm, which was established almost unexpectedly in 1977.

Political closure

Closure on the norm prohibiting the use of torture and other cruel, inhuman and degrading treatment or punishment was documented in Resolution 32/62 of the UNGA, which requested the Commission on Human Rights to prepare a draft Convention against Torture and other cruel, inhuman or degrading treatment or punishment.[144] Closure on the permissibility of the use of torture was achieved partly because the imperative switched to the problem of making the declaration against torture effective and partly because reports continued to mount from non-state actors about atrocities committed by governments around the world. The debates at the UNGA, which preceded the political closure, were focused on the question of whether there was a need for yet another legal instrument prohibiting torture.[145] On 28 October 1977, Sweden, one of the most active states on this issue, submitted a draft resolution – A/C.3/32/L.13 – to the General Assembly requesting that work on the creation of a convention against torture begin.[146] The discussions that followed at the meetings of the Third Committee took the form more of praise of the effort and commitment of support than of a debate between opponents. No opposition was raised in all four sessions of the committee that examined this question.[147] Forty delegations became sponsors and co-sponsors to the draft resolution; the latter was adopted without a vote by the Third Committee and then by the UNGA.[148]

The discussions at the Third Committee were quite revealing of the intentions and concerns of the participating states. The delegations of Sweden and the Netherlands pointed out that, although an agreement on the moral issue was achieved, their work was not complete until a legally binding international instrument was put in place.[149] Other delegations expressed their support, emphasising their deep regrets that torture was still taking place around the world, expressing concerns for some of the most extreme cases, which came to the attention of the world community (Chile, Steve Biko in South Africa, the conflict in the Middle East) and commenting on the need for an effective instrument that would induce urgent action.[150]

The build-up to the point of political closure was a lengthy process of arduous persuasion, but all the preliminary work done by NGOs, epistemic communities and professional organisations, along with the proactive states, paid off at this crucial stage. The norm prohibiting the use of torture under any circumstances, by any authority or individual was established and affirmed in the international normative context by the agreement of the members of the UNGA on the need to create a convention that would entail legal obligations. This agreement was solidly grounded in the norm-ative and scientific closures achieved earlier on in the campaign. These left little doubt about the effects of torture, cruel, inhuman and degrading treat-ment or punishment, and could not be ignored by policy-makers. The normative idea was situated within an existing normative context and cam-paigners had constructed a link between the broader concern for human rights and dignity and the issue of torture.

The case of *Filartiga* v. *Pena*, in the US, made legal history in 1980, but also reaffirmed the fact that political closure had taken place. The case was adjudicated by a US court under the Alien Tort Claims Statute, which allows US Federal courts 'to take original jurisdiction over tort actions brought by aliens "committed in violation of the law of nations or a treaty of the United Nations"'.[151] Both Dr Filartiga (the plaintiff, whose son was killed in police custody) and Pena (the defendant, a member of the police department) were from Paraguay, where the events unfolded. Since the Paraguayan legal system failed to charge the police department with the murder of his son, Filartiga and his daughter decided to try and use the Alien Tort Act against Pena, who was temporarily in the United States. The Court of the Second Circuit confirmed its jurisdiction over the pro-ceedings, stating '[a]mong the rights universally proclaimed by all nations ... is the right to be free from physical torture. Indeed ... the torturer has become – like the pirate and slave trader before him – *hostis humani generic*, an enemy of all humankind'.[152] This historical decision of the Second Circuit Court of the US officially confirmed that the norm prohib-iting torture had become part of the body of customary international law.

Once it was agreed that an effective prohibition of torture should be created, all efforts and discussions were concentrated on the wording and the construction of the convention, confirming that negotiations had reached a point of no return. The agreement on the existence of the norm was no longer questionable; derogation from the norm would incur public criticism.

Legalisation

The Swiss Committee against Torture put forward a proposal for a convention similar to the Geneva Conventions, allowing a designated international body to visit places of detention without requiring government approval well before the creation of CAT.[153] The International Commission of Jurists, however, sensing state resistance to such far-reaching measures, insisted that all efforts be concentrated on the creation of the strongest possible convention, with attempts for improving its effectiveness preserved for a later stage.[154] This decision was well calculated. Resolution 32/62 requested the Commission on Human Rights (CHR) to prepare a draft convention. Since discussions were foreseen to be prolonged and difficult, the CHR proposed that an open-ended working group be created to draw up the first draft of the convention.[155] Sweden and IAPL both submitted draft conventions. The proposal of IAPL reflected the work of NGOs and specialist organisations and was prepared at a Conference in Syracuse in 1977. IAPL worked closely with the ICJ, Amnesty International and the ICRC and later sought the opinion of a large number of experts.[156] It later became clear that IAPL's draft differed very little from the Swedish one.[157] This is not surprising, since the representatives of Sweden had attended almost all conferences organised or sponsored by Amnesty. Moreover, Amnesty International, the ICJ and the ICRC were represented at all meetings of the working group, preparing the draft convention under the Commission on Human Rights. This is yet another example of the close cooperation among state and non-state actors in this normative campaign.

The Swedish draft convention was an elaboration of the already existing declaration against torture. The discussions that took place in the working group of the CHR are available from the official records of ECOSOC – 34th to the 40th session of the Commission on Human Rights (1976 to 1984). The Swedish jurist, Justice Hans Danelius and the Dutch delegate to the UN, Herman Burgers, compiled a handbook on the Convention against Torture in which they describe in intricate detail the deliberations of the working group under the CHR.[158] Here I will focus only on those parts of the convention that have been influenced by the field work of the non-state actors and the scientific knowledge obtained by the professional groups.

In 1978, the CHR was concerned mainly with procedure for preparing the draft convention and with the presentation of the proposed drafts.[159]

It was not until the working group met in 1979 that substantive discussions on the actual text began. Article 1 of both the declaration against torture and the draft convention contain the definition of torture (and other cruel, inhuman or degrading treatment or punishment).[160] Needless to say, these were some of the longest discussions. The Swedish draft proposed that Article 1 be identical in the declaration and the convention. The delegations of the US, Portugal, Switzerland, Denmark and the UK all proposed that changes be introduced and the definition made both more elaborate and less open to interpretation (because interpretation can open the door to undermining of the prohibition).[161] The suggestions of Portugal and Switzerland both concerned the use of medical knowledge: Portugal proposed that the 'abuse of psychiatry' had to be included as a form of torture, while Switzerland insisted that 'medical or scientific experiments, if not serving any therapeutic purpose', can also be deemed torture.[162] It is impossible to deny that continuous reports of the abuse of psychiatry in the USSR,[163] the discussion of human experimentation[164] and the growing volume of medical knowledge regarding the after-effects of torture, all contributed to the concerns that these states voiced. The US representative raised the question of whether torture practised by public officials should be treated differently, and proposed that the term public official should be further specified. Amnesty has commented on the role of public officials in the practice of torture in a number of its reports.[165]

The Swedish delegation took into account the discussions and proposals discussed above and finalised Article 1, which was later adopted without a vote by the UNGA and became the opening article of the convention:

> For the purposes of this Convention, the term torture means any act by which severe pain or suffering, whether physical or mental, is intentionally inflicted on a person for such purposes as obtaining from him or a third person information or confession, punishing him for an act he or a third person has committed or is suspected of having committed, or intimidating him or coercing him or a third person, or for any reason based on discrimination of any kind, when such pain or suffering is inflicted by or at the instigation of or with the consent or acquiescence of a public official or other person acting in an official capacity. It does not include pain or suffering arising only from, inherent in or incidental to lawful sanctions.[166]

The discussion within the working group moved on to the question of the obligations of states, which are contained in Articles 2 and 3 of the original draft. While Article 2 of the Swedish draft obliged states to 'ensure that torture and other cruel, inhuman or degrading treatment or punishment does not take place within [their] jurisdiction',[167] other delegations pointed out that, while states can adopt measures to prevent torture, they could not ensure that torture would never occur. The final version of this article, adopted by the working group, reads as follows: 'Each State Party shall take effective legislative, administrative, judicial or other measures to prevent acts of torture in any territory under its jurisdiction'[168] (this is also the text of the paragraph as included in the convention of 1984). Article 2, paragraph 2, put an end to the deliberations as to whether torture could be justified in emergency circumstances, thus incorporating the decision of the European Court of Human Rights in the *Greek Case* and the *Irish Case*.[169] The lessons of the Nuremberg and Tokyo War Crime Tribunals are echoed in Article 2, paragraph 3, which announced that 'an order from a superior officer or a public authority may not be invoked as a justification of torture'.

The discussions at the working group continued by article and topic, including issues such as expulsion and extradition,[170] punishment for torture,[171] jurisdiction over the offence of torture[172] and further procedural issues, concerned more with the implementation of the norm than its substance. Some of the longest discussions concerned the issues of implementation[173] and universal jurisdiction,[174] both clashing with the principle of state sovereignty. The draft convention was ready by 1981, when only minor corrections were still being discussed,[175] and the question of torture itself was only briefly touched upon until 1984.[176] The stage of legalisation was completed by the adoption of the Convention against Torture by the UNGA on 10 December 1984. The General Assembly considered only the texts left in brackets by the Commission on Human Rights and ECOSOC and adopted the text almost as prepared by the working group.

Operationalisation

The Convention against Torture entered into force in 1987, but concerns regarding its operationalisation remained. One particular proposal for operationalisation was formulated by Jean-Jacques Gautier and put forward to the Swiss government in 1976.[177] Gautier's idea was based on the notion of creating a system of international visits to places of detention where torture often takes place in secrecy, in order to disrupt its use.[178] The Secretary General of the ICJ, Niall MacDermot, proposed that this particular mechanism be included in an optional protocol. There were fears that state disapproval towards an international visiting mechanism would slow down the already difficult negotiations on the text of the actual convention.

Effective operationalisation of the norm outlawing torture was indeed very slow, as the Optional Protocol of the Convention against Torture took ten years to negotiate and was only successfully adopted in 2002.[179] In 1984 Amnesty International published its report *Torture in the Eighties*, which drew attention to the fact that, while states were working on the creation and adoption of the convention against torture, some governments still resorted to this gruesome practice.[180] Amnesty, the Swiss Committee against Torture, the ICJ and the ICRC sponsored a colloquium in 1983 on 'How to Combat Torture', which marked the beginning of the campaign in favour of an optional protocol against torture. The colloquium was attended by representatives of governments who supported such a mechanism.[181] In the next year, Amnesty, CSCT and other NGOs formed a coalition against torture – the Coalition of International NGOs against Torture (CINAT), which aimed to keep attention focused on the issue as well as demand continued efforts from states to make the convention effective. The efforts of NGOs towards the creation and adoption of the optional protocol have been praised by the report of the Inter-American Institute of Human Rights and the Association for the Prevention of Torture.[182] Regional conventions against torture developed but those did not eradicate the need for an international mechanism to effectively monitor the ban. The most proactive states in the negotiations of the optional protocol were Costa Rica, Barbados, Nicaragua and Panama, supported by the countries of the European Union.

In June 2006 the Optional Protocol to the UN Convention against Torture finally received a sufficient number of ratifications and entered into force, which marked a historic moment for the prohibition against torture.[183] The OPCAT was a culmination of the efforts of both states and civil society to empower the convention prohibiting torture. Its entry into force signifies the resolve of states to create an effective mechanism to prevent torture and torture-like practices from being practised with impunity. Operationalising a norm grounds it more soundly into the international normative milieu and reflects the strength of the existing political consensus. Operationalisation in the case of CAT also meant the establishment of a subcommittee on the prevention of torture, which has been granted the power to visit places of detention and to gather information on the treatment of prisoners. The optional protocol makes provisions for the establishment of national preventive mechanisms, which would provide checks and balances at a level closer to those who are likely to suffer.[184]

Conclusions

The development of the norm prohibiting torture fits the theoretical model proposed in Chapter 2 fairly closely. The development of scientific knowledge required by the moral campaigners and the legal professionals induced increasing concerns over the use of torture and spurred many states (especially in Western Europe, which remained the stronghold of human rights during the Cold War) to take meaningful actions to curb this barbaric practice. Normative demands generated scientific knowledge, which, coupled with the principles of universal human rights and the pressure applied by some states and many non-state actors, helped to create a new behavioural norm. It was constructed in such a persuasive manner that even states who opposed the change to the normative status quo found it hard to exit the negotiations. In the case of constructing an effective ban, the components of the successful new norm included a strong and engaging ethical proposal, medical knowledge, which satisfied the requirements of scientific knowledge, legal expertise, which sided with the normative proposal backed up by the emerging scientific knowledge, and political support initially by a core of affluent and smaller states, which grew in membership to such a size that it became hard to ignore.

The creation of the norm banning the use of torture attests to the role and power of non-state actors in international policy-making. It also emphasises the importance of scientific knowledge even in areas that seem to be purely ethical in nature. Scientific knowledge and normative beliefs fused in such a way as to lay the foundation for a total ban on torture, cruel, inhuman and degrading treatment or punishment. This study provides further evidence of the effectiveness of combining the theoretical achievements of the social constructivists of international relations and the social constructivists of scientific knowledge – a connection worth exploring in further depth. The character of the closures achieved throughout the process of norm building did indeed reflect the strength of the prohibition imposed – a prohibition that to this day demands plausible justifications by anyone who decides to overstep it.

The political events in the years following the 9/11 terrorist attacks on New York, brought the problem of torture back into the social and political spotlight. Shortly after the attacks, the United States began a 'War on Terror', which resulted in some changes to domestic legislation and the curbing of civil liberties in some Western countries, as well as direct military action in Afghanistan and Iraq. The search for the leaders of the Al-Qaeda terrorist network renewed the normative debate on the 'ticking bomb' scenario and once more brought into question the utilisation of torture methods in situations and on individuals who are perceived to threaten national security.[185] Amnesty International, Human Rights First and other like-minded NGOs have continually expressed fears about individuals held without trial and about the treatment of prisoners in Iraq and Guantanamo Bay.[186] US policy-makers maintained that the methods of interrogation adopted did not constitute torture, although some caused stress and anxiety, and those included hooding, isolation and sleep deprivation. It is important to note here that the use of 'torture light' or 'nonlethal torture' has consistently been denied by the US government, which signaled that the Bush administration accepted the normative principle that torture was illegal, while looking for technical loopholes. Another high-profile US breach of the CAT has been the interpretation offered by the Bush administration to the effect that 'the ban on cruel, inhuman and degrading treatment under the UN Convention against Torture did not apply to Americans working overseas',[187] resulting in a policy of 'rendition', whereby CIA employees were allowed to engage methods of interrogation in foreign prisons, which would not be allowed in the United States.

The US came under sustained pressure and criticism from the EU countries and civil society groups for its rendition policy and during her visit to Europe in December 2005, Secretary of State Condoleeza Rice signalled a shift in the US position on the question. Analysts are still trying to determine whether this is a real shift in US policy, as Rice declared that 'US interrogators were barred from using cruel or degrading practices wherever in the world they were'.[188] A further development in US domestic politics is the successful vote in the US House of Representatives to ban cruel, inhuman or degrading treatment of foreign terrorist suspects, proposed by Senator John McCain.[189] How successful this policy would be in practice remains to be seen.

The principles of the CAT were reinforced even further by the decision of seven UK Law Lords on 8 December 2005 that evidence obtained by torture carried out abroad is inadmissible in court.[190] One of the members of the panel, Lord Carswell, stated that 'allowing torture to be used would involve the state in moral defilement'.[191] This decision, although expected, has far-reaching consequences, because it not only restates the UK position on the issue of torture, but also imposes a normative and technical obligation on other governments not to employ torture on detainees, because evidence obtained under torture will not be acceptable to the legal process. During his first few days in office, the new American President Barack Obama sent out a clear message that the 'harsh interrogation tactics' deployed post-9/11 are banned,[192] reaffirming the principles of CAT and curtailing any discussion of the permissibility of 'torture light'. These developments, although displaying some of the weaknesses of the Convention against Torture, have also emphasised its strength as a guiding principle on the issue.

4 Protecting intellectual property rights in the pharmaceutical industry

Norms prescribing the protection of inventions, innovations, products and technologies have existed for more than five centuries, the oldest ones dating as far back as Renaissance Italy. The protection of intellectual property (IP) was, however, considered an issue of domestic politics in the same way as the protection of physical property until the twentieth century. Although the first international conventions on intellectual property were signed in the nineteenth century (the Paris and the Berne Conventions), they only established general guidelines of international standards of IP protection, and provided no enforcement mechanisms. With the growth of knowledge-intensive industries such as the chemical and pharmaceutical industries, information technologies, computer software, and with the globalisation of trade and services, businesses began to demand higher levels of intellectual property protection and international safeguards for their scientific and technological breakthroughs.

In 1994 the member states of the General Agreement on Tariffs and Trade (GATT) signed an agreement on trade-related aspects of intellectual property (TRIPs), which established international norms for the protection of intellectual property rights under the mandate of the newly created World Trade Organisation (WTO). The TRIPs agreement regulates such diverse areas as the protection of patents, copyright, trademarks, utility models, industrial designs, geographical indicators, collective marks, certification marks and trade secrets.[1] One of the industries affected by the agreement is the pharmaceutical industry, which has attracted a lot of public attention in relation to the effects of TRIPs on the availability and affordability of essential medicines. The application and effects of the norm protecting all knowledge created in the pharmaceutical sphere has raised a number of issues of ethical, social, political, economic and legal character and has since 1994 not been completely implemented due to constant opposition from developing countries and various civil society organisations.

Several controversies lie at the heart of the debate over international protection of intellectual property rights in general and in the pharmaceutical industry in particular. Some involve principled issues, while others address normative concerns. First, there is the issue of definition – what exactly constitutes intellectual property rights, and whether intellectual property should be considered in the same way as individual physical property. It is one thing protecting trademarks, technologies, paintings, computer software, since all of these are tangible products; but it is a completely different matter protecting knowledge and ideas – establishing when they occurred or were created, their degree of novelty and who should own them. Knowledge and ideas may be said to have a communal character, because they are not exhausted by public usage and can be utilised by many simultaneously,[2] which makes the question of ownership and the regulation of use even harder to resolve.

Second, granting ownership over knowledge and ideas raises the question whether knowledge is a public or private good. Since knowledge is contextual and most new ideas are born in an already existing framework of knowledge, this would suggest that the products of the human mind are public rather than private goods,[3] entitling societies to share them instead of granting their owners monopolistic rights. The matter is further complicated by the availability of public funding for research in some areas now protected by TRIPs. Universities and government-owned laboratories often pass crude knowledge to private companies who then develop and market various products and patent this knowledge. Critics are outraged that societies are often made to pay for knowledge once through general taxation and a second time for the use of patent-protected knowledge.

Third, there is the controversy over whose interests should come first – the interests of innovators who are looking to recoup their costs of innovation or the interests of societies who cannot always afford access to new knowledge. Intellectual property rights should be about finding a balance between rewarding the innovators by allowing them some form of protection, while disseminating the new technology, knowledge or ideas, among members of society, which is not simply a matter of economic calculations, but has an inherently political character. If the former takes precedence over the latter, society will end up with monopolistic owners of knowledge and technologies who may abuse their position in the name of profit maximisation. If, however, new information is shared without regulation, then inventors are not rewarded for their effort and innovation and this, industries argue, is a disincentive to creativity, which is to the detriment of society.[4] According to some development specialists, such arguments put forward by industries are unreasonable and 'a negation of creativity ... generated by non-profit motives in both industrial and non-industrial societies'.[5] Constantine Vaitsos disagrees, arguing that the introduction of property rights in the sphere of knowledge and ideas creates an artificial scarcity that is aimed at generating an economic rent and securing control over markets rather than at creating incentives for inventive activity.[6] In economic terms, scarcity exists when 'needs and wants exceed the resources available to meet them ... and where the price mechanism usually offers the most efficient way to allocate scarce resources'.[7] When knowledge and ideas are socially constructed as scarce resources, consumers will learn to 'value' them,[8] thus avoiding the trap of non-scarce resources, which are usually free. In other words, Vaitsos argues that the proponents of IPRs are merely after increasing their profits and not so concerned with incentives for inventions.

The protection of intellectual property in the case of the pharmaceutical industry extends beyond the public vs private ownership-of-knowledge debate, because the products of the pharmaceutical industry have a direct impact on human life and health. The right to health is a fundamental human right[9] and access to medicines is closely linked to this matter. When medicines are patented and the generic competition eliminated,[10] drugs will become more expensive, and while multinational drug companies will begin recouping their research and development (R&D) costs, more medicines will be put out of reach of those in the underdeveloped world or indeed those without health insurance. Thus, a further problem specific to the pharmaceutical case is the reconciliation of the conflicting priorities of private business and public health.

This chapter examines the complex interplay between economic power, social concerns, technical knowledge and moral beliefs and the search for a common ground between them. I discuss how the economic might of international corporations backed up by the political influence of major developed states managed to offset the concerns and determination of developing countries to oppose trade policies that would hurt their populations. Further I discuss how the normative campaigners who drew attention to the ethical concerns for individual health and life managed to form coalitions with developing countries that were successful in securing changes to limit the scope of TRIPs in specific circumstances.

The development of the international norm for the protection of intellectual property needs to be examined in its specific historical, political and economic context, as the latter have further relevance to our understanding of the interplay of various factors that influence norm creation. Events that may seem unrelated to the new norm because of their character – such as the end of the Cold War, the terrorist attacks on the US, the changing image and relevance of the UN in world governance – have all played a role in the creation, modification and implementation of the

TRIPs agreement as it stands today. These political events have been a catalyst for political dynamics, which have changed the pace and final outcome of the TRIPs negotiations.

Historical patterns of intellectual property protection

Exclusive rights to practise a certain craft, privileges, monopolies and grants of authors' rights to limit the publication of books were awarded by the sovereign rulers in Florence and Venice in the fifteenth century.[11] Up until the nineteenth century the protection of intellectual property was a matter of domestic jurisdiction.[12] International instruments existed prior to the agreement on TRIPs, but these were only statements of principle and contained no enforcement mechanisms. Even the organisation that was created to overlook the application of the IP conventions, the World Intellectual Property Organisation (WIPO), was relatively powerless either to change any of the existing rules or indeed to ensure their implementation.[13] Intellectual property protection in the pharmaceutical industry was also limited to individual states' discretion, which many states chose to exercise negatively by prohibiting patents in this industry, due to the social implications that they might have.[14] The German Patent Act of 1877, for example, prohibited the patenting of inventions regarding medicines.[15] Many of today's developed countries only introduced pharmaceutical patents in the 1960s and 1970s, some of these restrictions coming into force as late as the 1990s.[16] In 1988 WIPO undertook a study for the negotiating group dealing with TRIPs in the Uruguay Round, which revealed that 49 of the 98 member states of the Paris Convention excluded pharmaceutical products from patent protection.[17] It is worth noting that the members of the Paris Convention include both developed and developing countries. In other words, there is a long history of keeping medicines and products of pharmaceutical research out of the reach of patent provisions, both domestically and internationally, and this is due partially, if not entirely, to the high social price of such protection.

The earliest instruments for the protection of intellectual property were passed by the Venetian Senate in 1474.[18] Another early system of patent law was set up in England in 1624.[19] The purpose of patent laws at that time was not to reward invention but to encourage new businesses to start up and to limit monopolies,[20] which is the opposite of the rationale for contemporary patent legislation. Patents up to the eighteenth century granted privileges and rights and were a symbol of approval by the sovereign.[21] In Europe these privileges mainly had to do with the right to print books, as they were considered to threaten the authority of monarchs and the Church alike.[22]

Growing industrialisation led to the improvement of the domestic machinery for the protection of copyright, patents and trademarks, while increasing volumes of foreign trade meant that in the absence of any international agreements, states had to work out bilateral mechanisms to protect intellectual property. When invited to the International Exhibition in Vienna in 1873, German and American inventors declined to participate due to fears that their inventions might be copied by other participating delegations and exploited commercially in other countries.[23] These fears, coupled with the growing concerns for the protection of domestic industries from increasingly successful foreign counterparts, led to the creation of the first international convention for the protection of inventions, trademarks and industrial designs – the Paris Convention of 1883.[24] In 1886 another international convention was created for the protection of literary and artistic works – the Berne Convention.[25]

The development of new knowledge-intensive industries such as the chemical and pharmaceutical industry, and agricultural research, which were all particularly strong in pre-First World War Germany, required the expertise of a large number of scientists. Big industrial cartels developed in the US after the war as well, as it was becoming clear that the basis of the economy was shifting from industrial design to the creation of scientific knowledge and information. The cartels relied on their ample resources to attract scientists and thus gain a competitive advantage. Since these organisations were primarily profit-oriented, they became interested in the protection of their industrial secrets and newly created knowledge, as that represented the basis of increased profits and competitiveness.

The First World War, coupled with the Great Depression of 1929 brought about two important changes in the attitude of the US towards intellectual property protection. After US companies came to regret their heavy reliance on the German chemical industry,[26] they had a vested interest in developing both their own knowledge and technologies and their own standards of intellectual property protection. The 1930s were also a time of growing suspicion towards international liberal economics, which led to 'greater government involvement in economic affairs and the vigorous assertion of economic nationalism'.[27] In the interwar years industries and government held the same position on standards of intellectual property protection.

Following the end of the Second World War, the US emerged as the predominant economic and technological power, which gave its corporations greater freedom to impose their terms of trade and to use their growing expertise in intellectual property rights to the best of their advantage.[28] Reconstruction funds, technology and knowledge started to flow from the US to Western Europe, Canada, South America and Asia. When setting up subsidiaries abroad, companies were careful not to disperse too much knowledge where they could employ their own specialists: for example, instead of training local workers, which might have provided them with 'expensive' technical knowledge, companies sent their native manager, in order to avoid creating opportunities for free-riding.[29] For many newly independent countries (mainly South America and some parts of Asia) this was the start of a cycle of dependency in which the US corporations managed to withhold knowledge and technological know-how while reaping high profits on the back of low-cost labour and natural resources.

The growing importance of IP protection in the twentieth century required a larger organisation than the United International Bureaux for the Protection of Intellectual Property (BIRPI) to handle an ever-expanding agenda. The convention creating the World Intellectual Property Organisation (WIPO) was signed in Stockholm in 1967 and in 1974 the organisation became part of the UN system with a mandate to administer intellectual property matters. WIPO inherited the work of BIRPI, administering the Paris and Berne conventions, and was also in charge of managing the work of other UN agencies in relation to intellectual property (UN Conference on Trade and Development (UNCTAD), UNESCO). Currently WIPO has 182 member states. Prior to the Uruguay Round of trade negotiations WIPO and UNCTAD were the only organisations administering IP issues at the international level. WIPO reached the capacity of its potential at the diplomatic conference to revise the Protection of Industrial Property.[30] The organisation hosted the negotiations of the revision of the Paris Convention, which ended in a deadlock. The developing countries led by the Andean Group,[31] Brazil and India tabled a proposal that demanded the Paris Convention be revised in such a way as to 'cater more effectively to the special needs of developing countries'.[32] Their intentions were simply to lower the standards of IP protection applicable to them and thus to gain a more equal start in the process of their own industrialisation and economic development. The Organisation of Economic Cooperation and Development (OECD) countries, influenced by the opinion of various national industry associations, were opposed[33] to the revision, holding that the demands of the developing countries were unreasonable and that the proposed change would not improve their development opportunities. In a forum such as WIPO, where every country has one vote, the united front of the Group of 77 (G-77) and the total opposition of the OECD countries created a stalemate that could not be resolved. Due to the inability of WIPO to settle disputes between developed and developing countries, to resolve negotiations that had reached a stalemate, or to enforce international agreements and under the influence of the industrial sectors of the US, Europe and Japan, the US government advanced a different solution to the problem of how to raise the international standards of IP protection.[34] It sought to change the forum and focus of the discussion in a way that might yield better results. This change was based on redefining the issue of IP protection as one that is closely related to international trade, and thus bringing the discussions to a forum where the G-7 states could exert more effective influence.

The economic crisis of the 1970s, fuelled by the rising prices of crude oil and falling prices of foodstuffs, helped developing states unite under a common agenda and attempt to shake up the international system with proposals for a New International Economic Order (NIEO) presented to the United Nations. US industries were hurt by the rising fuel prices created by the Organisation of Petroleum Exporting Countries (OPEC) and felt further pressure from the increasing technological production capabilities of Japan and Southeast Asia. Western Europe and Canada were concerned by the amount of influence US corporations had in their home economies, which led to debates with the US on issues of competition. The developing countries were engaged in a concerted effort to negotiate new economic rules, while the economies of East Asia and, most importantly, Japan were experiencing unforeseen growth.[35]

The campaign to create new rules for the international protection of intellectual property can be said to have begun with the failed attempt to create a code for the trade in counterfeit goods at the Tokyo Round of the GATT trade negotiations (1973–1979), where a conglomerate of US industries managed to persuade the US and the European Economic Community (EEC) delegations that international rules needed to be established limiting the effects of trade in counterfeit goods. This undertaking failed due to a lack of broader support, but it left a significant mark on the GATT agenda. It sent a signal to the corporate world that trade negotiations can be used to deal with questions of counterfeit goods and other issues of intellectual property and that the US and EEC governments were conducive to persuasion to address such questions. Issues of intellectual property were dealt with by the World Intellectual Property Organisation, which had limited enforcement mechanisms and hardly any power at all.

In 1982 an article entitled 'Stealing from the Mind' appeared in the *New York Times*, marking the determination of US corporations to stop what they called the theft of US knowledge and invention.[36] The initial campaign begun by US industry aimed to limit the trade in counterfeit goods.[37] Their approach towards the US government included lobbying and creating reports on lost revenues to countries that produce and trade in counterfeit products. Drahos and Braithwaite argue that, in the context of the early 1980s, the article by the president and chairman of Pfizer was a risky move, as there was no certainty what the reaction from the US government would be, nor was it clear how WIPO and the developing countries (many of which represented important markets for Pfizer) would respond to these accusations.[38]

The Uruguay Round of the ministerial meetings of GATT began in 1986 and took almost eight years to close. In those years important political changes took place in the international system. The Cold War, and thus the ideological opposition between East and West, ended in 1989. The triumphant liberal political ideology, with a strong emphasis on liberal economics, brought about an increased drive to liberalise international trade. The end of the standoff between the superpowers created a favourable environment for international institutions to take on an increased role, as well as an air of widening international cooperation. We have been experiencing rapid legalisation at the international level, where states have been creating more legal principles and aiming to improve the effectiveness of international law.[39] The international normative context was extending to take account of individual and human rights. Liberal norms similar to the ones advocated in American domestic politics – the right to protect private property, fairness, the support for innovation and so on – were becoming the basis of the developing new international norm for the protection of intellectual property.

The concept of intellectual property rights has dramatically changed its meaning over the centuries, reflecting the command of the sovereign at one point, the needs of industries at another and the need for protection of the vulnerable at yet another stage of economic development. The norm requiring the recognition of and respect for intellectual property rights has not been normatively consistent over the years, unlike the norm prohibiting the use of torture, where a steady progression towards the same goal had taken place. In the case of the norm prohibiting torture, the historical struggle for the establishment of the norm was mainly concerned with tightening the legal instruments, whereas in the case of the intellectual property norm there was no uniformity of meaning. Meanings changed with the requirements of the various stages of economic, social and political developments in different countries. The process of constructing IP protection might have come to a close, since only the scope of the protection awarded and the mechanisms of administering IPRs seem to have changed considerably over the past century.

The campaign for the creation and modification of the international norm protecting intellectual property rights in general and the case of the pharmaceutical industry in particular will be examined in further historical detail here in the context of the theoretical model of norm development proposed in Chapter 2. Box 4.1 below presents a timeline of events and agreements that have contributed to or influenced the process of norm development in this case study.

Box 4.1 Timeline for the creation of international and regional instruments for intellectual property protection of industrial patents and patents in the pharmaceutical industry

1474	Venetian Senate passed the first general patent law.
1557	Queen Mary grants printing privileges to a craft guild known as the Stationers.
1623	English Statute of Monopolies – England's early attempts to limit the scope of patent law in such a way as to add to the public wealth.
1711	First design patent statute passed in France to encourage creativity in the silk manufacturing guild in Lyons.
1793	US Congress passed the original Patent Act.
1836	New United States Patent Act entitled 'An Act to promote the Progress of Useful Arts, and to repeal all Acts and parts of Acts heretofore made for that purpose.'
1873	International Exposition in Vienna.
1883	Paris Convention for the Protection of Industrial Property.
1886	Berne Convention for the Protection of Literary and Artistic works.
1893	Bureaux for the Protection of Intellectual Property – established in Berne, Switzerland to overlook the Paris and Berne Conventions.
1952	The Universal Copyright Convention was drafted under the auspices of UNESCO in an attempt to include the US and other countries in South America in international treaties.
1967	The World Intellectual Property Organisation is established as one of the UN specialised agencies.
1973	European Patent Convention.
1973–1979	Tokyo Round of GATT negotiations – the US and EEC put forward a proposal for an anti-counterfeit code, which recommended that measures be taken internationally to curb trade in counterfeit goods.
1974	US Trade Act Section 301.
1978	The European Patent Convention created a European Patent Office in Munich to confer patents recognised throughout the EU (except Denmark and Ireland).
1979	The Advisory Committee on Trade Policy and Negotiation is created to institutionalise business advice to the president.
1980–1984	Diplomatic Conference for the Protection of Industrial Property – held under the auspices of WIPO and aimed at the revision of the Paris Convention.
1982	Harare Protocol on Patent and Industrial Designs within the Framework of the African Regional Industrial Property Organisation.

September 1986 Punta Del Este Meeting of Trade Ministers, culminating in the ministerial declaration opening the Uruguay Round of negotiations.

1986–1994 General Agreement on Tariffs and Trade – Uruguay Round of negotiations to establish the World Trade Organisation along with the creation of an Agreement on Trade Related Intellectual Property Rights (TRIPs).

April 1994 TRIPs agreement adopted at Marrakech as Annex C of the Final Act Embodying the Results of the Uruguay Round of multilateral trade negotiations.

January 1995 WTO agreement including the agreement on TRIPs entered into force.

1995 Ralph Nader and James Love create the Consumer Project on Technology (CPT).

January 1996 United Nations Programme on HIV/AIDS (UNAIDS) was developed.

October 1996 Health Action International organised the first major NGO meeting on health care and TRIPs in Bielefeld, Germany.

July 1998 'Bridging the Gap' – 12th International AIDS Conference, Geneva.

January 1999 Health GAP (Global Access Project) Coalition is created in the US.

March 1999 AIDS and Essential Medicines and Compulsory Licensing, Meeting sponsored by Médecins Sans Frontières (MSF), Health Action International (HAI) and Consumer Project on Technology, Geneva.

October 1999 MSF is awarded the Nobel Peace Prize, the money from which the organisation decides to spend on creating the Neglected Disease Fund.

November 1999 *Increasing Access to Essential Drugs in a Globalised Economy Working towards Solutions* – conference organised by HAI, MSF and CPT, Amsterdam.

May 2000 53rd World Health Assembly, Geneva – meeting of the World Health Organisation, which was attended by MSF, CPT and HAI.

July 2000 World AIDS Conference in Durban, South Africa.

2000 Andean Community Common Regime on Industrial Property.

February 2001 Oxfam, UK launches the 'Cut the Cost' campaign.

November 2001 Doha Ministerial Conference – Doha Declaration on TRIPs and Public Health.

March 2002 *The Crisis of Neglected Diseases: Developing Treatments and Ensuring Access*, New York, organised by MSF, CPT, Oxfam and HAI.

July 2002 14th International AIDS Conference, Barcelona.

Constructing IPR rules

Formulating the idea

The initial idea for introducing international standards of intellectual property (IP) protection to all industries (including pharmaceuticals) was formulated by a select group of some of the biggest US corporations in the early 1980s.[40] IP issues had been on the agenda of US business for the whole of the twentieth century,[41] but their application had been hampered by strong antitrust and monopoly legislation, as well as special considerations for pharmaceutical products. It was a combination of changing domestic legislation, a sense of decline in the US global economic position and developments in the international economic environment that made the US government more perceptive to the idea of introducing international intellectual property protection.

The move towards setting international standards of IP protection began from within the US domestic legal system. For most of the nineteenth and twentieth century, the principle of intellectual property protection was in continual competition with the antitrust policies.[42] There are identifiable periods of US legal history where the importance of patents was considered superior to concerns about monopolies,[43] followed by periods where this order was reversed.[44] The decisions of the US Supreme Court are a good indicator of the changing social perceptions, because it adjudicates and interprets the law in cases and controversies that arise under US constitutional law and set fundamental principles. Disadvantaged interest groups in the US, which are unable to pursue their causes through lobbying politicians, often rely on the Supreme Court as their 'sole practicable avenue ... to petition for redress of grievances'.[45] The Supreme Court agenda and attitudes to particular issues change as a result of the interplay of several factors – changes in the composition of the bench, for example, led to periods in which the court pursued alternatively conservative or liberal economic policies; changes of the character of the issues brought by litigants; changes brought about by broader socioeconomic processes.[46] The attitude of the Supreme Court to issues of patent law was amended in the 1980s and the direction of this change has not been overturned since, which makes it all the more profound.

In *Dawson Chemical Co.* v. *Rohm & Haas Co.* (448 US 176, 1980) the Supreme Court upheld the right to protection of patent holders against free-riding by denying allegations of patent misuse in the context of antitrust legislation, on the grounds that '[t]he incentive to await the discoveries of others might well prove sweeter than the incentive to take the initiative oneself'.[47] The Supreme Court's decision endorsed the crucial importance of intellectual property over antitrust and put the protection of the rights of inventors and/or patent holders above competition concerns. In the words of Susan Sell, there was a 'dramatically improved domestic environment for IP owners and a noteworthy redefinition of US interests in IP protection'.[48] These developments were reinforced by a change in the US economic position in international markets. During the 1970s and 1980s a 'policy discourse of a US in decline' developed among domestic political elites[49] due to a growing trade deficit. The private sector's move towards closer cooperation on IP issues across industries in the 1970s[50] helped industrial lobbying groups take advantage of the widespread concern that the US economy is not doing well. These groups managed to persuade policy-makers that the decline in the US economy is partly triggered by the losses suffered as a result of piracy, counterfeiting and free-riding on US knowledge.[51] These were the first steps towards linking intellectual property protection to trade issues, which later paved the way for the creation of the TRIPs Agreement. It was primarily research-intensive sectors such as pharmaceuticals, computer software, semiconductors[52] and the agricultural chemical industry[53] that were directly involved in lobbying the US government, as they felt that large proportions of their revenues were lost to piracy.[54] The success stories of developing economies and the rapid growth in India, Brazil and some states in Southeast Asia, including Japan, fed into these fears and allegations.[55] These economies were expanding swiftly, while the US economy seemed to be slowing down. Some of these trends were reversed following the oil crisis of the 1970s, but US industries were determined to pursue their agenda, by making a case for the protection of their most precious assets – new knowledge and technologies.[56]

Two important trends supplemented the reasoning of the corporate world. First, the transformations in the world trading system of the 1970s meant that the competitive advantage of companies was no longer determined simply by cheaper natural resources and labour, but rather by the possession of cutting-edge knowledge and technologies. Second, while research and development is an expensive undertaking, the increased speed of communications and technology transfer meant that information was dispersed more quickly and while R&D costs grew disproportionately higher,[57] product life-cycles in knowledge-based industries became shorter, thus impairing the ability of innovators to recoup their R&D costs.[58] Globalisation of trade, transport and communications was undermining the ability of industries to protect their innovations from free-riders, while the cost of free-riding was becoming insignificant.

The changing international environment, the pessimistic view of US policy-makers about the state of their economy, the new position adopted by the Supreme Court on the importance of intellectual property protection, and the determination with which US companies worked to prove the need for increased IP protection, all contributed to the creation of a receptive audience in the US administration for this new idea of internationally enforceable IP rights across industrial sectors. Businesses realised, however, that getting the US government on their side was going to be only the first step towards ensuring international protection. Money started to flow towards top lawyers in this highly technical and complex field, towards social science organisations to produce justification of the importance of IP principles, and towards professional lobbyists to persuade the US government of the need to press for international standards of intellectual property protection.[59] The foundations for the development of the norm protecting products of the mind were successfully laid, not just by means of the sheer size of the business resources committed to it, but also by investments in the creation of technical knowledge to back up the normative argument in favour of this norm.

Network configuration

Similar to the previously examined case of the norm prohibiting torture, network configuration and issue formulation (defining IP protection as a trade-related issue) occurred simultaneously. The difference in the process of network configuration in the case of IP protection was that the aim of the participants in the campaign was to stay out of the public eye as much as possible and to selectively engage only such actors who were likely to assist in pushing the trade agenda forward. Companies were striving to protect their chances of maximising profits and this was not an aim that would attract support or sympathy from the wider public.

Studies of the negotiations preceding the TRIPs agreement suggest that the idea for the creation of internationally binding intellectual property rules across industries came from the US private industrial sector.[60] As discussed earlier, the first unsuccessful attempt to introduce IPR concerns to the GATT was at the Tokyo Round of ministerial negotiations (1973–1979). The issue was formulated as a need to curb the trade in counterfeit goods, which was affecting trademarked products. Although the coalition of brand-producing companies was quite strong (comprising around 100 multinationals)[61] it only managed to persuade the US and the EEC to support its proposal; the much needed further agreement from other nation-states could not be generated before the end of the Tokyo Round.[62]

An increasing number of corporations complained that their profits were being eroded by breaches of trademarks, counterfeit goods and designs primarily in the developing world. The technologies to copy products were generally many times cheaper than the investment in R&D, which compromised companies' ability to recoup R&D costs. It was also becoming clear that significant reform of the Paris Convention under WIPO[63] was not going to materialise due to the deadlock between the opposing demands of the developed and developing countries. Multinational corporations like Pfizer and IBM realised that WIPO could no longer help developed countries regulate the 'knowledge game'.[64] Companies combined their efforts in an attempt to influence directly the policies of the US government by linking intellectual property protection to trade.[65]

Corporations were able to construct the link between IPR breaches and threats to US trade in two ways – by means of consolidating industry associations; and by actively participating in committees advising the US government on trade issues. The chief officers of Pfizer and IBM were represented on the Advisory Committee on Trade Policy and Negotiation (ACTPN), which is part of the office of the US Trade Representative (USTR).[66] Pfizer

> worked in Washington to multiply the [Advisory Committee's] efforts and strengthen its capacity to influence the multilateral policy agenda by calling on the membership of the Pharmaceutical Research and Manufacturers of America (PhRMA)[67] to put the protection of intellectual property high on its lobbying agenda.[68]

Pfizer, IBM, Monsanto and DuPont combined forces with the International Anti-Counterfeiting Coalition and the Copyright Alliance, which set them up for a breakthrough.[69] The Chemical Manufacturers Association also had an interest in increasing the protection of trade secrets.[70] In 1984 the International Intellectual Property Alliance (IIPA) was created to represent US copyright industries.[71] Although the copyright industries were initially satisfied with the protection afforded by the Berne Convention, the IIPA raised the issue of pirating and weak enforcement of the principles of the convention in the developing countries and thus became a strong ally in the coalition to increase IP protection.[72] A broad and very loose alliance was emerging among groups that lobbied separately for the protection of patents, trademarks, copyrights, software, music, movies and so on. The line of complaint was similar: heavy losses were incurred by companies working in various fields because of free-riders abroad. Industries' reports released figures of projected losses that echoed the need for universal norms that would help innovators and creators in any field recuperate their investments.[73]

In 1986, several months before the opening of the Uruguay Round of GATT negotiations, the executives of some of the biggest US-based corporations created the Intellectual Property Committee (IPC)[74] to seek international support and provide governments with advice for the creation of rules governing worldwide protection for intellectual property rights.[75] The IPC exerted its influence abroad through the CEOs of US companies, who were members of the committee. They would contact their counterparts in Europe and Japan to get them to pressure their governments into supporting the intellectual property agenda.[76] The governments of the European Community, Japan and Canada were further lobbied separately by the chairman of the United States Trade Representative. This group of countries became known as the Quad and consensus between them on the trade-round agenda was crucial.[77]

The process of network formation in the case of the international protection of intellectual property rights consisted of various industry-specific coalitions joining forces on an issue affecting them in a similar way. The network spread across borders, mainly between the governments of the most advanced economies in the world, shortly before the new round of trade negotiations opened in Uruguay. The support network, for the creation of an effective international norm for intellectual property protection has some specific characteristics. The aims of the organisations of multinational corporations and lobbyists were instrumental and concentrated on creating technical norms that would allow industries to increase their returns. These actors were not aiming explicitly to change any normative structures. Their efforts were put towards producing more effective rules that would bring about the desired results. Some normative arguments regarding the moral rights of entrepreneurs and creators were advanced, but corporations knew from experience that, unless there were stringent mechanisms to ensure compliance, normative structures would be ineffective.[78]

The actions of corporations were guided by a logic of consequences, which is demonstrated by the choice of avenues and the allies that corporations sought to achieve their goal. US corporations shared the expertise of their IP lawyers with various government agencies, but, unsurprisingly, were not as helpful towards the governments of developing countries. According to a study conducted by Susan Sell, 'the government relied upon IP experts, who were also advocates, to translate the complexities into political discourse ... therefore in this context, there [was] no neutral or objective group of civil servants in a position to counter-balance private demands'.[79] The success of the campaign was dependent neither on the number of supporters nor on the ability of corporations to get the public to back their position. Instead, success had to do with the level of economic and political influence that these companies could master. This campaign was not a public one; campaign records are limited and much information remains undisclosed. Large corporations with experience in lobbying employed all possible methods to engage policy-makers with their agenda. Corporations built networks among themselves, CEOs chaired advisory committees, organisations were created to liaise with the government and so on, until the message was heard loud and clear in the corridors of power. This message was carefully constructed in terms that were likely to engage the attention of policy-makers, which will be discussed in the next section.

Issue formation

Constructing a new norm requires a problem to be defined, within a given context, and its scope outlined. Agreement is thus needed on the technical, legal and normative parameters of the proposed norm. Reaching scientific (technical) and normative closures is central for the normative campaign, as it lays a more stable foundation for argumentation and political negotiations. Outlining the problem to be resolved involves the choice of context in which to position the issue,[80] the choice of an institutional forum in which best to address the issue at stake, establishing the cause and effect of the problem, and the proposal of solutions for its elimination. The proposed norm needs to be formulated in such a way as to be able to rectify the problem singled out in stage one, while at the same time remaining reasonable so that it would be easier to get conservative actors to support the new norm. The network promoting the development of universal norms of intellectual property protection provides a showcase example of how issue formation can be achieved most effectively.

'Conditions become defined as problems when we come to believe that we should do something about them.'[81] The paradox in the attitude to intellectual property protection in the US is that until well into the twentieth century, the government disregarded IP rights completely, in order to secure all the knowledge and technologies needed for a fledgling economy.[82] The issue of intellectual property protection was only formulated as a problem when large US businesses felt that others were making money by free-riding on their intellectual property. Pfizer's *New York Times* article 'Stealing from the Mind' outlined the concerns of many industries, stating that they were losing profits because no rules existed to protect their intellectual property abroad.[83] Economists constructed the 'appropriability problem'[84] – copying inventions is cheap but there needs to be a way to recoup expenses for industrial R&D, otherwise incentives for innovation will disappear, resulting in a 'suboptimal level of innovation'.[85] A campaign had begun to persuade policy-makers that this was an issue not only worthy of their attention but also one demanding decisive political action that would impact the welfare of many. Initially, the problem of intellectual property protection was constructed within the domestic economic context of the US. The support network formulated the issue as one of rights related to property ownership, fair rewards for labour and innovation. Since these concerns are part of the foundational principles of liberal economics, it was hard for the American government to disregard them.

Concerns for the state of the US economy were growing and this was a good time to present statistics that could explain why the trade deficit was soaring and propose solutions as to how corporations could do better in the future. Apart from knowing who to talk to and how to get through to policy-makers, multinational corporations knew how to make a persuasive case of their concerns. They used technical knowledge and expertise, which gave their arguments legitimacy and weight. A number of official studies (mostly industry-sponsored) were published to show that companies were incurring sizeable losses abroad due to foreign trade in pirated and counterfeit goods. The Automotive Parts and Accessories Association informed the Sub-committee on Trade of the United States House of Representatives that estimated losses of revenue incurred by the industry due to international trade in counterfeit automobile parts were as high as $12 billion for 1984.[86] In 1985, the IIPA published a report estimating that copyright industries lost over $1.3 billion to international piracy.[87] In 1986, the Intellectual Property Committee cited statistics prepared by the US International Trade Commission (USITC),[88] according to which US firms had lost $23.8 billion due to lack of international IP protection.[89] Other organisations such as the Office of International Affairs of the National Research Council also undertook studies into the global dimensions of IPRs in science and technology in response to concerns raised by US industry and US universities.[90]

Framed in this way, the issue of failing to protect intellectual property rights became a key explanation for the ailing US economy. The US trade deficit had, according to some, experienced a staggering increase of 309 per cent between 1980 and 1985.[91] Engaging standard methods of economic analysis, the advocates of strong international IP protection produced evidence that short-term losses due to strengthened protection would be outweighed by long-term benefits of increased innovation.[92] This economic analysis assisted the lobbyists in making a strong case in favour of improved worldwide protection. Once IP protection was constructed in technical terms as an issue not only of stolen knowledge and unfair enrichment, but also as a possible cause of future economic decline, it became much easier to mobilise US policy-makers to take international action. Technical closure was reached among the economic experts of multinational corporations, who were all of the same opinion. There were no actors with an opposing view to challenge this closure on any level and it became the basis of the campaign to regulate the use of 'products of the mind'.

The sustained pressure from various industrial associations and the information coming from a variety of advisory committees and think tanks prompted US policy-makers to take action. Steps were initially taken at the domestic level to amend legislation and enable companies, through the IPC, to reach beyond US borders and enforce protection of information and know-how. Amendments to the 1974 Trade Act – in particular Section 301 – enabled the president to impose bilateral trade sanctions and undertake retaliatory trade action against nation-states whose legal system was considered inadequate to protect the IP interests of US corporations (these changes will be discussed in more detail at a later point). The changes implemented by the US government were a catalyst for policy change at the international level as well.

Constructing the problem of IP rights as an issue of unfair trade helped US corporations make the case for their preference of the GATT as the appropriate institutional context for the new norms. Developing countries insisted that the organisation, which should be in charge of setting standards of IP protection, was the World Intellectual Property Organisation (WIPO). WIPO's failure to negotiate changes to the Paris Convention in three successive conferences between 1980 and 1982[93] convinced the US government and multinational corporations that this was one channel through which change was highly unlikely. WIPO had no enforcement mechanisms at its disposal, and each country holds one vote, giving automatic preference to the concerns of the developing states.[94] While the developing countries were attempting to persuade other WIPO members that IP protection needed to be relaxed, the developed countries (under pressure from industries) were concentrating on creating proposals for minimum standards of intellectual property protection.[95] Constructing IP protection in terms of its impact on trade was crucial, as the GATT had well-established enforcement procedures and a more solid organisational structure.

To conclude, the normative entrepreneurs in this campaign quickly built a network of support from other multinational corporations, across a wide spectrum of industries, to formulate a new norm, which would help them safeguard future profits more effectively. The message was skilfully presented as a case where the whole US economy was suffering because there were no international standards of intellectual property protection to safeguard US knowledge and technologies. The message was carefully woven into academic studies, reports from various associations, briefings with industries in Congress, the advice coming from organisations that facilitated the communications between industries and government like the Advisory Committee on Trade Policy and Negotiations. As so many sources confirmed the same information and as politicians were concerned with the state of the US economy, practical actions ensued. Although initially restricted to the domestic level,[96] these actions produced global implications through the bilateral trade agreements that the US government was negotiating with developing countries.

Dialogue with the conservative actors

The dialogue over the inclusion of norms on the protection of intellectual property rights on the negotiations agenda of the World Trade Organisation (WTO), preceding any form of agreement on their substance, was very problematic. The discussions were part of a larger framework of trade talks[97] and as such the outcome, some argue, was a product of linkage bargaining, and not genuine consensus.[98] The emergence of agreement was counterintuitive, because it materialised in an international context where most countries were net importers of knowledge and technologies. These legal rules favoured developed states and were agreed upon despite the significant rifts that existed among them.[99] The developing countries failed to mobilise in a coalition that spoke with one voice, largely due to the fact that they had different interests, pursued divergent foreign policy objectives, and did not take the issue of intellectual property protection very seriously.[100]

As early as 1982, a ministerial meeting was held to begin discussions of an agenda for the next round of trade negotiations.[101] By this time, US industry, led by Pfizer, had clearly indicated that WIPO was not the appropriate forum for negotiating effective IP rules.[102] The US submitted a proposal to include discussions on anti-counterfeiting practices in the upcoming negotiations, which would eventually lead to the creation of a code regarding actions on this matter.[103] The response of the developing countries was unenthusiastic – Brazil and India argued that 'GATT's jurisdiction was limited to tangible goods, and therefore, the GATT lacked legal competence to address an issue of the intellectual property area'.[104] Initially, the developing countries were unified in their position that IP issues were better dealt with by WIPO, but that consensus was not long-lived.

Two major developments occurred in 1984, which helped move IP issues forward on the GATT agenda. First, at the international level, GATT appointed an expert group to examine the effects of counterfeit trademark goods on international trade, thus practically admitting the possibility that these issues could make the GATT agenda.[105] The expert group was to work closely with WIPO representatives. In the next year, the expert group presented its findings and indicated that since some issues had remained unresolved, the GATT should decide whether a new round of multilateral negotiations was appropriate.[106] Second, a domestic development in US legislation was granted enough power to have international implications. The persistent pressure on US policy-makers, substantiated by various industries' reports that billions of dollars were lost to free-riders, theft of intellectual property and trade in counterfeit goods, proved successful in persuading Congress to take action. The 1984 Trade Act was passed, which adapted Section 301 of the 1974 Trade Act[107] and made it actionable by the president of the United States.[108] The president was effectively granted the right under domestic law to withdraw the benefits of trade agreements or impose duties on goods from foreign countries in cases when IPRs were not respected.

These developments sent a clear signal to the business community – their efforts had paid off and the government had confirmed in legal terms their support for the proposition that IP protection was indeed an issue intricately related to trade.[109] Unilateral action meant that the US government, backed by the knowledge and information supplied by its industries had the green light to take effective measures against any country that did not abide by the new American rules. The US government did not hesitate to demonstrate its readiness to use the mechanisms provided by Section 301 and the first countries that fell victim were South Korea[110] and Brazil[111] in 1985.

In 1986 the Preparatory Committee appointed by the GATT was given a broad mandate to determine the issues that were going to be discussed in the Uruguay Round.[112] The US delegation submitted a proposal to include all intellectual property issues, which largely reflected the US attitude to this matter. Japan backed the US proposal, while Brazil, India and Argentina expressed open opposition once again on the grounds that IP issues were outside of GATT's competence.[113] Since negotiations even on the agenda of future talks looked like they were going to end up in deadlock, the Swiss and Colombian delegates who were chairing the meeting of the Preparatory Committee put together a compromise proposal including the issue of intellectual property in the agenda for the future trade talks, as agreed by the US, the EC, Japan and some developing countries, which was later supported by more than 40 other delegations. Brazil submitted another proposal to exclude both services and intellectual property from the future negotiations, while the Argentinean proposal approved of IP issues but not of services being included in the GATT agenda. Brazil's position was supported by about ten delegations[114] but was outweighed by the Swiss–Colombian one, which became the basis of the Punta del Este ministerial declaration.[115] The Group of Ten was the core active opposition, which had the support of many other developing countries. The opposition was not consolidated enough and competing demands from some of its members made it easy to undermine.

The Punta del Este ministerial declaration seemed relatively harmless in itself, aiming 'to clarify GATT provisions and elaborate as appropriate new rules and disciplines'.[116] However, in the context of the increased determination of US industries to get results, these words should have rung 'danger', because of the broad spectrum of meanings that the term 'appropriate' can have. Developing countries failed to detect the actual scope of the mandate granted by the 1986 ministerial declaration. Their opposition to the creation of international norms for IP protection was undermined by the lack of unity among them. Some developing countries saw negotiating opportunities in areas where they needed to improve the existing terms of trade with their economically advanced counterparts, namely, textiles and clothing, agriculture, tropical products.[117] In 1987 the start of the Uruguay Round negotiations saw the developing countries still hanging on to the hope that they could limit the discussions of IP protection to trade in counterfeit goods.[118] At the same time, the US, backed up by Japan and Switzerland, made it clear from the start that they were willing 'to discuss substantive standards of IPRs such as copyright, patents, trademarks, designs, geographical indications, lay-out designs of semiconductor chips and trade secrets, by making detailed submissions on these issues'.[119]

In 1988 the negotiating group on TRIPs began to address specific proposals by various nation-states – the Nordic countries, Switzerland, the European communities, Thailand, Mexico, Brazil, etc.[120] The developing countries expressed concerns that intellectual property could be overprotected, slowing down the transfer of technologies and increasing the cost of agricultural and pharmaceutical products,[121] India and Brazil demanded that developing countries should be allowed to exclude pharmaceuticals, food and chemicals from patent protection.[122] Communications and tradeoffs between the US, Japan and the EC continued. Corporations from these countries were also liaising closely across borders.[123] Normative supporters had mastered enough political and economic power to push negotiations forward.

The United States government continued expanding its domestic IPR protection agenda by enacting the 1988 Omnibus Trade and Competitiveness Act, which included the Special 301 obliging the USTR

> to provide an annual report on unfair trade practices in foreign countries ... where investigations with regard to IPR infringements were to

be launched and action completed within statutory time limits ...
[t]his annual listing by the USTR follows detailed submissions by
interested US industry associations.[124]

The strengthening of bilateral actions under Special 301 began to break
down the foundation of the consensus between the G-10 because more and
more countries could not meet US national IP protection rules and as a
result faced the threat or the actual implementation of retaliatory trade
measures.[125] This showed the determination of the US government to push
ahead with IP protection. These coercive methods soon began to reap
results.

The mid-term review of the progress in the TRIPs negotiating group of
the Uruguay Round took place in April 1989 and the only agreement
achieved was on a 'general framework for future negotiations to cover
standards concerning the scope and use of intellectual property rights and
the means of enforcing them'.[126] The meetings of the negotiating group
that followed in 1989 consisted of proposals and counter-proposals by the
delegations who were actively participating in the negotiations.[127] These,
however, produced limited substantive agreements, namely, that additional
time should be allowed for less-developed countries to comply fully with
the regulations of the new agreement.[128] It was becoming obvious that
developing countries envisaged TRIPs negotiations as a threat and unless
this perception changed, agreement was going to be very hard to
achieve.[129] At this point, however, pressure exercised outside of the negotiating group and primarily by the bilateral trade actions of the US government proved very effective in bringing the negotiations closer to an end.

Developing countries began to signal their acceptance of the jurisdiction of GATT over the protection of intellectual property.[130] The most
important breakthrough in the months to come was the announcement
made by India in September 1989 that they accepted 'in principle the international enforcement of the trade-related aspects of intellectual property
rights within the framework of the Uruguay Round negotiations'.[131] This,
in turn, led to more developing countries adopting more flexible positions
on the future of this agreement.[132] The dialogue between the governments
in favour and against the new norm turned into a discussion of the parameters of this new norm where division lines multiplied. The persuasion
campaign on the need for such a norm, however, was complete. The coalition of developing countries had lost its major leaders – India had backed
down, while Brazil was heavily pressured into compromise by the sanctions employed by the US government under Special 301. According to
one author, 'developing countries came to realise that in reality [their]
choice was between GATT and USTR'.[133] Left with this option and in

view of possible gains from preferential regional agreements, many developing countries chose to support an IP protection norm in favour of broadened market access.[134] The dialogue with the conservative actors gradually evolved into bargaining over the content of the legal agreement. Although the pressure between developed and developing countries remained, new chasms were beginning to open among the industrialised countries – the US, Japan, the EC, Canada.

Political closure

When the states leading the opposition campaign against the creation of a particular norm signal their willingness to cooperate and negotiate the provisions of this new norm, one can conclude that political closure has been reached. This is a clear indication that a broad consensus exists on the need to create an international norm to regulate behaviour. Closure on the debate regarding the creation of an effective new international norm protecting intellectual property rights did not mean an end to the disagreements among the negotiating parties, but it did indicate a new phase in the development of the norm. Closure was reached partly on the basis of the economic logic and technical knowledge that were generated mainly by US corporations and their European and Japanese counterparts,[135] and fed into the norm-building process. And partly due to coercion – the unilateral policies and actions undertaken by the US government increased the economic pressure on already volatile developing economies. Many developing states that had experienced the determination of the US government to uphold its position on IPR protection by means of unilateral retaliatory trade measures were of the opinion that a multilateral solution could be less harmful and more flexible than bilateral talks with the US government.[136]

Some authors have argued that coercion alone could not explain the whole process of creating this norm.[137] Coercion played a large role, but there were other issues as well that made closure possible. Many developing country governments lacked a clear understanding of this highly technical and complicated subject matter, which led them to make commitments the scale of which they did not fully comprehend. The opposition to TRIPs – coming from public health agencies, consumer groups and NGOs – was not nearly as well organised as the campaign of the proponents of the new norm.[138] As discussed earlier, linkage bargaining meant that states, especially the members of the Cairns Group, were more interested in the immediate gains to be achieved in the sphere of agriculture and the textile industries than the long-term commitments that they were making.[139] In other words, the closure reached at the TRIPs negotiating committee was neither a result of genuine consensus on a plan of action regarding IPRs, nor of fair persuasion in which the best solution prevailed.

Although a consensus was reached on the need to create an international norm protecting IPRs, the negotiating parties continued to disagree on the scope, nature and enforcement of the new rights. These disagreements were not removed by the negotiations over the treaty language. The final agreement, as we will see, reflected primarily the interests of private companies within the developed countries. This in turn meant that the foundations of the IP protection norm were built on a narrow consensus, which struggled to endure the test of time and public pressure. Closure, at least with regard to the intellectual property provisions protecting the developments in the pharmaceutical industry, was challenged and reformulated to incorporate concerns about public health.

Legalisation

Upon closure, the discussions with the conservative actors over the need for a new norm evolved into a debate over the form of the agreement and the institutional arrangements. In March 1990 when the EC tabled a draft agreement on TRIPs[140] in treaty language that covered standards, principles and enforcement issues, this marked the beginning of the process of legalisation.[141] By May, four more proposals were submitted, respectively, by the United States, Japan, Switzerland and India (the latter was backed up Argentina, Brazil, Chile, China, Colombia, Cuba, Egypt, Nigeria, Peru, Tanzania and Uruguay).[142] The proposal submitted by the developing countries still demanded that the issues of trade in counterfeit goods should be separate from other intellectual property protection issues.[143] Negotiations were heading for a complete breakdown with states' interests and demands pulling in different directions.

Since compromise was hard to come by, the chairman of the TRIPS negotiating group, Ambassador Lars Anell of Sweden, presented the chairman's draft.[144] The draft was a report summarising the positions of the negotiating parties and comprised of two parts, reflecting, respectively, the proposals of the developed and the developing countries.[145] Ambassador Anell's draft signalled that some agreement was in sight. According to Jayashree Watal,[146] the most important and effective negotiations took place in the second half of 1990 in informal meetings. Drahos and Braithwaite point out that membership in the informal groups was chosen on the basis of the expertise of the delegates and most important decisions were often taken in the smallest groups.[147] Since these meetings were informal, they left no record and this hinders further studies of the changing positions of different governments. The proposals that were put forward have no recognised source, impeding a better understanding of the dynamics of these negotiations.[148] Analysis is thus likely to miss out on some developments and changes in positions.

Although hopes were high that the Uruguay Round could come to a close at the ministerial meeting in Brussels in December 1990, they quickly disintegrated as negotiations broke down due to deadlock over agricultural subsidies between the European Community, the Cairns Group[149] and the United States.[150] Disagreements existed among all actors – between North and South, among nations in the industrialised North, among countries in the developing South. Economic might, although not irrelevant, became insufficient to resolve differences; the way forward for the negotiations' progress lay in the weight of numbers. Jane Ford notes that the role of developing countries was changing, in that they were becoming negotiators rather than just passive receivers of policies.[151] Once the ministerial meeting in Brussels failed to reach its objective of concluding the Uruguay Round, it became clear that even states with relatively little economic power were in a position to derail the negotiations by adopting an uncompromising position on key issues. This development dispels the conventional understanding that economic might and political pressures alone can push a large number of unwilling members of the international community into signing agreements that run counter to their interests.

The Uruguay Round of trade negotiations was restarted in February 1991 and the GATT was looking for more flexible approaches as it became clear that this would be the only way towards closing the negotiations. The initial 15 negotiating groups were restructured into seven groups.[152] The negotiating committees sought effectiveness by 'keeping the negotiating process constantly under review and supervision'[153] and by introducing informal meetings to foster consensus. The Director General Arthur Dunkel recognised that states were not finalising their positions and were not pushing on with the negotiations on TRIPs because they were waiting for the outcomes in two other spheres of trade negotiations – agriculture and textiles.[154] Director General Dunkel, in his final attempt to salvage the Uruguay Round, put together the Dunkel Draft, which compiled the results of negotiations and 'provided an arbitrated resolution to issues undecided by the negotiators'.[155] Negotiations continued throughout 1992 and 1993 with the US and India tabling proposals for changes to the Dunkel Draft.[156] Once the conflict over agriculture was settled, however, the member states agreed to the whole package of the newly created World Trade Organisation, one part of which was the agreement on TRIPs.[157] The Uruguay Round of trade negotiations was concluded on 15 December 1993, the final act was signed in Marrakech on 15 April 1994 and the WTO agreement was scheduled to come into force on 1 January 1995.

The conclusion of the Uruguay Round was influenced by external factors and the state of the international economy, while the completion of the TRIPs agreement was almost entirely circumstantial. Authors give different weight to the exact factors that brought about the WTO agreement. According to Gail Evans, the slowing down of the world economy increased fears of protectionism and rising levels of national debt,[158] which pushed nation-states into signing the final WTO agreement. Moreover, the round of trade negotiations had become too costly to let agreements slip away. Jayashree Watal claimed instead that it was political events – the collapse of the Berlin Wall, the crumbling of the Soviet Union, and the success achieved in the First Gulf War – which influenced the closing of the Uruguay Round. The US had emerged as the undisputed hegemon in the world, and that made developing and developed states alike unwilling to oppose the global superpower when so near to reaching an agreement at the end of the negotiating round.[159] Watal thus proposed that political factors were the catalyst for the completion of the Uruguay Round, and not the consensus reached in the other spheres of trade, discussed at the trade round.

The success of the TRIPs agreement is partly based on the disproportionate power of the US government and corporations, which was further supported by the lack of a strong unified position on the part of the developing countries. US industries successfully employed rhetorical action, which persuaded the government to protect their interests worldwide. The US government took full advantage of Section 301 of its Trade Act, thus breaking up a relatively strong group of developing countries who dared to stand in opposition.[160] The developing countries' actions were further limited by the lack of expertise and a clear understanding of the full scale of consequences stemming from this new international norm. Furthermore, the package offered at the end of the Uruguay Round negotiations – including concessions on trade in agricultural and textiles products, was too good to miss. The possibility of future gains in areas that deeply concerned the developing countries, coupled with the prospects of having to deal with the unilateral pressure exercised by the USTR,[161] acted as incentives to vote in favour of international minimum rules for the protection of intellectual property rights.[162] Citing a US trade negotiator in his study of the developing countries and their position in the international IP standard-setting process, Drahos observes that TRIPs represented less a negotiation and more a 'convergence of processes', as the opposition of the developing countries was not met by argumentation and reasoning, but was instead diluted through bilateral negotiations and unilateral trade sanctions.[163] The position of the developing countries was further undermined by the fact that African states were not significant players in these trade negotiations even though their development prospects and the welfare of their citizens would be inevitably affected by the decisions of other states.[164] NGOs were also marginalised, as the position of the GATT was that if any actors other than nation-states wanted to put their agenda forward, they should do so through their respective governments,[165] many of whom were disinclined to pay heed to civil society activists.

Closure in this case was based on coercion and not on consensus, or any shared need for legalisation. The character of the closure was reflected in the process of negotiating the legal text of the new norm. Negotiations were exclusive and highly specialised. There was no agreement on the way in which TRIPs would be implemented and many developing states lacked the expertise and resources to make IP provisions a part of their domestic legal context. The TRIPs agreement represented rather a shaky foundation for the creation of a functional international intellectual property regime and that showed in the years to follow.

Operationalisation

Operationalisation of a norm refers to the stage at which the actions of states become norm-compliant, with any behaviour not consistent with the norm condemned or sanctioned. The TRIPs agreement came into force on 1 January 1995, giving developing countries until the end of the year 2000 to comply, while the least-developed countries (LDCs) received an initial extension until the end of the year 2005. The IPR regime for the pharmaceutical industry diverged here by granting developing countries until 2016 to comply.[166] The pressure for operationalising the TRIPs agreement in the pharmaceutical sector raised much concern and opposition. The political closure on TRIPs in the pharmaceutical sector became undone, due to normative pressure brought to bear by developing countries and global civil society.

The actors who were most eager to operationalise the norm protecting intellectual property rights in the pharmaceutical industry were the large corporations like Pfizer, Bristol-Myers, GlaxoSmithKlein, along with the other members of PhRMA, who initiated the whole IPR campaign. The US government had vested interests in enforcing IPRs, which were perceived as a mechanism to decrease the trade deficit. Both industry and the government were in favour of much stricter minimum rules of IP protection at the Uruguay Round, and while developing countries believed that the TRIPs agreement was the lesser evil compared to unilateral trade sanctions by the US, their hopes that the USTR would lessen the pressure on their fragile economies were in vain. The US government continued to pursue higher standards of intellectual property protection with the same vigour[167] and via the same methods. Since the late 1980s, the United States had included requirements for the provision of adequate IP protection as a prerequisite to the conclusion of Bilateral Investment Treaties (BITs) and by 1987 BITs had been signed with 11 developing countries.[168] Peter Drahos discusses in some detail the complementary use of BITs and Section 301 in the case of Nicaragua (1995), which resulted in Nicaragua implementing IP protection policies in 1998 prior to its TRIPs deadline in the year 2000.[169] The US continued to use extensively the provisions of its domestic legal principles, while taking full advantage of the WTO dispute-settlement mechanisms as well. The US filed the first six complaints for TRIPs violations in 1996 against Japan, India, Pakistan, Portugal, Turkey and Indonesia, followed in 1997 by dispute-settlement procedures against Denmark, Sweden, Ireland and Ecuador.[170]

Discontent with the increasing demands of the pharmaceutical industry and the actions of the US government was brewing in the late 1990s. There were several overlapping concerns, which formed the foundation of a relatively powerful opposition to IPRs for pharmaceutical products. First, many developing countries felt they did not get a fair deal out of the TRIPs negotiation process to start with (due to its lack of transparency, asymmetries of power and the isolation of African countries, as discussed earlier). Second, developing countries were not fully availing themselves of the transitional provisions, compulsory licensing provisions and parallel imports provisions granted by the TRIPs agreement. Moreover, developing countries were often sanctioned by the US government, which sought the speedy implementation of the new agreement. Third, NGOs were beginning to actively pursue the issue of access to essential medicines (the case of HIV/AIDS is a particularly strong example) and the problem of the creation of drugs for neglected diseases (tuberculosis, malaria, etc.). All three of these campaigns benefited from the attention that each of them attracted, and that helped in gaining critical mass and wider public support. Although a norm had already been created, there was growing pressure for the revision of this norm in a way that would allow it to cover a broader spectrum of issues, such as social justice, the right to health, sustainable economic development. A coalition was beginning to emerge, bringing together a variety of actors, including developing country governments, NGOs, civil society activists, medical professionals, lawyers and economists. Due to the growing opposition, political closure regarding the need for effective IPRs protecting pharmaceutical products came undone. The resolve of some states to support the agreement weakened, opening the possibility for further negotiations. Discussion of implementation was reopened and normative concerns were taken into account. It should be kept in mind that the process of renegotiating the parameters of this norm began only as a result of sustained pressure and well-calculated political action by the partners of the coalition against this norm.

There was nothing 'natural' or inevitable in the process, which resulted from the convergence of normative campaigns among relatively powerless actors. Since resistance towards the implementation of IPRs in the pharmaceutical industry grew, not without the help of the public in the industrialised world, policy-makers were forced to reconsider and renegotiate the TRIPs provisions in relation to public health. A norm-revision process was set in motion as a result of nongovernmental organisations revealing the negative consequences of TRIPs on the already poor state of health care in developing countries and in the context of the worsening HIV/AIDS pandemic.[171] The power of coercion may have worked in previous stages of this campaign, but bullying countries to prematurely adopt TRIPs rules while they were struggling to provide drugs and medical care angered public opinion. The level of mobilisation and determination of civil society was quite unusual.

Challenging the new norm

Configuration of the network of normative opposition

There was a history of domestic campaigning within the United States for affordable treatment for HIV/AIDS. The ACT UP campaign, which officially began in 1987 with the creation of the First Working Document setting out its objectives and structure, was continuously drawing attention to the 'drug development bottleneck' and the greed of pharmaceutical companies when creating treatments for AIDS.[172] In 1993 Ralph Nader and James Love, founders of the Consumer Project on Technology in 1995, in testimony before the Special Committee on Aging of the US Senate,[173] drew attention to the fact that pharmaceutical companies in general and Bristol-Myers Squibb (BMS) in particular were benefiting from government-sponsored R&D. They argued that corporate profits were made on the back of the taxpayer, because some of the knowledge used by these corporations was produced in government-sponsored research institutions. These two activists opened the debate on fair pricing of and access to medicines that had been discovered with taxpayers' money.[174] US NGOs were further concerned with the availability of medicines to the marginalised groups in society.[175] The traditions in campaigning on these issues were useful when similar concerns were raised at the international level.

New and existing international organisations were getting involved with normative issues stemming from IPRs in the pharmaceutical industry, the availability and affordability of drugs not only for HIV/AIDS, but also for a list of 'neglected diseases'[176] primarily affecting developing countries. The Consumer Project on Technology (CPT) was created in 1995 to address the issue of the high cost of pharmaceuticals.[177] In 1996 the Amsterdam group Health Action International (HAI)[178] organised the first major conference for NGOs regarding issues of health care and TRIPs.[179] In 1998 the highly influential Médecins Sans Frontières (MSF) sought the acquiescence of CPT and HAI to join their campaign for access to medicines.[180] The support of MSF was even more important in 1999 when the organisation was awarded the Nobel Peace Prize, the money from which MSF donated to the Neglected Disease Fund, which was set up to fund projects related to neglected diseases and access to medicines. Another very active coalition of NGOs was consolidated in March 1999 – the Health GAP (Global Access Project) Coalition. Health GAP was started by a New York physician and became a meeting point for human rights activists, people living with HIV/AIDS, public health experts, fair trade advocates. Activities were centred on campaigning for access to affordable, life-saving medicines as a way to control the AIDS pandemic. A growing number of NGOs engaged with health issues and access to medicines. A loose network began to emerge among these NGOs, medical professionals and developing states.

NGO activities were bolstered by political events and social research, which made the claims of the advocates of civil society all the more persuasive. After the coming into force of the TRIPs agreement in 1995, the developing countries faced increasing pressure to stop importing generic drugs that could combat widespread and growing epidemics of curable diseases.[181] In late 1998, a high-profile lawsuit was filed by 39 of the biggest pharmaceutical companies against the government of South Africa. The South African government had passed the African Medicines and Medical Devices Regulatory Authority Act, which allowed it to revoke patents and to use compulsory licensing for purposes of averting a health crisis due to the high number of HIV/AIDS patients in the country.[182] This case, which was dropped by the pharmaceutical giants in 2001,[183] generated much negative publicity for the pharmaceutical industry, turning into a terrible PR disaster; it also helped NGOs and developing countries mobilise public opinion in favour of their cause.

The network of opposition was most clearly delineated at the Geneva Meeting in March 1999, which was organised by MSF, HAI and CPT and comprised more than 120 delegations from 30 countries.[184] The meeting brought together representatives of national governments, NGOs, international organisations and industry delegates. Attention was focused on the issue of compulsory licensing as a means of making drugs more affordable in poor countries.[185] The Access to Essential Medicines Campaign continued to grow, with Oxfam UK joining it in 1999, thus contributing to increased civic activism. The interests of otherwise separate campaigns overlapped in their constructive opposition to the TRIPs agreement. Less powerful actors found strength in numbers and were able to make their concerns heard by the governments and the industries of the developed countries alike.

Formulation of the issues raised by the opposition

The need to revise the TRIPs agreement in such a way as to address public health concerns was outlined by NGOs and developing countries, against the backdrop of claims by pharmaceutical companies that without full compliance with TRIPs they would go out of business.[186] NGOs and developing countries organised a number of conferences to discuss issues of access to and availability of essential medicines and medicines for the neglected diseases. Following a pattern, similar to that in the campaign against torture, conferences served to formulate the problem at hand, to consolidate the positions of various actors, and to attract public attention.

Concerns of a medical character along with ethical questions were juxtaposed with economic interests, within a political and judicial context, which was not necessarily suited to the needs of the poor. Science was accused of following markets and funding in setting research agendas, while disregarding the needs of the poor. Richer states and private corporations put profits before normative concerns and that attracted much criticism.

> How we phrase the problem defines the solutions we seek ... AIDS, the TB, the malaria, the sleeping sickness epidemics are not simply global public health crises – they are obscene acts of political negligence that cannot go on.... Trade law around intellectual property rights for pharmaceuticals, the political process around their application, the deification of profit over people, and the fact that trade has become a barrier to health of literally billions of people is nothing short of the most profound obscenity.[187]

These succinct but powerful words of Dr James Orbinski – the functioning president of MSF International in 1999 – summarised the way in which the opposition to full-scale TRIPs rules for pharmaceutical products defined the issues that MSF was trying to resolve.

The scale of the problem, as highlighted by the opponents to TRIPs, was indeed daunting. UN estimates from 1998 indicate that 26 million of the estimated 33 million people infected with AIDS live in sub-Saharan Africa and approximately 95 per cent of the worldwide cases of HIV are in the developing world.[188] MSF argued that most of the patients with HIV in Africa have no access to antiretrovirals at all, while only about 1 in 100 patients in Southeast Asia can afford the drug cocktails.[189] Communicable diseases were responsible for the deaths of 14 million people around the world in 1999 and most deaths were in developing countries,[190] while around 0.2 per cent of pharmaceutical research is devoted to infectious diseases like acute respiratory infections, tuberculosis (TB) and diarrhoea.[191] Malaria exists in 91 countries, which puts around 40 per cent of the world's population at risk – from the 500 million cases that are recorded, around 90 per cent are in Africa where up to 2.7 million die from the disease.[192] And while one-third of the world's population has no access to pharmaceutical drugs, the industrialised countries hold 97 per cent of all pharmaceutical patents worldwide.[193] These medical statistics compiled by various IGO agencies and NGOs paint a completely different picture to the one presented by the pharmaceutical giants, which had simply chosen to ignore the state of the health of individuals in the developing and least developed countries.

The ethical issues relating to access to essential medicines, neglected diseases, and social justice raised by the civil society campaigns attracted the attention of UN agencies. In 1996 the World Health Assembly Report pointed out that 'poverty exposes hundreds of millions of people to the hazard of infectious diseases in their everyday lives … half the world's population lacks regular access to the most needed essential drugs'.[194] This in turn would worsen health concerns further deepening inequalities and the health crisis that humanity is facing. Once the TRIPs agreement is fully operational generic drug producers would not be allowed to export their products to countries which do not have the capabilities to produce their own pharmaceutical products, affecting the supply of affordable drugs.

The ethical concern over the treatment of curable diseases in developing countries and the affordability of medicines is exacerbated by the foreign trade policies of the US government. Its bilateral agreements in the form of BITs and Free Trade Agreements (FTAs)[195] are eroding the ability of developing countries' governments to provide much needed health care for their citizens.[196] The campaigners for revising the TRIPs agreement have, by means of publicising the decisions and policies of the US government, constructed an ethical problem. They question the morality of policy-makers and businesses alike and seek to 'reveal injustice, to provoke change, and to locate and insist on political responsibility', in the words of James Orbinski.[197] To tackle the problem with access to medicines, Oxfam initiated the Cut the Cost Campaign in February 2001. While making the case for affordable drugs, Oxfam together with MSF, HAI, CPT, ACT UP and others began to deconstruct the argument made by the pharmaceutical companies that 'without patents, [some drugs] would not even exist'.[198] The normative framework thus approached the problem from both a normative and a technical angle. This is another instance where the combination of ethical concerns and technical knowledge laid the foundation of an effective campaign.

Pharmaceutical companies initially constructed their concern with IPRs as an economic issue of life or death for the industry: 'innovative pharmaceutical companies are in business to make money, as well as to market new medicines, and, unless they do both, they would be out of business, and the flow of new medicines would be reduced', said the CEO of Merck & Co Inc.[199] Lee Gillespie-White from the International Intellectual Property Institute stated that '[i]t is only from the protection of the intellectual property invested in new drug development that the incentive to innovate arises. And without this incentive, new drugs will not be produced and the right to health care will be increasingly insecure'[200] and further 'IP is being asked to shoulder too much of the burden of the right to health care. [And since the system is unable to do this] new drugs will not be produced and future advances in health care will be jeopardised'.[201] The estimated cost of discovering a new medicine and bringing it to the market, according to studies within the pharmaceutical industry, has risen from around $54 million in 1979, to $231 million in 1987 US dollars, and to as much as $802 million in 2001, which, after being supplemented by the cost of failed projects ($114 million) and the inflation figures, has been put up even higher.[202] The pharmaceutical industry further argued that there was no causal link between relaxed intellectual property rules and improved access to medicines.[203] Patents were not considered to be the principal impediments to supplying patients with medicines because the impediments were more practical, such as lack of 'refrigerators and clean water, needed for administering complicated anti-HIV regimes'.[204] Thus the industry sought to downplay the causal link between IP protection and access to medicines, because if these were perceived as unrelated, pharmaceutical corporations could hold onto a positive public image, while continuing the pursuit of higher profits.

NGOs and developing agencies have been working hard to produce evidence that countered the reports of industries, aiming to show that these were manipulated and one-sided, seeking to justify higher profits at the expense of the needs of the poor. According to Oxfam, the pharmaceutical industry has some of the highest operating profits already, standing at around 20–23 per cent on investment.[205] At the same time, the whole of sub-Saharan Africa accounts for only a minute fraction of the global market for medicines – $1 billion of a $343 billion US industry.[206] If the markets of the developing countries are so small, then even more lax IPR rules in these parts of the world would not profoundly affect the R&D capacity of the pharmaceutical industry. On the question of the causal link between IPRs and innovation, various authors have argued that it does not exist. According to the UNDP *Human Development Report*, 'studies have found that the competitive markets are the biggest influence on research and development, not patents'.[207] Research and development is driven by the prospect for profits and the size of the market for new products and not by the availability of restrictions on knowledge.[208] According to the Commission on Intellectual Property Rights (set by the Department for International Development in the UK),

> stronger patent protection in poor countries is unlikely to lead to significant increases in *global* innovation for neglected diseases. This is because the key disincentive for international companies to develop intellectual property of use to developing countries is not the lack of patent protection in those countries but the lack of market demand and profitability.[209]

This argument is at the centre of the campaign to modify the trade rules of TRIPs in such a way as to make them more responsive to the needs of the poor in the realm of health care and pharmaceutical products.

The NGO campaign highlighted the related problem of the treatment of neglected diseases and the direction of scientific research, where 'Science follows the market', as argued by Jeffrey Sachs in an article about the state of the world's poorest populations.[210] According to the UNDP report of 1999, 'tighter control of innovation in the hands of multinational corporations ignores the needs of millions'.[211] Médecins Sans Frontières conducted a survey in 2001 that included the 20 largest pharmaceutical companies in the world and some of these findings have helped to further outline the ethical problem of neglected diseases. None of the companies responding to the survey had in the past five years brought to the market a drug for the most neglected diseases.[212] Furthermore, for 25 years only 15 new drugs for tropical diseases and tuberculosis were brought to the market, compared to 179 new drugs for cardiovascular diseases, where tropical diseases and TB make up 12 per cent of the global disease burden and cardiovascular conditions make up 11 per cent.[213] These figures helped raise awareness about the disproportionate burden of disease in many developing countries, which is worsened by the fact that pharmaceutical companies are not interested in consumers who cannot afford to pay. Non-governmental organisations worked to mobilise governments to take action and resolve the conflicting rights to private property and to life and health.[214]

Oxfam constructed the problem of access to medicines as an issue relating to economic development as well. The organisation drew attention to the global health divide, where 'widespread sickness acts as a brake on economic growth'.[215] The HIV/AIDS epidemic combined with the Asian economic crisis in the late 1990s is said to have had a detrimental impact on development in the region since it hit the most productive members of society and began to reverse the development gains.[216] The problem of HIV/AIDS and access to medicines for neglected diseases is even worse in Africa, where, according to the World Bank, 'AIDS has already reversed 30 years of hard-won social progress in some countries'.[217] Jeffrey Sachs also warned that disease and short life expectancy in the developing countries are not 'just a result of poverty, but also a powerful cause of impoverishment'.[218] By linking the issues of access to and availability of medicines to economic development, NGOs were able to appeal to a larger audience, since the problem of development has been on government and international institutional agendas since the call for a New International Economic Order of 1974.

The network of normative opposition to the newly legalised norm of IPR protection has managed to reveal a multilayered normative problem in its vast complexity by publicising and problematising various aspects of this new norm – such as human health, access to medicines, affordability of medicines, economic development, and the weighing of individual rights to health and life against the rights of companies to exclude individuals and governments from the advances of pharmacology in the name of higher profits. The underlying normative theme, however, has been centred on the issue of social justice. Initially, TRIPs were created under the influence and with the assistance of experts representing industries and this is reflected in the inflexible, instrumental character of the agreement, which aims at ensuring that royalties flow to the patent holders and free-riding on registered patents is kept to a minimum. The powerful normative message constructed by the opposition campaign and developing countries, however, managed to effectively mobilise public opinion worldwide and demand a new consideration of IPRs for pharmaceutical products, which pays closer attention to the broader implications of the norm.

*Proponents and opponents of full-scale implementation of
TRIPS for pharmaceuticals*

NGOs and developing countries formed the network of normative opposition, formulated their issue of concern and led a dialogue with those actors who supported the full-scale implementation of the TRIPs treaty in the years between 1999 and the present as the efforts are ongoing. In this section, I analyse the key events that brought about a change in the provisions of the TRIPs agreement relating to the products of the pharmaceutical industry, and the changing positions of the stakeholders in the debate.

As discussed earlier, campaigns for access to HIV/AIDS medicines were well underway in the US in 1996 with CPT and ACT UP leading the way. In March 1996, the World Health Organisation published a report of the World Health Assembly, entitled 'The State of World Health – A Fatal Complacency'. The report drew attention to problems related to the struggle for control over infectious diseases such as malaria, respiratory diseases, AIDS, hepatitis, some cancers caused by viruses and the potential for global pandemics due to increased amounts of air travel and the development of drug-resistant strands of bacteria. In January 1996, UNAIDS was created to manage and coordinate the work of six other UN agencies – UNESCO, UNDP, UNFPA, UNICEF, WHO and WB.[219] Also in 1996, HAI organised the first conference on public health and TRIPs, held in Germany.

The actual dialogue between non-state activists, developing countries, the pharmaceutical industries and the governments of the Quad countries (US, EU, Japan and Canada) did not become visible to the public until 1997. In 1997, the South African case discussed previously outraged many and drew attention to the issue of IP protection. In 1999 NGOs began to mobilise for the upcoming 3rd WTO ministerial conference in Seattle, as this was a chance to get the issue of access to medicines on the governmental agenda. A number of NGO conferences were held, including AIDS and Essential Medicines and Compulsory Licensing – held in Geneva, 25–27 March, and sponsored by Médecins Sans Frontières, Health Action International and the Consumer Project on Technology, and Increasing Access to Essential Drugs in a Globalised Economy Working Towards Solutions (conference organised by HAI, MSF and CPT, in Amsterdam, 25–26 November). These brought together not only NGOs but health professionals and governmental officials from developing countries.

In 2000, UNAIDS reached an agreement with five of the biggest pharmaceutical companies to supply cheaper AIDS drugs to some African countries.[220] The 53rd Meeting of the World Health Assembly attracted trade and IP experts representing states and international organisations.[221]

The meeting was focused on confronting the HIV/AIDS epidemic and on taking swift actions to match the political commitments that many developed countries had made.[222] President Clinton issued an executive order to make AIDS drugs available far more cheaply throughout sub-Saharan Africa.[223] In other words, although NGOs and developing countries were not negotiating directly with pharmaceutical giants and developed country governments, the dialogue between them was taking place on the pages of academic journals, in the discussion forums of various UN agencies, at international conferences and in the public space. The debate was made very public and pharmaceutical companies were trying to promote an image of themselves as 'caring and sharing' members of society, while holding on to their demands for the strict application of the TRIPs agreement, but this proved impossible. Companies began to make concessions by means of donating drugs to developing countries and by selling medicines at discounted prices.[224] NGOs pointed out that such ad hoc measures were not a solution to the problem of access to medicines, nor to the implementation of the TRIPs agreement, which is rather rigid in its provisions and disregards the needs of many in the developing world.[225]

The year 2001 witnessed fast developments and changes in the dialogue between the actors on issues of public health and access to medicines. Oxfam UK launched its Cut the Cost campaign, joining MSF, CPT, HAI and Voluntary Service Overseas (VSO) in their efforts to generate enough public attention to influence policy-makers into taking practical action and making commitments on these issues. Public pressure was also mounting in view of the continued court case between the South African government and the pharmaceutical companies. MSF launched an internet petition to collect signatures asking drug companies to drop the case.[226] Under increasingly negative public exposure and in view of the commitments made by President Clinton in 2000, the pharmaceutical firms dropped the lawsuit. This was an important moment for the campaigners because it confirmed that their tactics could bring results. Campaigners felt the need to engage expert knowledge in order for their arguments to be taken seriously.

The normative campaigners to undo TRIPs regulations of pharmaceutical goods began attracting their own pool of experts – legal scholars, economists, medical personnel. They provided technical analysis, which showed that in many situations the arguments advanced by the experts of the pharmaceutical industry were only aimed at protecting its economic interests. Legal scholars like Frederick Abbott and Peter Drahos, medical experts like Nathan Ford (MSF) and economists like Carlos Correa solidified and validated the arguments put forward by the activists of civil society. The dialogue among experts revealed the complexity of the problems posed by the current intellectual property legislation – including ethical issues of access to medicines and profit levels of pharmaceutical companies, legal issues of whose rights should take precedence – individual rights or rights to intellectual property, political issues between developing states and most often the US with its practice of bilateral trade agreements. The actors in this case study were of different economic calibre – volunteer NGOs vs the top pharmaceutical companies,[227] but they were equally unified around their arguments, which makes the success of the civil society campaign all the more interesting.

The dialogue between the supporters of full-scale enforcement of the TRIPs agreement and the supporters of changes to the agreement culminated at the 4th WTO Ministerial Conference in Doha, Qatar (November 2001). The conference was preceded by intense political and social activities. The World Health Organisation together with the WTO, the Ministry of Foreign Affairs of Norway and the Global Health Council organised a workshop on differential pricing and financing of essential drugs.[228] The African countries, virtually left out of earlier TRIPs negotiations, became united in their demands for the revision of the agreement and submitted a proposal to the TRIPS council requesting that the issue of IPR protection be examined in conjunction with the problem of access to medicines.[229] The council accepted this proposal, which was later examined in the meetings of the TRIPs negotiating group. The dialogue between North and South at the Doha Ministerial Conference was further mitigated by a number of external factors. The unsuccessful lawsuit of the 39 pharmaceutical companies against the government of South Africa gave more power to Western NGOs and caught the attention of Western media and public opinion. The increasing amount of scientific research on the influence of patents over the availability and affordability of various drugs,[230] which was conducted independent of industrial groups like PhRMA, took the sting out of an otherwise highly influential study by Amir Attaran and Lee Gillespie-White,[231] undermining its 'aura of scientific objectivity'.[232] The anthrax attack in the US immediately following the 9/11 attacks on the World Trade Center in New York had made the US government consider compulsory licensing in case of a public emergency, which was the same move that the US was trying to deny to the developing world.[233] The preceding NGO campaign had influenced public opinion in the OECD governments, that they could not afford to disregard public demands for concerted actions to improve the availability of medicines in developing countries and afford their governments the right to look after the health of their citizens in situations of public health crisis.[234]

Discussions at the Doha Ministerial Conference were by no means easy, but governments had agreed that 'TRIPs should not be part of the problem but part of the solution ... and that countries should not be put under pressure bilaterally or in the WTO to limit their use of the flexibilities built into the TRIPS Agreement'.[235] After prolonged discussions in Doha, the TRIPS Council produced the Declaration on the TRIPS Agreement and Public Health[236] (hereafter referred to as the Doha Declaration).

The Doha Declaration represents a limited *political closure* in a debate that continues today. The declaration signals closure on the issue of the need for action on the HIV/AIDS pandemic, on government responsibility to address this problem together with the issue of neglected diseases. Attention was also drawn to the disproportionate public health burden on developing countries' governments and agreement was reached that concerted government action should be taken.[237] Developed countries recognised as legitimate the problems of developing countries without production capabilities for generic medicines, which would be unable to import cheap generic drugs after the agreement is fully in force, and requested the council for TRIPS to find an expeditious solution.[238] The declaration postponed the entry into force of the agreement for the least-developed countries until 1 January 2016.[239]

The Doha Declaration did not completely close the debate over TRIPs between industry and civil society. It may have partially moderated the TRIPs-related foreign policies of the US towards the rest of the world, but it neither resolved problems of public health, nor established any long-term mechanisms that would ensure that TRIPS would not get in the way of any possible solutions to problems of access to medicines, availability of R&D for neglected diseases and the treatment of HIV/AIDS. The debates over the best possible policies continue on the pages of academic journals,[240] in various conferences and workshops,[241] and by different civil society actors.[242] One last development that took place in August 2003 seems to have concluded, at least for the moment, the legal and political battle over the permissibility and the extent of IPR protection of pharmaceutical products. A decision was taken by the council on TRIPs to make it easier for developing countries to import cheap generics made under compulsory licensing if they were unable to manufacture the medicines themselves.[243] The member states of the WTO had planned to reach an agreement on permanently incorporating the Doha Declaration waiver into the TRIPs agreement by the end of June 2004; however, this has not yet been achieved, as negotiations have become bogged down in details. This issue remained unresolved at the WTO ministerial meeting in Hong Kong in December 2005.

Conclusions

This chapter examined norm development and knowledge creation in the context of the emerging norm protecting intellectual property rights in the pharmaceutical industry. The empirical evidence that was obtained shows that the process of norm creation is not necessarily a linear one. When consensus among key actors becomes unattainable, the processes of normative network configuration and issue formulation may take place anew to frame the normative issue in a way consistent with state interests and public normative demands. It has further become apparent that reaching political closure does not always signify the end of normative, scientific and political negotiations. The process of creating a norm is a dynamic one, and it continually interacts with the normative, scientific and political contexts of the time. It is this interaction that can lead to unpredictable results – such as the opening and closing of controversies, reaching swift agreements or prolonging negotiations.

The case study of IPRs in the pharmaceutical industry is particularly interesting because of the interplay among political, normative and economic power. The outcome of these negotiations defies the conventional wisdom that 'might makes right'. Although prevailing at first, economic interests then had to give way to more important normative concerns and developed countries have been constrained to give in to the demands of the developing ones, for more lax principles of intellectual property protection of pharmaceuticals. The way in which knowledge and normative concerns were framed afforded valuable insight into the patterns of their interplay.

Economic power and political power are very important determinants of the direction in which international norms evolve; however, these alone may not always determine the direction of normative change, because moral campaigns have the potential and ability to overshadow economic and political power. Scientific knowledge is another influential resource in the creation of norms and is useful in backing up practical and ethical arguments alike. Public opinion is an understudied force in international norm creation because, when mobilised, it may speak louder than economic power, especially in cases when the price of economic progress in one part of the world costs human lives in another. This is certainly not the case in every situation and there are still numerous examples of economic actors abusing their power, but this case study shows the potential of public opinion even against some of the largest corporations in the world. The number of actors and the strength of their union are also crucial in the negotiations of the parameters of a norm. Although developing countries, for example, do not have influential economic leverage, they can sometimes accumulate political leverage in international negotiations when they stand together in difficult negotiations.

An important conclusion stemming from this historical reconstruction of the events leading up to the current norm of IPR protection of pharmaceutical products is related to the nature of closure in international politics. Initially, political closure leading to the TRIPs agreement was reached via coercion and was based on partial scientific closure, stemming from the reports of Northern industries. The normative closure was also one-sided in that it only took account of the normative concerns of fairness that industries put forward. Political closure was based on rhetorical action and coercion, and proved to be unstable as a result. Since the industrialised states were faced with difficulties and strong normative upheaval among civil society networks and developing states, political closure was reversed and the debate over the scope and character of the new norm reopened. This empirical study thus shows that coercion is not always effective and that, when political closure is based on one-sided technical knowledge and normative concerns, it may become unstable and susceptible to challenges.

The developments leading up to the creation of the TRIPs agreement and the negotiations that followed it fit well into the negotiating stages proposed in the theoretical model of norm creation. Although the normative process was specific to this norm (with the reopening of political debates), the negotiations' dynamics were characteristic of the same theoretical stages. Studying the negotiating processes in more detail clearly reveals the different types of power at play in the international system and shows that more traditional theoretical approaches, which limit their understanding of power to that of state power, are missing out on vital developments in the international system. The negotiating networks develop their own methods of cooperation and lines of agreement, which become the foundation of more peaceful coexistence and regional collaboration. The interaction between governments and scientific communities, lobby groups, civil society organisations, advocacy networks paves the way to more transparent and democratic international governance. This case study shows that normative concerns play a large part in international policy-making and that the general public is capable of applying political pressure on moral grounds when properly mobilised. The developments post-Doha also raise hopes that the international community can address issues in a way that is sensitive to the needs of individuals in the developing world. They also raise the question whether individual human rights are taking centre stage in the politics of the global village, or if they still come second to what is perceived as the 'strategic interests' of states.

5   Protecting the atmosphere to avoid climate change

> Humanity has the ability to make development sustainable to ensure that it meets the needs of the present without compromising the ability of future generations to meet their own needs.[1]

The norm advocating economic development in harmony with our natural environment was first spelt out in the Report of the World Commission on Environment and Development in 1987 and became the normative foundation for continuous legislation in the realm of international environmental politics. The chairman of the commission, Dr Gro Harlem Brundtland, emphasised that while until the 1980s humanity has been concerned with the effects of economic growth on the environment,

> we are now forced to concern ourselves with the impacts of ecological stress – degradation of soils, water regimes, atmosphere and forests upon our economic prospects.... Ecology and economy are becoming ever more interwoven ... into a seamless net of causes and effects.[2]

This report, submitted to the UN General Assembly, marked the entry of environmental issues on to the international political agenda, which was an important first step towards generating international environmental norms in the future.

The sphere of international environmental governance is very broad – comprising every aspect of our natural environment; and very complex – due to the high degree of interconnectedness between all natural elements and our insufficient understanding of these links. Legalising environmental politics is a difficult task as it involves numerous actors whose interests may collide irreconcilably or pull in different directions. Amidst the multitude of environmental concerns, this study focuses on the emerging norm for the protection of the atmosphere from increasing greenhouse gas concentrations, which are perceived to lead to changes in global climate. The process of constructing the problem of global warming involves continuous scientific debate, strong normative beliefs centred on inter-societal and intergenerational justice, and the powerful economic interests of the energy-producing industry. This case study provides abundant material for the study of the interplay between technical knowledge, normative ideas, economic and political power; as well as for the changing spectrum of actors who partake in international decision-making and the powers they exercise. The problem of global warming is of great magnitude and importance because of the scale of its possible consequences for all activities of humanity and its natural habitat.

There is an ongoing scientific debate about whether global climate change is occurring, undermining the tentative political agreement that action needs to be taken. Scientific opinion has varied widely and some authors have attributed this variation to the interests of those who fund the research. The politicisation of science has undermined scientific neutrality and objectivity, and opened space for resistance to scientific advice. Scientists still lack a complete understanding of the ways in which the elements of our environment relate to and influence each other. Some sceptics, however, argue that more science may not necessarily lead us to the right answers if such exist at all, or even if it does, that it might not necessarily result in better policy.[3] The complexity of natural processes and the interplay between the various parts of the environment stand in the way of ascertaining whether the problem of global warming is real, what the direction of climate fluctuation is,[4] what consequences we can expect, and if there is anything that can be done to modify these consequences. The scientific community seems unable to reach an unequivocal agreement on any of these issues. The lack of scientific closure has in turn affected political negotiations and thus political closure, as it allowed actors to make arguments against meaningful political action on the basis of that scientific uncertainty.

Like science, industries have been divided over the existence of climate change and on the need for immediate action to avert possible crisis. Businesses that are directly implicated in fostering climate change – the fossil fuel industries and those who rely on their products, for example – are in direct opposition to any meaningful action being taken at present, as any action is likely to come at a great cost for them. At the same time, the insurance sector, the renewable energy and the green technologies sector have seen a window of opportunity to unite their efforts and counter the actions of energy producers in order to improve their market positions. Insurers are increasingly worried about the rising costs of the aftermath of natural disasters, which are predicted to increase in both frequency and intensity,[5] while the green energy lobby has an opportunity to bank on alternative energy sources.[6]

Among states, the North–South debate was magnified and deepened by the climate change negotiations, where disagreements were centred around the allocation of costs and responsibilities. The G-77 countries, although a very diverse group, were united in their position that the developed world should take the lead in lowering emissions and should furthermore pledge resources and technologies to assist the developing world in fulfilling its obligations towards future generations. Since the consumption and life-style patterns in developed countries are perceived as the main cause of current environmental problems, the South has found it easier to consoli-date its stance.[7] The developing countries further insist that they should be given an equal opportunity to develop economically and should not be held back.[8] At the same time, OECD countries predict that China, India and the rest of the developing world will produce 60 per cent of green-house gas (GHG) emissions by the year 2050,[9] and insist on the inclusion of developing states in environmental negotiations. A further complicating factor is that environmental degradation in general and climate change in particular are predicted to have a most notable impact on developing coun-tries – affecting patterns of agriculture, food production, the availability of fresh water, etc., which would undermine the prospects of future economic development in these parts of the world.

Nongovernmental organisations, advocacy networks and social move-ments are also heavily involved with the climate change campaign. Their numbers have been growing exponentially over the last decade, while only a few of the largest ones have managed to make a noticeable differ-ence by means of cooperation with governments and businesses. A large part of environmental NGOs have remained on the fringes of the policy-making process, due to political subjectivity, lack of a clear agenda and the use of dubious campaigning techniques. The United Nations and its agencies engaged with the issue of climate change have been accom-modating of a variety of NGOs, and have welcomed their contributions to the campaign. Non-state actors continue to participate in governmental negotiations and to provide useful information, but the fact that their network is very loose and disjointed has affected their power to put pressure on states. UN agencies have also come under criticism for their role in coordinating and managing the environmental regime in general and climate change negotiations in particular. Supporters of their work have indicated that the perceived problems of the United Nations Environ-mental Programme are rooted in limited political will on the side of states to unambiguously commit to environmental protection and effective governance.[10]

Achieving an international response in a world of sovereign states, conflicting corporate interests, clashing civil society demands, and uncertain scientific knowledge is unlikely to be easy. The consequences and effects of global climate change and enhanced greenhouse gas concentrations are likely to affect societies to varying degrees. They would not necessarily be confined to the states that produce higher emissions, but are likely to affect the vulnerable, poverty-stricken societies of the South, exacerbating already existing inequalities and negatively affecting development. Wedged between the issues of scientific uncertainty and limited political will is also the problem of the lack of urgency, as climate change was initially predicted to take place after hundreds of years (these predictions are currently being modified). Previous examples of effective environmental agreements have had two features in common, as illustrated by the regulations on ozone depletion, biodiversity (the Mediterranean, tropical rainforests, extinction of species), acid rain – first, there was an immediate need for action; and second, the causal relations were clear and straightforward. The effects of the build-up of greenhouse gases in the atmosphere may take decades to manifest themselves, while action to combat increasing levels of greenhouse gases is likely to be costly and have unpredictable effects, even with the best intentions. Concerned scientists have emphasised the need to take decisive action on climate change before it is too late. The growing body of evidence, documenting some irreversible changes to our planet has so far been insufficient to induce resolute international political action.

The study of environmental politics is probably the one area where the need to bridge the social constructivism of IR and SSK, is becoming most obvious. Analysis of the practice of knowledge creation with regards to the norm for the protection of the atmosphere has been much more extensive than in other fields of international politics. There has been growing criticism that climate change has become an area in which knowledge has followed finance, in search of continued attention and relevance.[11] Different types of power have been utilised by a broad spectrum of actors and processes of the social construction of meaning have been affected in the process. The interests and identities of states have been influenced by the norm construction process, while public opinion has struggled to reflect the resolve of non-state actors in demanding meaningful political action.

The aim of this chapter is to begin untangling the complex web of processes leading to the construction of the norm to control climate change. I begin by identifying the actors involved in the creation of this norm, their normative positions and the tactics that they engage to achieve their goals. Close attention will be paid to the methods of argument and persuasion that actors have chosen to get this issue on the international agenda, to sustain the interest in it and to persuade states to produce binding legal principles capable of changing the parameters of appropriate behaviour.

Greenhouse gases are essential in keeping the earth inhabitable, as it has been estimated that, if they were not in the atmosphere, the earth's surface would be approximately 33°C cooler.[12] There are six main gases that make our atmosphere act as a greenhouse, according to the Intergovernmental Panel on Climate Changes. These gases are opaque and trap the heat reflected from the earth's surface, as opposed to letting it escape back into space. Scientists argue that industrialisation, mass deforestation and the increased use of agricultural fertilisers increase GHG concentrations in the earth's atmosphere. Sceptical scientists believe that there isn't enough evidence to prove that human activity is capable of causing global warming, because there are mechanisms that regulate the greenhouse effect. Some are natural – CO_2 'sinks',[13] and some are man-made – sulphur, soot, ash, dust, which reflect heat back into space and thus create a cooling effect.[14] Some evidence suggests that there is much more natural CO_2 trapped in the tundra and the world oceans than humans have produced, which would in other words make the human impact negligible.

The changes that global warming could bring about are profound, in that it could directly threaten the ability of humanity to produce food, retain access to fresh water and survive. Although it is difficult to predict the exact scale of the problem and thus its exact consequences, increasing the temperature of the earth's surface is likely to change the plant life, agricultural activity and food production, precipitation patterns and climatic zones, thus disrupting familiar patterns of human existence.[15] Scientists have further suggested that climate change is likely to affect developing countries worst because of the high financial and technological costs of adapting to the new conditions, which would take funding away from direct economic development.[16] Ecological imbalance, stress and resource scarcity can swiftly become the leading causes of violent conflict in politically volatile areas, which has further engaged the interest of policy-makers at the international level.[17] All these factors make research into climate change urgent and vital.

History of climate change research

The inception of climate change research was almost entirely accidental – global warming was discovered in the process of searching for the causes of the Ice Age.[18] Although theories about the warming of the temperature at the earth's surface were available as early as the nineteenth century, the issue was not constructed as a problem until much later. Scientists have been instrumental in conceptualising and theorising this issue, and drawing attention to it. Having communities of scientists guiding the policy process has had an impact on the political dynamics of the process of norm build- ing, which as will be demonstrated, has been quite different from the proc- esses in the preceding case studies.

It was not until the eighteenth century that some European scientific societies began keeping a more structured and standardised record of weather and weather fluctuations.[19] A series of international conferences and publications of climatologists and meteorologists established the need for standardised record of temperatures, precipitations and general weather conditions, which later became one of the requirements of the scientific approach to climate issues, to ensure consistency across the world.[20] Con- sistent climate monitoring records have only been compiled over the last two centuries, which leaves contemporary scientists without direct histor- ical data, reducing their chances of recreating a reliable picture of the climate changes that the earth has experienced.[21] Climate change occurs in long cycles and the lack of older records has left scientific hypotheses without solid evidence to prove either the lack or the imminence of global warming.

In the nineteenth century, scientists and people with general interest in the natural world were researching the causes of the Ice Age, when results from experiments and calculations pointed out that the earth's atmosphere was warming up and retaining heat from the sun. Jean Baptiste Joseph Fourier is considered the first author to compare the function of the earth's atmosphere to that of 'glass in a greenhouse' as early as 1824.[22] Later, John Tyndall studied the transparency of the gases of the atmosphere and discovered that, while oxygen and nitrogen were transparent, the gases produced by the burning of coal, like CO_2 and methane, were opaque and able to absorb heat.[23] Tyndall was concerned with the scenario where the concentration of the opaque gases drops and the surface of the earth cools down, leading to another Ice Age.[24] While he is considered to have coined the term 'greenhouse effect' in his 1859 publication, Tyndall's work was not concerned with global warming.[25] Further research on the greenhouse effect and the possibility of a new Ice Age was conducted by Svante August Arrhenius. He produced a mathematical model to reflect and predict the amount of temperature change related to the change of the atmospheric concentration of CO_2 and conducted extensive calculations. Arrhenius's calculations were prompted by the eruption of the Krakatau volcano on the island of Palau in Indonesia.[26] As the volcanic dust was spread around the world by winds, scientists predicted the possibility of temperatures falling and the advent of a new Ice Age. One of Arrhenius's most popular publications is entitled 'On the Influence of Carbonic Acid in the Air upon the Temperature of the Ground',[27] and is often cited as the inception of the climate change discussion.

Scientists have been probing numerous hypotheses over the years, regarding both the causes and consequences of a change in earth's climate. Some of these have been more plausible than others, but none has emerged with overwhelming certainty. The variability of climate has been attributed to spots on the sun,[28] to the movement of continents,[29] to human activities, to the complexity of the interaction between the various parts of the natural environment,[30] to the changing orbit of our planet. Some of the works were based on scientific evidence while others were purely speculative, but the debates were nowhere near to a conclusion. The first publication arguing that fossil fuel burning causes increases in the temperature of the earth's atmosphere was George Callendar's article 'The Artificial Production of Carbon Dioxide and Its Influence on Temperature', published in 1938.[31] The author examined data from 200 weather stations around the world between 1880 and 1934 and concluded that temperatures were on the rise already.[32] The early scholars of climate change believed global warming to be beneficial. They projected that warmer weather could improve plant growth and food production, and make more places inhabitable in a world of ever growing population.[33] The debate on the causes of the Ice Age, as well as the question whether the earth was warming up or cooling down, continued in the first half of the twentieth century.

Despite scientific reports, articles and debates regarding climate change, little political or social response was generated until the 1960s. There was a confluence of external factors that brought the issue onto the political agenda. These include changes in the relationship between science and politics, social changes and growing public concerns, civil society engagement, the work of the United Nations, natural disasters, and the generation of better scientific understanding. It took several decades for the issue of climate change to get enough public attention, and even that has not been sufficient to get the policy process moving more efficiently.

Science was not taken too seriously by politicians up until the middle of the twentieth century. It was perceived as incompetent and subjective. The use of the atomic bomb at the end of the Second World War and the unfolding of the arms race in the early years of the Cold War helped politicians realise the potential benefits of scientific research, which became directly associated with issues of national security.[34] After the end of the war, science also became part of the new industrial complex; research attracted more public and private funding and became the foundation for developing the postwar economy.[35] In the politically charged atmosphere of the Cold War, science was seen as objective, neutral and practical, based on hard facts and precise calculations.

The use of nuclear weapons at the end of the war, nuclear testing and proliferation raised public concerns about its effects on human health and its potential to cause long-term environmental damage. Atmospheric pollution also became a problem in the context of the blooming industrial development during the 1950s when London became known for its 'killer smog'.[36] The press reflected these concerns in articles discussing apocalyptic scenarios of rising sea levels, loss of habitat and changing agriculture zones that would hinder economic development.[37] These events, together with temperatures peaking (for the century so far) in the 1950s, changed an important part of the public perception about the natural environment – namely, that human activity could have a substantial impact on the environment in general and on climate in particular.[38] Sensitivities were reflected in the oft-cited book *Silent Spring*, by Rachel Carson (1962), which discussed the effects that agricultural pesticides (DDT) had on wildlife and particularly on birds. Changes in public perceptions were a key source of questions about responsibility towards the natural environment, the damage caused by human activity, and the causal relationship between economic development and environmental degradation.

Public concerns coupled with the emergence of social movements. These became more active in the 1960s when the campaigns of ecological groups overlapped with groups protesting nuclear proliferation and the arms race.[39] It was clear that science alone was not sufficient to raise the environmental issues to the international level. There was growing social pressure on politicians to find solutions to both pending and future problems related to the earth's climate. Droughts that affected India, Russia and the American midwest and the famine that hit Africa during the 1970s assisted in drawing the attention of the general public to environmental issues.[40] Environmentalist social movements were created around the world – most notably, 1969 saw the inception of Friends of the Earth, with Greenpeace founded two years later in 1971. The activists of these organisations were taking direct action in protest both against government activities and against the ignorance of the wider public on issues such as biodiversity, deforestation, nuclear energy, protection of the oceans. These campaigns, along with the coverage of the droughts, attracted much-needed media attention,[41] which in turn assisted in mobilising the wider public in support of environmental policies. The civil society response to the evolution of green parties in the domestic political space of the UK, Germany and New Zealand,[42] was the emergence of not-for-profit think tanks.[43] They were prepared to provide less biased advice to policy-makers compared to mainstream scientific communities, which had compromised their objectivity and diminished their neutrality in an attempt to secure public funding from the Reagan administration.[44]

In the meantime, scientific knowledge concerning atmospheric changes continued to evolve, supported by conferences and the work of national scientific unions. The Conservation Foundation produced a report in 1963 indicating in figures the relationship between CO_2 emissions and climate change.[45] In a 1965 report of the US president's Science Advisory Committee, respected scientists put the greenhouse-induced warming on the domestic US policy agenda.[46] In the same year, a scientific conference in Boulder, Colorado, became a forum for scientists of different fields to discuss the problem of global warming.[47]

The rapid improvement in climate change science was partly due to the increasing capacity of technology. One of the main methods to project the extent of climate change was through General Circulation Models (GCMs), which were based on extensive calculations of the interaction between various elements of the natural environment. The improving computing power and sophistication of these models led scientists to conclude that 'there is no reason to doubt that climate changes will result and no reason to believe that these changes will be negligible'.[48] Although the voice of science was becoming more determined, the inherent complexity of the natural environment made it very difficult to reach scientific consensus, because the global temperatures were indicating a consistent decline between 1945 and the 1970s.[49] Science, according to Andrew Jamison, was becoming more professionalised and a process of institutionalisation of knowledge production took place during the 1970s, thus excluding those who could not afford to participate or were not educated to the required level.[50]

These developments were magnified by the work of the United Nations. The UN Conference on the Human Environment (UNCHE), which took place in Stockholm in 1972, managed to elevate environmental concerns to the level of global politics. Environmental issues thus became embedded in international politics as the UNCHE conference drew attention to and problematised various aspects of the human environment.[51]

Public, political and scientific attention to the issue of global warming grew exponentially in the late 1970s and the 1980s. An increasing number of international scientific conferences took place to reflect the changing research agenda.[52] Politicisation, professionalisation and specialisation characterised the field of environmental studies of the 1980s.[53] Nongovernmental organisations and environmental social movements became more active. Environmental departments were created within larger companies to defend their interests,[54] while policy-makers were asking for more conclusive scientific knowledge. The 1980s were a decade of ever growing environmentalism, which paved the way for the political achievements of the 1990s.

All these developments hinted at some of the problems that climate negotiations would come across and would have to resolve in the future, as the negotiations were not only political, but also scientific, economic and social. Political consensus appeared difficult from the start for a number of reasons. The scientific community had not reached closure on the debate of global warming, prompting continual arguments among scientists from different backgrounds and political inaction based on these disagreements. Although the Intergovernmental Panel for Climate Change was established to foster consensus, the scientists outside of it questioned the scientific value of the conclusions reached by this organisation. North–South disputes over economic development, responsibility, humanitarian ethics and resources began to appear on the international agenda in the 1970s and became one of the major dividing lines in world politics after the end of the Cold War. The size of the fossil fuel industry alone and the alliances and resources of the oil-producing countries enabled both the industry and states to stand in the way of political agreements. All of this meant that the future of the climate change negotiations was not one of easily negotiated treaties and general consensus.

To begin untangling the negotiating processes and examining the actors involved and the sources of their influence, I will begin to reconstruct the historical developments of the international norm for the protection of the atmosphere from increasing GHG concentrations, and discuss the significance of the resulting developments. Box 5.1 below reflects the chronological sequence of the unfolding political events.

Stages of evolving climate change regulation

Formulating the idea

The idea that greenhouse gas emissions need to be controlled to avoid catastrophic climate change was formulated over a protracted period of time. Scientists began exploring the earth's atmosphere in the nineteenth century, but it was not until the mid-1950s that they formulated the hypothesis that the increase of CO_2 from industrialisation could have extreme consequences for the whole of our environment. This was a decade when the Northern Hemisphere experienced unusually high temperatures, and the popular press used that to spur fears that the world was getting warmer.[55]

In 1957 Roger Revelle and Hans Suess stirred the scientific circles by showing that the widespread belief that oceans would absorb the excess CO_2 from the atmosphere was incorrect, or at least not to the degree proposed by previous studies.[56] In 1957–1958, during the International

Box 5.1 Timeline for the creation of international and regional instruments to control climate change

1827	Baron Jean Baptiste Joseph Fourier showed that the earth's atmosphere traps heat in a similar fashion to a greenhouse.
1859	John Tyndall discovered that some of the gases in the atmosphere are transparent and let heat escape into space, while others are opaque, trapping heat and keeping the earth warm.
1896	Svante Arrhenius proposed a link between human activity such as fossil fuel burning and the increase in earth's surface temperature.
1938	British scientist G. S. Callendar suggests that human emissions are sufficient to alter climate significantly.
1957	Study of Man's Impact on Climate, International Council of Scientific Unions (ICSU) concluding that the build-up of carbon dioxide is potentially a major threat.
1957–1958	International Geophysical Year – the first major international plan to develop a better understanding of the atmosphere, co-organised by the WMO and the International Council of Scientific Unions (ICSU).
1965	'Causes of Climate Change' Scientific Conference in Boulder, Colorado.
July 1971	First major International Meeting of Scientists 'Study of Man's Impact on Climate', in Wijk, Sweden begins to establish the state of scientific understanding regarding the impact of human activity on regional and global climate.
1971	First International Conference on Environmental Futures, Finland.
1972	UN Conference on the Human Environment, Stockholm.
15 December 1972	UNEP was established by UN General Assembly Resolution 2997.
1977	The Beijer International Institute, Stockholm, was established under the auspices of the Royal Swedish Academy of Sciences to foster interdisciplinary work on environment, economics and development.
February 1979	First World Climate Conference, Geneva.
1979	World Climate Programme (WCP) was launched by the WMO, UNEP, UNESCO and ICSU.
1980	First WMO/UNEP/ICSU Meeting of Experts on the Assessment of the Role of CO_2 on Climate Variations

	and their impact, Villach, Austria. WMO and ICSU Agreement on the World Climate Research Programme.
1985	Scientific Report UNEP, WMO, International Council of Scientific Unions (ICSU).
October 1985	Second International Conference on the Assessment of the Role of Carbon Dioxide and Other Greenhouse Gases in Climate Variations and Associated Impacts held in Villach, Austria. Organised at the initiative of UNEP, WMO and ICSU.
May 1987	Brundtland Report.
1987	Developing Policies for Responding to Climate Change workshops held in Villach (Austria – October) and Bellagio (Italy – November).
June 1988	The Changing Atmosphere: Implications for Global Security, Toronto.
November 1988	World Congress on Climate and Development, Hamburg.
November 1988	The Intergovernmental Panel on Climate Change (IPCC) is established by UNEP, WMO and ICSU.
December 1988	UNGA Resolution 43/53 Protection of Global Climate for Present and Future Generations of Mankind.
February 1989	Conference on Global Warming and Climate Change: Perspectives from Developing Countries, New Delhi.
February 1989	International Meeting of Legal and Policy Experts on the Protection of the Atmosphere, Ottawa.
May 1989	UNEP Governmental Council Decision 15/36 to prepare for negotiations on a Framework Convention on Climate.
July 1989	G-7 meeting was held in Paris and was dubbed the 'green summit'.
September 1989	Tokyo Conference on Global Environment and Human Response towards Sustainable Development.
November 1989	Small States Conference on Sea-level Rise, Maldives.
November 1989	Ministerial Conference on Atmospheric Pollution and Climatic Change, Noordwijk, the Netherlands (representatives from 72 countries), producing the Noordwijk Declaration on Climate Change.
May 1990	Bergen Conference – preparatory meeting for the UN Conference on Economic Development.
January 1990	Global Forum on Environment and Development, Moscow.
November 1990	Second World Climate Conference, Geneva.
February 1991	Intergovernmental Negotiating Committee (ING) holds the first session towards the creation of a Framework Convention on Climate Change.

June 1991	Beijing Declaration on Renewable Energy for Sustainable Development resulting from the meeting of 40 developing countries.
July 1991	International Meeting of Scientific and Technical Experts on Climate Change and Oceans, Malta.
October 1991	World Bank, UNDP and UNEP jointly establish the Global Environmental Facility (GEF) to provide funding for research into the protection of the environment in developing countries.
June 1992	United Nations Framework Convention on Climate Change (FCCC) signed at the United Nations Conference on Environment and Development, Rio de Janeiro.
April 1995	Conference of the Parties (CoP-1), Berlin produces Berlin Mandate.
July 1996	Conference of the Parties (CoP-2), Geneva produces Geneva Ministerial Declaration.
December 1997	Conference of the Parties (CoP-3), Kyoto – Kyoto Protocol.
November 1998	CoP-4, Buenos Aires.
November 1999	CoP-5, Bonn.
November 2000	CoP-6, The Hague.
November 2001	CoP-7, Marrakech.
November 2002	CoP-8, New Delhi.
December 2003	CoP-9, Milan.
November 2004	Russia ratifies the Kyoto Protocol.
December 2004	CoP-10, Buenos Aires.
February 2005	Kyoto Protocol comes into force.

Geophysical Year, under the initiative of the World Meteorological Organisation (WMO), systemic measurements of the carbon dioxide concentrations began.[57] This marked the beginning of a structured campaign to gain more knowledge of the problem. Governments in Western societies actively sought and encouraged the construction of new knowledge, which assigned natural sciences a new social position.[58] Governing elites demonstrated growing confidence in the ability of climatologists and meteorologists to address complex issues. This change in attitude, however, did not automatically translate into a preparedness to take meaningful action.

Improving General Circulation Models (GCMs) in the 1960s prompted a paradigm shift in scientific understandings of our environment. An accidental discovery of wide variation in results after introducing small changes in the numerical model of simulating weather patterns had a huge impact in changing the perceptions of scientists. By displaying errors and mismatches in predictions in GCMs which used different components of the natural environment, these models indicated that there were many more elements that needed to be incorporated into the calculations in order to improve the understanding of the way in which the natural environment functions. Edward Lorenz of the Massachusetts Institute of Technology (MIT) concluded that 'orbital patterns, wind patterns, melting ice sheets, ocean circulation – everything seemed to be interacting with everything else ... [and that] the planet's environment was a hugely complicated structure'.[59] This changing perception prompted more uncertainty about the effects of climate change and undermined the ability of scientists to spur government action.

At the Stockholm Conference in 1972, the International Council of Scientific Unions (ICSU) presented the position that there was a causal link between growing concentrations of CO_2 in the atmosphere and extreme weather conditions.[60] Even though the understanding of the changing concentrations of greenhouse gases in the atmosphere was improving in the 1970s, the decade was also marked by a slight loss of public interest in the issue of global warming. Research showed that average global temperatures had actually dropped in the period 1945–1970,[61] which in turn increased fears that a new Ice Age might be about to set in.[62]

Scientific opinion was tentatively consolidating around an agreement on the existence of a causal relationship between human industrial activities and growing concentrations of greenhouse gases in the earth's atmosphere, and, further, that the growing amounts of GHGs could lead to global warming, which in turn might have undesirable consequences for the human environment and world's climate. The 1970s was the decade in which consensus was reached to problematise the enhanced greenhouse effect and to conduct further studies into the components of the proposed causal links – i.e., to research the relationship between human economic activity and increased GHGs in the atmosphere, as well as the probable effects of this increase on the overall climate of our planet, and the future consequences of this climate change. Scientific uncertainties remained high, but the issue was officially on research agendas across the world, as became apparent at the first World Climate Conference in 1979. The conference was organised by the World Meteorological Organisation and held in Geneva, where it concluded that:

> it could be said with some confidence that the burning of fossil fuels, deforestation and changes of land use have increased the amount of carbon dioxide in the atmosphere ... it appears that an increased amount of carbon dioxide in the atmosphere can contribute to a gradual warming of the lower atmosphere, especially at high latitudes.[63]

The initial idea regarding global climate change was formulated almost exclusively by communities of scientists, whose work was brought to the fore by media, public interest and active social movements. Politically, the need to construct an international norm regarding environmental sustainability, responsibility and equity was formulated much later. However, the 1972 UN Conference on the Human Environment marked an important watershed. Perceptions of global climate as being stable and unaffected by human activity were challenged. The conference outlined the causal link between human activities and the state of our environment. The trials and tribulations in formulating the problem of climate change continued throughout the process of norm development. Unlike the campaigns in the other two case studies, formulating a political demand for action was not the driving force behind the efforts of scientists. Their aim was to gain a better understanding of complex processes and inform policy-makers of possible scenarios. Political and social interest in the realm of environmental governance varied, scientific uncertainty was high and the formulation of the problem remained tentative.

Network configuration

The network of support for the reversal of climate change is loosely knit. It encompasses an incredibly large number of actors[64] with a broad spectrum of vested interests – political, normative, ideological, economic or scientific. An interesting characteristic of the normative network of support to limit climate change has been the disconnectedness between its normative and scientific partnerships. Unlike the networks in the case of outlawing torture or those in the intellectual property debate discussed previously, actors in this case engaged with more than one aspect of the new norm. Technical knowledge, for example, was constructed not only by scientific communities, but by businesses, NGOs and IOs, which made it extremely difficult to rely on scientific objectivity and/or neutrality. Scientific knowledge became so politicised that it was clearly reflecting the interests of its creators, which in turn undermined its credibility.

Studies of the evolution of the climate change issue have classified the actors participating in the norm entrepreneur networks into states, international organisations, NGOs, epistemic communities and corporations.[65] All of these actors were equally concerned about the outcomes of international political negotiations. Since the problem at the heart of this normative campaign was primarily scientific, most actors chose a knowledge-creating strategy to persuade policy-makers of the merits of their cause. The contributions of the fossil fuel industry were primarily obstructive, seeking to destabilise scientific consensus and thus contribute to scientific uncertainties. Green industries, NGOs and think tanks, on the other hand were concentrating on decreasing uncertainties and gaining useful knowledge to back up policies that could reverse the enhanced greenhouse effect.

This case study differs from the previous ones in two major respects. First, there were two distinct networks from the very beginning of the norm development process, and the conservative ones formed a clearly outlined lobby. One of the networks was made up of actors who believed that climate change was a problem that needed to be tackled and the second one propagated against. It is necessary to emphasise once again that the two networks were not closely connected. Second, the process of network configuration was continuous even during state-level negotiations – actors joined and left the process of norm development. The membership of the networks of support kept changing, making this case study particularly complex and dynamic.

The network in favour of the need for political action to control climate change was configured during a number of conferences and scientific meetings. Some of these conferences were organised under the auspices of the UN – the UN Conference on the Human Environment and the First Meeting of Experts in Villach (Austria). Others were convened by communities of scientists – such as the First International Meeting of Scientists in Wijk (1971), Sweden and the First International Conference on Environmental Futures in Finland. The initial stages of the configuration of this network were confined mainly to scientific circles in the US and Western Europe. These scientific communities were working within meteorological organisations and prestigious universities – the Weather Bureau of the US, Princeton University, UCLA and the UK Meteorological Office. The Scientific Committee on Problems of the Environment was established in 1969 to provide expertise and scientific advice to nation-states, other scientific communities and the UN General Assembly and to contribute to assessing human influence on the environment. Scientists worked closely with other intergovernmental and nongovernmental organisations.

The Massachusetts Institute of Technology conducted influential studies and became fundamental to the UN Conference on the Human Environment in 1972.[66] These studies provided the basis for the establishment of the US Environmental Protection Agency.[67] The agency was to lead the nation's environmental science, research, education and assessment efforts. Another national scientific community, which later became a prominent international actor, was the Beijer Institute of Ecological Economics, established in 1977 under the auspices of the Royal Swedish Academy of Sciences to study issues of energy and development. These scientific communities were initially doing work at the national level, addressing domestic issues and influencing national governments. It took time for them to develop international connections and to aim to influence policies at the international level.

Environmental NGOs employed direct action and spectacular campaigns to get their ideas through to policy-makers and engage public opinion. However, their efforts were dispersed on different environmental issues, and since there was no coordination, the NGOs failed to master the critical voice and mass needed to be persuasive and effective in influencing the global political agenda. In the 1980s some green NGOs were consolidating at the regional level – the African NGO Coalition was created in Nairobi in 1982; the Asia-Pacific Peoples' Environment Network was founded in Malaysia in 1983; the Asian Society for Environmental Protection (ASEP) was founded in Germany in 1984. The work of these organisations was better organised and focused on providing training and a resource point for professionals and organisations in the region.

The Climate Action Network was established in 1989 as a forum, at which NGOs could specifically discuss strategies for action, exchange information on climate change and construct policies to be offered to nation-states. The organisation generated a much-needed impetus for the consolidation of the NGO agenda. In 1989 a number of international lawyers created the Foundation for International Environmental Law and Development (FIELD) in London, to deliver advice to governments, intergovernmental organisations and NGOs. The Stockholm Environmental Institute was established in the same year at the initiative of the Swedish government with the aim of developing an international environmental research organisation. Although these groups communicated, they were not actively involved with each other. Their work was mainly concentrated on influencing governments, or on assisting them with expertise and scientific knowledge during international negotiations.

The second major normative network argued that there was not enough clear evidence that global warming was taking place, and that changes in the atmosphere and global weather represented natural fluctuations of climate. This network was made up primarily of the industries (and later nation-states) that produced or relied heavily on fossil fuels. The non-governmental organisations associated with the above actors were referred to as 'grey NGOs' and were coordinated by the International Chamber of Commerce.[68] These actors contended that any change of policy with respect to global warming would have undesirable consequences on the international economy and could cause major instability, as the latter is still largely dependent on burning of fossil fuels. The 'grey' lobby centred its position on the lack of scientific certainty about the causality between human activity and increased concentrations of GHGs in the atmosphere, about the effects of global warming on the environment and finally about what action would be appropriate to avoid catastrophic consequences.

Economists claimed that the price of scientific uncertainties is too high, because, while little is known about the way in which nature will react, quite a lot is known about the price of adjustment and/or abatement costs and their effect on the economy.[69] Industries created the Global Climate Coalition (GCC) to mobilise their financial and political clout and enable them to apply more structured pressure in domestic politics.[70] The GCC hired professionals to lobby the governments of the Organisation of Petroleum Exporting Countries (OPEC) and the United States.[71] This network used the usual tactics of persuasion – lobbying, knowledge construction, data and research collection. The scientists employed by the GCC, united by their relations to the fossil fuel industry, produced sceptical reports about the findings of mainstream scientists. For purposes of clarity, I will designate these as the 'politicised' scientists to differentiate them from the scientists who were engaged with research without an economic agenda.

The agencies of the United Nations provided a much needed forum for debates, as the interests of the two normative coalitions collided irreconcilably. The World Meteorological Organisation was one of the most active participants in the formulation of the norm to protect the atmosphere. WMO undertook, coordinated and summarised research into climate change,[72] and helped to create international standards for measuring and recording various aspects of the world's climate.[73] The First World Climate Conference was held under the auspices of the WMO in February 1979. The organisation became a focal point for early climatic research and was particularly useful in emphasising the interconnectedness of all elements of our natural environment. The WMO instituted an international framework for cooperation on the complex issue of climate change and gave policy advice to both fellow UN agencies and nation-states.

The United Nations Environment Programme (UNEP) was established following the recommendations of the UNCHE Conference in 1972, to generate interest and support for environmental governance. It became another important hub for scientific communities and expert organisations, as it dealt with a large array of environmental concerns. Together with the WMO, the UNEP helped set up the Intergovernmental Panel on Climate Change in 1988, which is an intergovernmental body of scientists, whose primary objective is to supply balanced information on climate change to states and other actors. The IPCC was established to assist the achievement of scientific consensus on climate change by drawing together knowledge from different fields – economics, politics, environmental studies and the social field.

The institutional structure in the climate change regime was formed parallel to the consolidations of the networks supporting and opposing the creation of a new norm. UN agencies furnished an institutional framework within which the debate could continue in a more productive manner, and which called for objectivity and the balance of interests against demands for development, the alleviation of poverty and the protection of humanity and its habitat.

Although many actors became involved in the climate change campaign and the actors already involved were interested in projecting their influence into the realm of international politics, these networks remained highly decentralised. The large, diverse and relatively disconnected group of social movements supporting green policies was often torn by conflicts and disagreements between Northern and Southern NGOs, between mainstream and politicised scientists, over different priorities, conflicting objectives and strategies, resulting in its powerlessness. According to Mark Valentine from the US Citizens' Network, NGOs 'barely scratched the surface of official documents [at the UN Conference on Environment and Development in 1992]', while Larry Williams of the Sierra Club admitted that '[NGOs] had almost no impact' at these negotiations.[74] Scientific communities were more successful in influencing the agenda and the direction of the negotiations, but analysts have concluded that the heart of the problem of climate change is deeply political in nature and so too would be the solutions to it.[75]

Issue formation

The campaign for the creation of a norm to control climate change is very different from the two cases considered in the previous chapters. This was not a decisive campaign committed to achieving a particular goal, but rather a collection of normative campaigns related by the common theme of the effects of climate change. This characteristic is reflected in the issue formulation process, which was decentralised and where the separate campaigning normative networks proposed different parts of the future norm.

Constructing an issue, which requires political action, is ultimately a political process, which cannot be advanced by means of scientific knowledge alone. The problem needs to be framed in such a way that it would attract and sustain the interest of policy-makers and would justify political attention. This process requires information and data gathering, research and analysis, sensitivity to the overall social and normative context of the times and sympathetic public opinion. The final decision on whether a norm will be created or not lies ultimately with policy-makers, which means that national interests and national priorities are likely to play a role.

The multifaceted nature of the problem of climate change was reflected in both the broad spectrum of actors involved in advocating a global policy and in the manner of constructing the core concern of their campaigns. The need to curb climate change was formulated from the vantage point of four thematic layers – nature and biodiversity; human well-being, equity and justice; economic development and sustainability; and scientific knowledge and uncertainty.

During the International Geophysical Year (1957–1958)[76] laboratories were established to begin measuring CO_2 concentrations in the atmosphere. Studies of the human impact on the environment were commissioned and scientific activity was underway to develop knowledge that would improve the understanding of the complex issue of climate change. In the 1960s the assumption that climate is inherently stable and that any fluctuations are natural and short-lived was altered.[77] There was growing evidence of the impact of human activity on the environment, affecting the loss of species and habitat, due to agricultural needs, industrial pollution and incidents. Issues of biodiversity and the health of the environment were fused with the larger concern of gaining a better understanding of the causes and consequences of climate change.

Normative concerns were not confined to the problems of the biosphere and wildlife. Following the pronouncement of the need for a New International Economic Order, economic development and international distributive justice emerged as dominant issues on the international agenda. Within this politico-normative context, research showing that the worst impact of possible global warming would be experienced by the poorest regions of the world[78] brought about demands for unconditional international cooperation, equitable distribution of responsibility and improved principles of international justice. These demands were voiced by a number of NGOs and environmental institutes, such as the International Institute for Environment and Development in London and Buenos Aires; the International Institute for Sustainable Development of Canada; the Stockholm Environment Institute of Sweden, etc.[79] The predominant number of NGOs, however, were based in industrialised countries and this gave rise to controversies between Northern and Southern NGOs, and to criticism that Northern NGOs lack sensitivity to the real needs of the developing South.

The culmination in the formulation of the economic aspect of the future norm for controlling climate change came with the report of the independent World Commission on Environment and Development (WCED). *Our Common Future*, authored by the Prime Minister of Norway Dr Gro Harlem Brundtland was published in 1987.[80] It coined the objective of sustainable development, which was based on the duty of current generations to use resources in such a way as to not compromise the ability of future generations to meet their development needs.[81] It also called for the more affluent to make sensible use of natural resources,[82] spelling out the principle of equitable distribution of responsibility. At the state level, the contentious issue of distribution of responsibility later became a negotiation impasse between North and South. The Brundtland report overturned the belief that human economic development and environmental protection were a zero sum game.[83] It argued that protecting the environment does not have to compromise economic development and would not necessarily result in economic stagnation.[84] The old view, however, was so deeply rooted in social constructions that these two opposing beliefs gave rise to competing policy recommendations on climate policy, which I will discuss at a later point.

Scientific knowledge lies at the core of the campaign to curb climate change. Knowledge has been constructed by means of research, conference discussions and publications. Scientists in the sphere of climatic research have had to play the role of both providers of knowledge, and the normative entrepreneurs – advocating political action to limit potential consequences. The second role has not come easy, because scientists have continually admitted that they lack explicit certainty about the exact dynamics of global climate change. Scientific consensus was tentative and slow to emerge.

The conference assessing the role of CO_2 and other greenhouse gases in climate variation held in Villach (Austria) in 1985, under the auspices of WMO, UNEP and ICSU, reached a tentative consensus on the dangers of climate change and was the first one to prescribe actions for governments.[85] The conclusions of this workshop warned that 'the accumulation of greenhouse gases posed a great risk to the earth's natural equilibrium'.[86] The conference was authoritative in its conclusions, as it gathered top scientists from 29 industrialised and developing countries.[87] The two main strategies to deal with climate change were outlined at this conference – adaptation and mitigation. The former included the calculation of anticipated expenditures that would need to be dedicated to adapting to the effects of climate change – adapting infrastructure, coastal defences, freshwater supplies, irrigation systems, etc. – while limitation/mitigation strategies would incur the limiting of GHG emissions, which would also involve high costs.[88]

Inspired by the conclusions of preceding scientific conferences, policymakers and more scientists took part in the Toronto conference of 1988. Consensus at the conference swiftly became elusive – policy prescriptions were issued but no mechanisms were created to ensure that the ambitious targets would be met, nor were institutions created to monitor compliance and provide policy advice; and ultimately none of the recommendations were applied.[89] The Toronto target was based on much enthusiasm and little in-depth understanding of the complexity of the issue. The consensus was unstable and unproductive because it was not founded upon a solid closure to the scientific debates that made up this issue. Many unresolved controversies remained among the actors involved.

Scientific uncertainty has been the main justification for political inaction. It is examined here as part of the issue formation process, because it is an integral part of our understanding of climate change politics. The argument that the sceptic scientists have put forward is based on the notion that apart from human-produced emissions of carbon dioxide, nature has its own sources of CO_2 as well as natural mechanisms that absorb these gases (CO_2 sinks) to balance off the sources. Since modern science does not have a proof of all sinks and sources, and their capacity to increase or reduce CO_2 concentrations in the atmosphere, it is difficult to predict the level of future GHG concentrations.[90] Moreover, there are natural negative feedback mechanisms, which influence the magnitude, timing and patterns of climate change. Sulphur particles, clouds, volcanic dust and water vapour can offset the effects of global warming;[91] changes in the temperatures of the oceans and the thickness of the polar ice sheets will have an impact on the scale and regional distribution of the effects of climate change, including sea-level rise.[92] Compounding these uncertainties is sufficient to undermine the limited scientific consensus on the human-induced changes to the global environment.

In constructing their case against the need for regulation of climate change, the 'grey NGOs' coupled the issue of climate change with that of energy policy. This move was quite effective and slowed down the policy-making process because energy concerns are directly linked to national security. When issues are effectively coupled with national security, international consensus tends to break down.[93] Economic analysis of adaptation costs, the cost of the research into new and cleaner but unreliable energy sources, the cost of slowed-down economic development not only in industrialised countries, but also in poorer countries, all managed to sway the opinion of policy-makers in their consideration of the possible options.[94] Corporate actors, like the Global Climate Coalition, were better equipped to lobby governments at the national level because of their experience and connections with government agencies, and were thus more effective in getting their message through.

The debate on the relevance of climate change concerns finally swayed in favour of the supporters of regulation at the UN Conference on Economic Development (1992), after the IPCC produced its first scientific report in 1990. The conclusions that were reached in this report indicated a level of scientific consensus that 'the increase in global-mean temperature over the coming century was likely to be of the order of 2°C but might be as much as 4.5°C ... noting that such warming was likely to have severe adverse consequences for mankind and recommending that GHG emissions should be cut by at least 50 per cent'.[95] The UN also set up the Intergovernmental Negotiating Committee (INC) to negotiate the Framework Convention on Climate Change in 1990, thus embedding the issue further on the international political agenda.[96] At the first meeting of the INC held in December 1990, the executive director of UNEP said that 'the mounting evidence of global warming and climate change gave urgency to the present negotiations'.[97] Global warming as a threat to humankind and as a result of human activity was officially confirmed in the Second Assessment Report by the IPCC, published in 1995, which stated that 'the balance of evidence suggests there is a discernible human influence on global climate'.[98] The IPCC downplayed the scientific uncertainties discussed earlier in order to foster scientific closure on the basis of which meaningful political action could be taken. Thus, the scientific closure reached was institutional rather than based on true scientific consensus and the nature of this closure would haunt the political negotiations that followed.

The politicisation of science for the purposes of climate change negotiations tainted the perceived objectivity of scientists and made science much more open to criticism for siding with some political actors and not with others. The problem of institutional scientific closure undermined scientific efforts to gain a better understanding of the nature of the problem and the appropriate remedies. In the process of formulating the norm for the prevention of climate change, science lost some of its aura of neutrality and the perception that scientists worked for the greater good. This has added confusion and intensity to scientific debates and has undermined the foundation of future political agreement related to the norms and instruments of improving our natural environment.

Dialogue among states

The problem of climate change cannot be resolved by research alone. Some interests would have to be sacrificed for the greater good; costs would have to be borne by businesses or societies, or both; economic development might have to change pace and direction. These concerns involve issues of responsibility, just distribution of resources, and they need to be addressed by states at the global level, to make a sizeable difference. The global character of the problem of increased concentrations of greenhouse gases in the earth's atmosphere means that the action of one, or a number of states, or indeed for that matter, any combination of states short of the whole international community promises to be short of effective.[99] Although this principle has been made very clear by mainstream scientists, it has had very little effect on any progress towards consensus about the mechanism through which this problem needs to be addressed.

This section will explore the political position of states, as the key decision-makers in the global system. States require specific attention not only because they are the only actors who can create international law, but also because they are responsible for implementing it, measuring compliance and ensuring that their international obligations are met. It is difficult to establish which states formed the conservative group, because almost all of them expressed reservations regarding different provisions of the climate change regime. The main dividing line ran between North and South, primarily due to unequal economic power, varying prospects for development, divergent needs and economic interdependence.

The North has been 'keen to emphasise that whilst it has contributed most to the problem historically, the future emissions of Southern countries will counter the global effectiveness of any action the North takes to offset climate change', and thus the South should commit to a level of effort to partake in climate change mitigation.[100] The problem of global warming is bound to put the South in an even more disadvantaged position whatever policy course the industrialised countries choose to take. Adaptation policies would require large amounts of money to be put into defences against sea rises, into adapting agricultural technologies to new weather conditions, and dealing with an increased number of natural disasters. All of these costs would come on top of the costs of development and poverty alleviation. Mitigation policies presuppose investments in new cleaner technologies, and in training specialists how to use them, which will make economic development even harder to achieve.

A secondary dividing line among states involved in these negotiations was between the producers and consumers of fossil fuels, where the former were doing their best to slow negotiations down, while the latter were keen to create effective principles to control climate change, which would encourage R&D into green technologies and renewable energy sources.

Outlining the conservative actors in these negotiations is an awkward task because of the nuanced positions that states took in relation to the complex and dynamic problem of climate change. Their varying demands and conditions of involvement resulted in a spectrum of 'conservativeness', which produced unusual alliances and had the Organisation of Petroleum Exporting Countries (OPEC) at one end and the Alliance of Small Island States (AOSIS) at the other.

OPEC was opposed to the whole process of regulating GHG emissions and the very norm of controlling climate change. Any attempts to curb CO_2 emissions would imply limiting the use of oil and petroleum products and cutting into the main source of finance for their economies. Although the OPEC countries are members of the G-77, their position is determined by their heightened dependence on oil revenues. OPEC's position in negotiations has been to question the need for strong action and to emphasise the economic cost of scientific uncertainties.[101] This group of states has also made use of the scientific and policy proposals made by groups of scientists and other professional organisations, who have been looking to lobby sympathetic states.[102]

At the other spectrum of the negotiations was the Alliance of Small Island States, which was in favour of the new norm and its timely operationalisation, as some islands continue to be in danger of disappearing as sea levels are rising globally. Many of these states are likely to be entirely submerged under water if sea levels rise even a few metres. Some islands are already battling high tides, losing income due to disappearing beaches, and have to deal with freshwater shortages. Their vulnerability has made small island states virulent supporters of concerted international political action and they have made extensive use of the support of international NGOs and legal professionals (FIELD) who provided them with helpful scientific and professional advice and cooperated closely on negotiating positions and the drafting of resolutions.[103]

Another Southern coalition is the one emerging among China, Brazil, India and other newly industrialising countries.[104] These countries are united in their ambitions for improved economic growth. They have demanded that their responsibilities under climate change conventions be postponed in time, so that their opportunities to achieve higher levels of economic development are not sacrificed. This coalition has been defending such principles of international customary law as equitable distribution of responsibilities for environmental degradation, the polluter pays and the principle that states should ensure that they cause no harm to other states.[105] Their focus has been not so much on the environment but more on issues of justice, development and pragmatic solutions that are suited to both their needs and economic capabilities.[106] India, China and Brazil have been particularly vocal in these negotiations and have stood their ground against the pressure from OECD countries to commit to targets that even industrialised countries avoid.[107] It has become obvious in the first decade of the twenty-first century that these countries are expected to commit to future emissions cuts, with China in particular having surpassed the United States as the largest CO_2 emitter in the world.

The remaining G-77 countries are mainly LDCs and they have been primarily active at the national and regional level, partly due to limited resources and partly to the specific character of the problems that they were facing – drought, desertification and floods. Their main contribution to the debate has been confined to developmental issues and searching for financial assistance for any commitments required under the new international environmental roles.[108] LDCs are also expected to be hit hardest by any climate fluctuations, not only because of their dire poverty, but also due to their vulnerable geographic position. Overall, however, the developing countries were in favour of a new norm, but against any binding obligations that might affect economic development.

Consensus has been lacking among industrialised countries as well. The US, Canada, Australia and Japan did not oppose the creation of a new norm, but were against extensive responsibilities to control GHGs, which could harm their industries, while the EU was in favour of the new norm and new responsibilities, as long as the provisions of the norm were effective. The United States, in particular, opposed concrete targets and timetables,[109] basing its arguments mainly on the lack of solid scientific consensus on the issue. The US has been a rogue state in these negotiations and continues to play this role today by not respecting the responsibilities set by the Kyoto Protocol. The economic position of America, combined with its high dependence on burning fossil fuels,[110] goes some way towards explaining the practical aspect of this opposition. The European Union took the role of a normative entrepreneur, but could not always find a single voice – with the Scandinavian countries being very enthusiastic and proactive, and Southern Europe trying to pull away from strict guidelines and specific policies.[111] This divisiveness even among industrialised countries is a major impediment to constructing effective agreements to curb climate change and limit its effects.

The positions of these coalitions and groups of states clashed at the meetings of the Intergovernmental Negotiating Committee on Climate Change (INC)[112] in the lead-up to the UN Conference on Environment and Development, held in Rio de Janeiro, 1992. The INC was charged with the task of drawing up a convention on climate change that would be signed by political leaders at the Rio Summit.[113] One might wonder why coalitions of nation-states whose interests clash so dramatically, and are in some cases completely irreconcilable, demanded a climate change convention when it was obvious that consensus was unlikely to be reached. This discussion goes some way towards a comment that was made at the beginning of the study – non-security norms emerge despite state politics and not because of them. States realised that if any political action is to have practical effects of slowing down or reversing climate change it would have to be based on broad international consensus and cooperation.

The task of bridging the differences among the coalitions listed above and of finding a solution among the noise of scientific theories and expert opinions was daunting to say the least. Following the UNEP Governmental Council Decision 15/36 of May 1989, preparation began for negotiations of a framework on climate change. In February 1991 the INC held its first session.[114] Finding a solution to the problem of climate change, which incorporates other priorities like economic development, energy production, national security and ultimately survival, requires a political solution capable of reconciling these competing demands. The United States was the strongest dissenting voice in these negotiations and the hardest bargain maker. They entered the negotiations resolved to avoid being 'trapped' into any explicit commitments, including deadlines and specific reduction targets,[115] as well as to include developing countries in the international response to climate change, even if in a limited manner.[116] The developing countries, on the other hand, were resolved to stick to their position that the developed countries were responsible for the CO_2 problems and refused to undertake specific commitments.[117] The available records from the meetings of the INC, however, are not verbatim records of the discussions that took place and rarely mention the positions of particular states.[118] Information about state positions is only available from publications by individuals who have participated or observed these negotiations.

During the INC meetings, consensus was slow to develop and the European Union was at the forefront of the effort to foster cooperation. The EU made the first move to bridge differences with Japan and later with Canada, Australia and other OECD countries.[119] The G-77 members were also attempting to reach a unified position, centred around issues of poverty, economic development and countering the power of the OECD coalition.[120] The US position was proving difficult to negotiate around and its interests were closest to those of the OPEC countries. Differences had to be narrowed within this triangle of world political power. The only possible way forward was to water down the provisions of the future climate convention. Some observers argue that there was pressure of expectations on the national delegations at the INC meetings to come up with an agreed text of a climate convention for the Rio Summit, because 105 heads of state were going to attend and the meeting had to be a success.[121] These observations are in tune with similar developments in different issue areas, where consensus was reached hastily and positions compromised in unexpected ways at the end of prolonged and difficult negotiations. The dialogue among states thus shifted focus from working out a solution to the issue of climate change to finding the smallest common denominator among a group of actors who had very different needs and wants.

Political closure

After long hours of negotiations and hard bargaining prior to the Rio Summit, the resulting proposal for a climate change convention was ambiguous, set no specific targets for emission cutbacks, avoided shifting responsibility to developing states[122] and established the Conference of Parties to negotiate, review and implement further particulars of what specific actions would be taken and when.[123] The Framework Convention of Climate Change (FCCC) was signed at the Rio conference in 1992 and entered into force in 1994. The signing of this convention constituted political closure on the problem of climate change. It is unusual that states agreed in such a short period of time to create a framework convention with such far-reaching consequences, but it is not surprising that consensus was easily reached. The FCCC 'established a non-binding goal and policy framework for the industrialised countries to pursue various voluntary measures to limit their emissions of greenhouse gases to 1990 levels by the year 2000'.[124] Even though the convention was based on limited consensus among the negotiating partners, resulting in hardly any practical change, it still reflected an agreement that greenhouse gas emissions, climate change and global warming were interconnected, problematic issues that needed to be addressed at the international level.

Political closure was evidenced by the fact that 'science ha[d] not been very relevant in the post-Rio negotiations. Most of the issues facing negotiators [were] either not scientific or only very narrowly so',[125] which signified that the debate over whether climate change was a problem was now closed. The UNFCCC also recognised that the framework convention reached some kind of political closure and classified this as 'a major accomplishment'.[126] The secretariat of the UNFCCC argued that 'recognising that there is a problem … was no small thing [in 1994]', especially in view of the fact that it is very difficult to get states to agree on and adopt a common approach to anything in world politics, especially if it is a complicated issue with unforeseen consequences.

The political closure that was reached on climate change is characterised by instability due to continued scientific debates over the causal relationships between human activity, GHG concentrations and climate change. This is demonstrated by continuing negotiations and discussions of these problems post-Rio, post-Kyoto and up to the present day. However, what this tentative political closure indicates is that the place of the issue of controlling climate change has been secured on the political agenda and its technical and normative parameters agreed on a very basic level, which closed off the debate between the normative entrepreneurs and the conservative actors as to whether this issue is a problem at all. Even in the face of significant scientific uncertainty, the need for meaningful international action had been recognised and accepted. Political negotiations moved on to issues of institutional and procedural mechanisms related to climate change.

Legalisation and operationalisation

The political closure on the problem of controlling climate change was very rudimentary and did not involve any substantial agreement on how to protect the atmosphere and reverse global warming. This was partly due to the continuing scientific debates on causality and partly due to the difficulties that faced the negotiating parties in their attempts to find consensus. The dialogue among states continued with the same fervour as prior to the FCCC and the positions of states did not change much. A deeper level of agreement and commitment was needed to produce an effective legal instrument that would be accepted by the majority of states.

The processes of *legalisation* and *operationalisation* were taking place simultaneously. States attempted to reconcile their conflicting views as they were creating legal principles with specific enforceable guidelines. The Framework Convention on Climate Change, which was signed at the Rio Summit (1992) and came into force in 1994, was the main legal document, on the basis of which the processes of legalisation and operationalisation began.

Following the adoption of the FCCC, the climate change debate moved on to practical questions of how this norm for the prevention of global climate change would be implemented. The FCCC established five institutions: the Conference of the Parties (COP), the secretariat, two subsidiary bodies to deal with questions of implementation and advice on science and technology, and a financial mechanism. The Global Environmental Facility (GEF) was established in 1991 to help developing countries fund environmental projects; its functions were later utilised on an interim basis under the FCCC as financial mechanisms.[127] COP became the supreme decision-making body of the climate change convention, responsible for the review and implementation of the convention provisions.[128] Negotiations among states on commitments and mechanisms under the FCCC continued in the INC. The developing countries were united in their demands for 'common but differentiated responsibilities'.[129] The countries most concerned with the problem of global warming – the AOSIS coalition – submitted a proposal for a protocol on climate change in 1995, which was met well by most states, apart from Saudi Arabia and Kuwait.[130] At the end of the 11th meeting of the INC and prior to the first Conference of Parties, some states and NGOs were not pleased with the progress made in these negotiations, but appreciated the successes in beginning the process of operationalising this thorny issue.[131] The first meeting of the Conference of the Parties took place in Berlin in 1995.

According to Yamin and Depledge, the mere establishment of international institutions by states 'signals acceptance that the pursuit of a shared goal is better achieved through a permanent mechanism to facilitate cooperation'.[132] Each of the COP yearly meetings resulted in the preparation of a mandate. The Berlin Mandate was mainly organisational and administrative in character, emphasising the need for the creation of stronger legal documents that would outline adequate commitments to alleviate human effects on the earth's atmosphere.[133] The Berlin COP meeting established the Ad-hoc Group on the Berlin Mandate (AGBM), which was left in charge of delivering an authoritative legal document, outlining the obligations of the parties to the convention.[134] These are the first institutions that can support the policy process and assist implementation in the future.

COP-2 took place in 1996 in Geneva and brought together 1,500 delegates and observers. Three important developments took place at this meeting, which further established the direction for the efforts to implement and operationalise this new norm. First, the Geneva Declaration endorsed the IPCC reports as an authoritative and exhaustive scientific appraisal of the issue of climate change and confirmed the conclusions of these reports that continued GHG emissions would 'lead to dangerous interference with the climate system'.[135] This enhanced the credibility of the IPCC and removed, at least partly, the basis for a sustained scientific uncertainty debate. Second, the declaration encouraged the AGBM to intensify the negotiations to create a legally binding instrument for the adoption of steps towards limiting GHG emissions in the atmosphere. The third important development was the change in the US position on climate change and the instruments that should be adopted: the US government agreed on the need for a 'realistic, verifiable and binding medium-term emission target'.[136] The latter was only superficial, as the United States is to date not active in the climate change regime, even though President Obama has signalled a change in policy.

The third COP meeting held in Kyoto, Japan in 1997 produced the Kyoto Protocol, which was based on the work of the AGBM and was created after long and complex negotiations among actors with conflicting interests. The protocol was negotiated in an overnight session on the last day of the conference[137] and although most analysts perceived it as a major achievement signifying the creation of practical mechanisms for the protection of the earth's atmosphere, some declared it as insufficient in light of what was needed to avoid future climate change.[138] The Kyoto Protocol to the Framework Convention on Climate Change remained unimplemented until 2004 when Russia agreed to sign it and thus achieve the number of signatures needed to make the protocol binding.[139] The COP meetings after Kyoto continued with debates on the problems of and solutions to climate change. Even though these meetings take place every year, they have not managed to change the attitudes of states, nor have they produced any effective mechanisms to implement the norm to control climate change.

After Hurricane Katrina hit the US in 2005, fresh fears of the impact of global warming rekindled the debate. With the coming into force of the Kyoto Protocol, states in Europe are growing concerned about whether they can meet their obligations under the watchful eye of NGOs and scientific communities, which continue to rely on bleak scenarios to sustain the public interest on the issue. The United States, however, continued to refuse to follow the guidelines set by Kyoto, and stayed out of climate change negotiations, demanding that China and India become more involved. The US delegation walked out of the 11th meeting of the Conference of the Parties held in Montreal (28 November–9 December 2005).[140] Some journalists argued that President Bush and his administration were isolated at home for their climate change policies and that local action had been taken by more than 140 city mayors to curb GHG emissions.[141] Saudi Arabia and Kuwait continue their sustained opposition to the Kyoto targets as well. However, the combined opposition of these states has proved insufficient to prevent the process of operationalising the protocol. COP-11 produced one of the most important instruments in the history of controlling climate change, hailed as the 'rule book' to operationalise the Kyoto Protocol.[142] The Kyoto Protocol is due to expire in 2012 and efforts are already underway to negotiate a replacement treaty that would ensure more meaningful international engagement. While the current financial crisis may undermine negotiating efforts, the increasing number of freak weather conditions and natural disasters may speed them up. The European Union is engaged in a concerted effort to foster stronger commitment to alleviating climate change. If US policy changes under President Obama, and if G-20 cooperation gets underway as planned in 2009, there may be enough institutional support for an improved climate change treaty. The process of legalising and operationalising the norm for the prevention of detrimental climate change is not yet complete.

Conclusions

This chapter studied in some detail the development of the norm to control climate change by reducing the emission of GHGs into the atmosphere, since these are believed to be capable of upsetting the heat balance of the earth, leading to changes in climatic conditions, some with potentially disastrous consequences. The process of creation and negotiation of this norm has been unusual, prolonged and extremely complex, reflecting the character of the issue itself.

A vast quantity of information is available on this issue. Analysts have studied many aspects of the problem, the science, the social concerns, the economic issues and the politics of climate change. The literature on climate change reflects a complex, diverse and loosely knit social network of support for the new norm, which shares concerns about the impact of human activity on the atmosphere and the resulting impact on natural weather conditions. The issue of climate change as discussed throughout this chapter is riddled with uncertainties, continual negotiations of meaning, implications and political discussion of consequences. Even today scientists cannot explain with sufficient clarity the exact causal links between human activity and GHG concentrations, between the change in GHG concentrations and natural climate, and cannot predict how exactly climate will change and with what effects. There is further uncertainty over whether more research will resolve the above questions and whether humans are at all in a position to understand the intricate balancing mechanisms of nature, which make the physical environment relatively stable over time, let alone to try and influence these complex mechanisms.

Two important conclusions can be drawn from this detailed historical reconstruction of the events leading up to the creation of a norm to control climate change. First, the complexity of the issue of atmospheric pollution and climate change, of its causes and effects, has resulted in very difficult political negotiations at the international level. Nation-states have had different degrees of involvement with this issue and taken varying degrees of responsibility for this problem. These complexities, combined with often irreconcilable national interests, have led to states being unable to agree on a meaningful and effective solution to the problem. Since controversies over whether climate is indeed changing have not been settled with overwhelming scientific evidence, and because national interests influence states to choose policies carefully, it has been difficult to identify who the conservative states are. States have been conservative on some issues and cooperative on others. The climate change negotiations are very densely layered and affect different spheres of economic, political and social life, which makes them complex for analysis by the social sciences. Some of the agreements reached have not been based on genuine consensus, but on bargaining and trade-offs, which will ultimately affect the implementation of these agreements.

Scientific uncertainties have provided further basis for difficulties in reaching political closure. Scientific consensus has been undermined by scientists who have been financed to look after the interests of the fossil fuel industries. The findings of these scientists, however, cannot be dismissed, because of the lack of overwhelming proof that one or the other network of scientists is right. Tentative and partial scientific closure has supplied poor foundations for political closure and causal relationships are continually re-examined, questioning the basis of closure.

Former US president Bill Clinton made a powerful assertion at the COP meeting in Montreal in December 2005, stating that 'there is no longer any serious doubt that climate change is real, accelerating and caused by human activity' and that is sufficient evidence to demand state action on this problem, even in view of the continued scientific uncertainties, regarding some aspects of the issue.[143] Scientific uncertainties have been part of the reason for hesitant policy-making, which has been insufficient to limit greenhouse gas emissions and to reverse global warming if such a process is indeed underway. Clashing interests among states and other non-state actors have managed to limit agreements to a minimal common denominator, which has been celebrated by some but declared thoroughly inadequate by others. It is unclear whether policy-makers will be able to reach more meaningful agreements and implement effective mechanisms to tackle the issue of climate change. It is also unclear when climate change is likely to manifest itself and whether humanity can handle the consequences of it or not. The international resolve has not been strong enough to foster meaningful political action and the lack of a feeling of impending urgency has fostered a more lax attitude among states towards this truly global problem. The COP meeting in Montreal reached what has been celebrated as an outstanding political achievement, to extend the Kyoto Protocol beyond its initial deadline of 2012. The United States agreed to hold informal talks, which was a further breakthrough after consistent opposition on its side to participation in any such negotiations.[144] However, even these steps may prove insufficient in the global and far-reaching context of this problem. Many NGOs continue to call for a more determined approach to the issue of climate change, claiming that the current political agreements reflect too little action, which is coming too late and is insufficient in terms of the resources committed to it.

6 Conclusions

International non-security norms are a product of complex social processes and the interplay of scientific knowledge, normative beliefs, economic, political and social power. Norms are constructed by means of multilayered negotiations, involving different levels of analysis, and actors with conflicting interests and demands. The process of norm construction has a direct effect on the character, strength and binding power of the emerging norm. Norms based on consensus and genuine closure tend to be more effective, characterised by higher levels of compliance. Even though scientific knowledge and normative beliefs lie at the core of international norms, the norm construction process is deeply political. Behavioural norms are products of their time, reflecting power structures, dominating interests and beliefs, but not necessarily determined by them. This study has demonstrated that in the realm of non-security norms, traditional state power may not always yield the desired results. Norms are generally constructed to respond to specific problems, which tend to be contemporary or which are perceived to have consequences in the near future. The attention of governments is usually drawn to the need for constructing regulation by a wide variety of non-state actors, including scientific experts, NGOs, businesses.

This study has sought to reconceptualise norm development by reconsidering the elements of the process of norm building, adding the assumption that all non-security norms have a core of technical knowledge and normative beliefs, and demonstrating that norms have similar patterns of development by revisiting existing theoretical models. This is done by combining the insights of the sociologists of scientific knowledge and the social constructivists of international relations. These two approaches provide the research tools for rethinking norm development as a dynamic process and examining the stages of this evolution. A number of theoretical and empirical studies have contributed to building an improved understanding of the process. The two theoretical approaches have examined the concept of closure, which is useful in understanding the dynamics of norm development. Building on this idea, the current study introduced the notion of normative and scientific closures, which contribute to the achievement of more stable political closure. The character of the political closure, in turn, is likely to influence the levels of implementation and compliance with the new norm. Based on the empirical findings of the sociologists of knowledge and social constructivists, and to address the problem of issue-specific norm research, this study offered a reconceptualisation of the way in which states and non-state actors interact, network and build coalitions in the context of the norm-constructing process. This has been crucial in adjusting normative research to the complexities of world politics and making it more pragmatic and relevant.

Norms are socially constructed and emerge in a relatively defined logical sequence, which raises a number of substantive questions. How do scientific knowledge, political power and normative beliefs interact to lead to successful norm creation? What circumstances favour the development of new norms? What factors induce change in social perceptions? How is consensus built among actors of different calibre, different social roles and diverse aims and not necessarily harmonious interests? Who are the actors best positioned to attract the attention and support of policy-makers for the creation of new norms? The goal of this research has been to seek answers to these questions, as these could improve our understanding of global governance and the everyday conduct of international politics, as well as the role and the type of power that various actors wield in the international system.

International norms are increasing in number and scope. Scholars of international relations have used a multitude of approaches to explain their presence and relevance in global politics. This study argued that to gain a better understanding of why norms exist, we need to take another look at how they come into existence. The sections that follow examine in turn the way in which we theorise normative change, the actual patterns of norm construction and normative change in the broader context of world politics, and the implications of the current research for building a better understanding of norm development.

Theorising normative change

Combining the insights of conventional constructivists of international relations and the sociologists of scientific knowledge has proven rather helpful. These two approaches have much in common, as they both examine social processes in which perceptions, shared knowledge and ideas play important roles. They have produced detailed studies of how changes in social constructions take place and of the processes that lead up to these changes. Sociologists of knowledge and constructivists, alike, have examined power relationships that influence the process of creating social norms and scientific facts and the tools that actors use in their work towards shaping social perceptions – persuasion, argumentation, coercion, knowledge creation.

Constructivists have studied the influence that norms have on state behaviour. They have also asked why states comply with international norms, how international norms affect state behaviour, and how specific norms have evolved and have been internalised. Constructivists have analysed the way in which norms shape and are shaped by state actions and identities. A further constructivist contribution to IR theorising is the study of how various actors bring about change in the social environment and what processes of advocacy, persuasion or coercion take place before a norm is created.

The sociologists of scientific knowledge, on the other hand, have argued that science and scientific knowledge are both socially constructed, in a way that reflects hierarchical power networks and vested interests. SSK theorists have studied in great detail the social processes leading up to the construction of scientific facts and the closure of scientific debates. The sociologists of knowledge have questioned the objectivity and neutrality of the natural sciences and have outlined ways in which emerging scientific knowledge is conditioned by politics and social expectations. They have emphasised the importance of adopting a dynamic approach to the study of the evolution of facts, which has become a central assumption in this research.

Having analysed the theoretical proposals and the variety of case studies presented by constructivists, my purpose was to synthesise a more comprehensive and flexible theoretical model of norm development, based on recurring social processes. The synthetic theoretical model proposed in Chapter 2 above, examines the links between norm construction and studies of norm compliance by showing in some detail how the process of norm development influences the character of the emerging norm and possibly the levels of compliance with this norm in the future. The current research analyses recurring patterns of interaction, the influence of social, political and economic context, the power and methods of argument and persuasion that influence norm construction and make up this complex, multilayered, social process.

The theoretical model of norm development, proposed at the outset of this research, was based on the hypothesis that international non-security norms are constituted by technical knowledge and normative beliefs. This hypothesis has held true across all case studies and is an important contribution to the understanding of the nature of norms, and their patterns of evolution. This view of norms is a departure from mainstream constructivist thought, which has tended to divide norms into principled and causal ideas, which would in turn be handled and advocated by the actors believed to hold these ideas – epistemic communities, transnational social movements and moral movements.[1] Empirical research has demonstrated that there is no such rigid division between actors and norms. Communities of scientists and professional advocates have participated in the creation of the norm against torture, and NGOs have played a major role in the negotiations of climate change policies. Scientific and technical knowledge are in continual interaction with normative beliefs. They are co-constitutive and shape each other in the process of norm building. Actors use them in different ways and proportions, in an attempt to put forward balanced normative ideas that are justified, fair and projected to be effective in addressing the problem at hand.

The core of this research is the synthetic theoretical model of norm development, which is based on a combination of existing constructivist theoretical and empirical studies and the research of the sociologists of scientific knowledge. The model consists of seven main stages of evolution which have a causal character, meaning that the completion of one stage leads to the next. After conducting the research on the three case studies presented above, it has become apparent that the evolution of some norms may go through some of the same stages more than once, until an agreement is reached between the proactive and conservative actors. The presence of such loops in the model is not undermining the assumption of causality between the stages, but instead reflects the complex processes of negotiation among a great variety of actors in the global system. The proposed stages are artificial and at the beginning of a norm-building campaign, may take place simultaneously. They have been conceptualised as separate parts of a complex process to outline key dynamics. A theme that runs throughout the model is the interaction of technical knowledge and normative beliefs, which in combination with power dynamics, economic and social interests propel the process of norm building.

The first stage of norm development is the formulation of the initial idea to regulate behaviour in a particular sphere. Ideas for norms are usually framed in the context of a crisis or an impending calamity. Norms emerge for reasons that are time- and context-specific. One cannot fully understand the growth of an initial idea if it is detached from the immediate political, economic and cultural environment. As argued previously, norms are not created as part of an overarching process of 'civilising' world society; instead, they are constructed to respond to a particular concern or crisis. Their emergence is not predetermined, and usually at the start of a normative campaign, the outcome is not clear.

The formulation of the initial idea is closely followed by stages two and three of the synthetic model – network configuration and issue formulation. These two processes generally take place simultaneously but are examined separately to reflect in more detail the dynamics of interaction between the actors involved. Constructivists have studied some aspects of these two processes and have hinted on their importance for understanding norm construction.[2] However, these studies have been largely incomplete, not very detailed and based on the differentiation of actors into states, epistemic communities, advocacy networks and NGOs. The current research has unpacked and studied these processes in more detail in order to understand the bargaining and argumentation that takes place. By closely examining the behaviour of various types of actors, one can also begin to understand how normative networks are being formed, the types of power that non-state actors use and the ways in which these actors interact.

One of the central hypotheses of this research held that different actors – states, scientific communities, NGOs, etc. – come together to form normative networks and to take advantage of each other's strengths and bargaining skills in the process of norm development. This has been confirmed by all three case studies, as discussed in more detail below. Actors come together in coalitions according to their negotiating aims, and not according to the character of their goals – instrumental goals, shared causal ideas or principled beliefs. The variance in membership to a norm-entrepreneurial network has been related to higher chances of an impact on state policy-making, since the differing backgrounds and capabilities of the actors involved allow them to address both issues of normative beliefs and scientific knowledge. Normative entrepreneurs need technical and scientific expertise to substantiate their claims of injustices that need to be addressed by policy-makers. Scientific experts need normative entrepreneurs to help formulate a problem in normative terms. It is the combination of these two sides to a proposed norm that has made for successful and productive normative campaigns, as will be discussed below.

In the process of issue formulation actors define the technical and normative scope of the proposed new norm, and position it within the broader normative context. The scope of the norm is typically expressed in terms of a working definition. Actors need to define relationships of cause and effect that lead to problematic consequences or behaviour. Agreement may sometimes take a long time to achieve. Such agreement is signified by reaching normative and scientific closures. It is at various conferences and forums, in working groups, and at workshops that normative and scientific closures are reached. If there is no closure the development of the norm is not necessarily discontinued, but the reaching of political closure is made all the more difficult, as opponents to the emerging norm will always try to exploit scientific or normative uncertainties – as demonstrated in the case of the protection of the atmosphere. The concept of closure is borrowed from the sociologists of knowledge here and will be discussed in more detail below in relation to political closure. The empirical evidence in this research has shown that the process of creating norms is based on a continuum of closures through which the debates are moving forward, overcoming controversies that with time help norms evolve and reach the point where they are uncontested and their existence seems natural.

Once the norm entrepreneurs formulate the problem that needs a policy solution, they begin seeking ways of putting this problem or normative proposal onto the political agenda. There are usually states that are supportive of the development of a new norm, and are even actively involved in normative campaigning, as well as states that are either not interested at all or actively oppose proposals for a new norm. The task that normative networks face is to persuade or coerce the 'conservative' actors who are to a larger or lesser degree in favour of keeping the status quo. Once again, this stage of norm development has been acknowledged by some constructivists,[3] but has not been studied in enough detail, and the politics of the dialogue with the conservative actors is just too dense to miss out in the overall analysis of the nature and effect of norms. The way in which states and non-state actors reach an agreement to create a new norm has been demonstrated to affect aspects of the new norm – its strength, the level of compliance and the way in which the norm is internalised by states.

The dialogue with the conservative actors concludes with reaching the moment of *political closure*. This moment marks the end of the controversy over whether a certain normative principle needs to be constructed and endowed with the power to regulate behaviour, i.e., the moment when a new norm becomes a part of the normative context within which actors interact. If closure is not reached, a loop may open in the model where actors go back to the preparation stages to amend either the norm proposed, or their normative campaign. The studies of the sociology of knowledge have contributed greatly to our understanding of the moment of closure, which is referred to as the 'tipping point' of norm development by constructivists in IR.[4] The empirical case studies in this research have revealed important shortcomings in our understanding of closure. One such deficiency is in the available tools of measuring closure and in the lack of a mechanism of establishing when closure has been reached. Pinpointing the moment of closure is a difficult task in the midst of multilateral political negotiations, which often include a number of equally thorny political issues. The causes of closure have not been isolated with certainty, because in international negotiations it is often the case that some states are coerced into accepting a norm, or lured with trade-offs in spheres they consider of higher importance to their national interests; closure sometimes happens unexpectedly under the pressure of deadlines to complete negotiations. Understanding the processes that lead up to closure more clearly will help us understand why some controversies are resolved, others reopened, and yet others ignored altogether. There is a need for further inquiry into the mechanisms of reaching political closure and into the ways in which closure can be measured and defined, as this is one of the crucial moments in the processes of both norm development and knowledge creation.

The next two stages of the synthetic model – legalisation and operationalisation – do not necessarily take place in relation to every norm. The process of legalisation entails the creation of treaties, conventions, covenants and other written rules of international law, referred to as 'international conventions' in Article 38 (1) of the Statute of the International Court of Justice, which establishes the sources of international law.[5] Some scholars argue that treaties are increasingly beginning to replace customary international law, meaning that generally speaking more norms reach the legalisation stage. Constructing the legal language of the obligations that states agree to undertake is a process of difficult negotiations, which is increasingly involving not just states but non-state actors as well, both directly and indirectly. Consensus on the limits and legal language of the new norm may take a long time to achieve. Negotiations often reach deadlock, as none of the parties that present drafts of the new norm are willing to give way to other drafts. It has become apparent from the empirical studies in this research that negotiations are often concluded due to pressing negotiation deadlines, with states signing up to final drafts that come short of their initial demands and comprise elements from the various proposed drafts. This is an interesting finding that needs to be researched further, as it might have far-reaching implications for our understanding of how international negotiations are concluded.

Even though some norms evolve so far as to be legalised, states might need extra help to make the legalised norms functional, for example, by creating institutions that oversee norm compliance, or by constructing optional protocols that offer mechanisms to verify norm implementation and compliance. The operationalisation of norms is another stage of norm development where the work of non-state actors is again focusing on attracting public attention and pressuring states into upholding their normative obligations. A specific feature of the public campaigns at this point is that they already have a legal basis and it is much easier to shame states into norm compliance. The stage of operationalisation supplies the link between norm development and norm internalisation. The issue of how states adopt norms and why they choose to follow them is closely related to the way in which norms have been negotiated and constructed. We may not be able to ascertain why states comply with norms until we understand why these norms have materialised in the first place.

This synthetic theoretical model, based on the theoretical and empirical research of social constructivists in IR and the sociologists of scientific knowledge, was compared to three empirical studies. I have historically reconstructed the events leading up to the creation of three international non-security norms, which have been constructed in the relatively recent past. This detailed historical reconstruction has been quite insightful with regards to the validity of the theoretical model. Alongside the theoretical findings, I have also tried to examine the process of norm development in its dynamic form by comparing records of the same process kept by the different actors taking part in it. This research has resulted in detailed empirical and theoretical examinations of the development of three norms from different fields of international relations – the norm outlawing the use of torture, cruel, inhuman and degrading treatment or punishment, the norm protecting intellectual property in the pharmaceutical industry and the norm for the protection of the atmosphere from increasing levels of greenhouse gases. All examples studied here have been marked by the strong influence of normative beliefs, which has not necessarily resulted in the creation of 'good' norms. Technical knowledge has been instrumental in pushing forward the normative campaigns, but it has also provided the main source of contention in the case of the protection of the earth's atmosphere.

Following normative change in world politics

Initial ideas in world politics, as argued by the theoretical model in this research, are constructed as a result either of a crisis or out of a feeling of an impending disaster. The evidence from all three case studies has confirmed this hypothesis. The development of international norms is neither predetermined, nor natural and often at the beginning of a normative campaign, norm entrepreneurs may not be able to predict the scale of the impact of their campaign. In the case of the creation of a norm to outlaw torture, the campaign that Amnesty International began had aimed to draw the attention of policy-makers to an age-old practice, which as Amnesty demonstrated in a series of reports was taking place in enormous proportions and was in breach of basic human rights. The way in which the campaign for the protection of intellectual property rights began was also incidental in the sense that, although the multilateral corporations involved wanted to have worldwide protection, they took a gamble by accusing developing state governments of allowing the theft of intellectual property to take place.[6] This approach was risky because developing states were important markets for the corporations and the whole matter could have turned against vital corporate interests leading to large-scale losses of revenues. The campaign to control emissions of greenhouse gases experienced a prolonged period of consolidation, as the interest in the protection of the atmosphere fluctuated under the influence of external factors. One of the catalysts keeping this idea going was the continual fear that humans might soon come to pass the point of no return at which damage to the world climate might be permanent.

All three empirical cases suggest that when a normative idea has gained enough momentum, the actors promoting it begin to configure networks of support. Contrary to more traditional constructivist beliefs, the process of network configuration draws a variety of actors – global civil society organisations, advocacy networks, communities of scientists, professional networks, industries, even states that are sympathetic and supportive of the proposed norm. Evidence of this is available from conference records that documented the configuration of the normative network against torture, from reports and existing literature on the development of the norm protecting intellectual property rights, reports and conference papers delivered by scientists, green energy producers and some interested states in the case of the norm for the protection of the atmosphere. It is important to note that actors group together according to their vested interests and in the search of not only critical mass, but also expertise and effective access to policy-makers. Actors who are interested in the technical language and scientific logic of a norm seek others who can add a normative spin to that knowledge, providing evidence that all norms contain a technical and a normative component, prescribing what is appropriate in the normative context of society and what is effective, given the laws of science.[7] The case of the norm outlawing torture illustrates this point, with the network of support for the new norm comprising the International Commission of Jurists alongside Amnesty International, the British Medical Association, the World Council of Churches, the Danish Medical Group, and so on. Two important empirical conclusions emerged from this case study – first, that networks of support can be in a perpetual state of flux, with actors coming to the forefront of the campaign when their expertise was needed and taking a backseat when questions outside their competence were discussed. Second, the different parts of this campaign were interlocked, in the sense that findings from the medical and legal field were logically connected and provided a solid ground for the technical argument related to the norm.

Technical and normative campaigners are not always on the same side of the debate over the need for the creation of a new norm, as was demonstrated by the case of the development of a one-size-fits-all type of norm for the protection of intellectual property rights. The industry network leading the process of norm development created close ties with the governments of economically developed states by setting up expert committees and industry-wide associations, which supplied expertise to governments on issues of concern. The network avoided the attention of the wider public and concentrated on lobbying governments. The normative entrepreneurs of the campaign against this norm had to deal with the well-developed arguments of the economists supporting a blanket norm. Actors attempted to engage in debates to reconcile their differences and find plausible solutions, but no consensus could be reached. If no consensus is reached, then a norm may either not emerge at all, or emerge in a form only addressing the concerns of one side, which in turn could lead to that norm being continually challenged by the group whose concerns were not addressed. In this particular case, while attempting to operationalise the norm reflecting industry sentiments and actively hurting individuals in poorer countries, the continuum of norm creation opened a loop – there was a second instance of network configuration for the network opposing the blanket norm and demanding a norm more sensitive towards the needs of the underprivileged.

The case study of the campaign for the protection of the atmosphere from greenhouse gases presents a different scenario of network configuration where two opposing normative networks developed simultaneously. Both of these were loosely connected and the normative and scientific partnerships did not work very productively together. The contributions of developing scientific knowledge were pulled together by the World Meteorological Organisation, which coordinated and summarised research to produce some common standards for measuring and recording various aspects of world climate fluctuations.

The process of formulating the problematic issue had been taking place simultaneously with the process of the configuration of the network of support in all three cases reconstructed in this research. The aim of this process is, by reaching scientific and normative closures, to come to a definition of the nature and scope of the problem and propose solutions. Part of the proposed solution is the creation of a new norm, which would ameliorate the problematic consequences of certain behaviour. The normative network needs to determine the substance and limits of a norm and position it within the appropriate context, so as to demonstrate to policymakers the benefits that it can bring.

The three case studies of this research yielded further insight into the dynamics of the stage of norm development. The campaigners against torture were determined not to repeat the mistakes of previous campaigns and to formulate the norm in a way that would not leave any room for justification for the use of this practice. Normative closure and determination to create the norm was at the heart of the normative campaign, the stage of issue formulation was dedicated to the technical definition of torture, cruel, inhuman and degrading treatment or punishment. The discoveries made by medical professionals working with torture survivors concerning the full extent of the consequences of torture gave great impetus to the normative campaign, which ran parallel to campaigns for the creation of codes of ethics for medical personnel. In the legal field various national courts confirmed the existence of a customary principle of law against the use of torture. Legal professionals worked towards a tighter definition of torture with a more universal reach. The scientific closure was marked by the unified position of non-state actors rallying for a new norm on torture.

The case study of the norm of intellectual property protection outlined the importance of an appropriate choice of institutional forum, in which best to address the needs of the norm entrepreneurs. Formulating the issue of the protection of intellectual property rights as a problem of unfair trade practices secured the attention of the US government and the governments of other industrialised countries. The proposed forum for intellectual property-related trade grievances was the GATT (and later WTO), an organisation with more enforcement mechanisms than the World Intellectual Property Organisation. The various industrial associations emphasised the normative character of their campaign – fairness and the protection of private property (including ideas and products of the mind) – and carefully formulated the technical parameters of their normative proposal in close cooperation with the US government.

Formulating the issue at the heart of a norm for the protection of the atmosphere and for the prevention of climate change took place in a number of different forums and over a long period of time. The loose character of the normative networks proposing the creation of competing norms led to a decentralised process of issue formulation, resulting from the work of a number of different campaigns. The construction of new knowledge about the relationship between different aspects of climate and human activities was in high demand, meaning that scientists were not the only actors engaged in knowledge construction. This case study illustrates most clearly the socially constructed character of scientific knowledge. Some critics claimed that scientific knowledge was produced to respond to certain concerns, depriving this knowledge of objectivity and neutrality. The separate campaigns on the protection of the environment reached their own normative closures regarding biodiversity, the protection of the atmosphere, fairness, the right to development, etc. There was no overall scientific closure, however, meaning that scientific uncertainty remained a source of opposition throughout the process of norm development. The only reason why states came together to discuss climate change and to try and work out a solution to the problem was the constant pressure from UN agencies – the World Meteorological Organisation and the United Nations Environment Programme.

The dialogue with conservative actors is one of the most important stages of norm evolution. This is the stage at which enough political will needs to be generated to create a new behavioural norm. All three normative campaigns echoed a common concern – that the problematic issues that they addressed ultimately boiled down to questions of political will. When normative campaigners reach the stage of dialogue with the conservative actors, they have to make their case stand out among all other issues on the world political agenda. This is a crucial social moment when policy-makers have to make a normative judgement as to whether the problem in front of them requires regulation and the creation of a new norm. The empirical findings of this research show that the dialogue with conservative actors can take different forms, from the near lack of normative opposition in the case of the norm against torture, to the abundance and varying success of opposing groups in the case of the norm protecting the earth's atmosphere.

The normative dialogue with states unwilling to change the human rights status quo began with Amnesty's petition of more than 1 million signatures. The proactive states that played the role of norm entrepreneurs engaged persuasion and argumentation at the UN General Assembly and in the Third Committee to push forward the creation of a new norm. The conservative states (many non-aligned states led by Chile and Yugoslavia) downplayed the seriousness and extent of torture and claimed that their sovereignty would suffer if such a norm were created, but did not oppose the norm directly. Normative opposition was difficult due to the nature of the problem and due to the fact that no state wanted to openly support the use of torture. The overall international normative climate was conducive to the creation of a more structured and extensive prohibition on torture. Agreement developed in a functionalist manner – starting from agreements to create professional standards of ethics – for policemen, doctors, medical personnel, prison officers, etc., all of which incorporated the belief that torture is inexcusable, and finished with overall agreement to create a convention against torture, inhuman, cruel and degrading treatment or punishment.

When proposals for the creation of a one-size-fits-all norm protecting intellectual property rights were tabled at the Uruguay Round of trade negotiations, India and Brazil immediately formed a coalition of developing states to oppose the creation of such a norm. The discussions to construct this norm, however, were part and parcel of a larger framework of trade talks, where the coalition of transnational corporations had the right partners – the industrialised states. The normative leader among the negotiating states was the US, later supported by the European Union countries, Japan and Canada. The US government signalled how dedicated it was to creating this norm by changing domestic legislation in such a way as to allow US companies to punish foreign governments for not upholding US domestic principles of IPR protection abroad. It was mainly due to coercion, linkage bargaining, and trade-offs in other spheres of trade that the industrialised countries emerged victorious from these negotiations. The leaders of the opposition campaign – India and Brazil – were both coerced and enticed by US trade policies into agreeing to negotiate the TRIPs agreement.

The most complex case in terms of reconstructing the dialogue with the conservative actors was that on the prevention of climate change. There was not a single state that was totally dedicated to the creation of this norm. Some states played the role of normative leaders – such as the Nordic states of Europe – but they would only agree to the new norm if its provisions were constructed to be effective, which of course could not be guaranteed. The Southern member states of the EU, however, were not as keen. The US, Canada, Australia and Japan did not oppose a new norm, in principle, but were not eager to agree to one, which imposed extensive responsibilities to control greenhouse gas emissions. Some developing countries were concerned with issues of development, social justice and responsibility, while others were worried about the consequences that global warming might have on their natural environment; for some like the states from the Alliance of Small Island States, this was a question of survival. The OPEC countries were understandably concerned for their future income from the production and use of oil and other fossil fuels. In other words, the dividing lines of opposition among states ran on so many levels, and states brought along so many of their personal demands that the resulting agreement for the protection of the environment emerged in a very weak, watered-down form. The dialogue in this case was based on conflicting scientific reports and the agreement reached bore fairly little value. It was only with the help of the UN agencies that debates were sustained for long enough so states could agree to take legislative action.

In the successful process of norm development the dialogue with the conservative actors completes once political closure has been reached. Political closure is an understudied stage of normative development and it carries valuable information about the strength and effectiveness of the emerging norm. The issue of closure was examined in greater detail by the sociologists of scientific knowledge, who have conducted extensive research and produced an in-depth analysis of different types of closure.[8] These observations are particularly relevant to the study of the development of norms, as it seems that social norms emerge in a similar process to scientific knowledge, and under the influence of similar factors. This research applied the concept of closure to the development of behavioural norms and has suggested a link between political closure and the strength of the new norm.

The empirical evidence gathered shows different political dynamics leading on to closures. In the case of the creation of a norm prohibiting the use of torture, inhuman, cruel and degrading treatment or punishment, closure was reached fairly quickly at the UN General Assembly, where a UN resolution was put together requesting the Third Committee, which deals with pressing concerns on human rights and social welfare, to prepare a draft convention against torture. Things went fairly smoothly in the case of the creation of a norm on the protection of intellectual property rights too. Once the opposition of India and Brazil was thwarted by a series of coercive measures, economic sanctions and trade-off bargains, the discussions at the ministerial meeting turned to the technical scope and the wording of a new norm. This is a sign that political closure had been reached. The closure, however, was not a stable one, as it was neither a result of genuine consensus nor of fair persuasion. Fundamental disagreements remained among the negotiating partners and that undermined the prospects of making the norm functional.

Another reason to relate closure to the future stability and effectiveness of an emerging norm is illustrated by the evidence from the case study on the norm for the protection of atmosphere. Closure here emerged as a product of circumstances and expectations rather than as a result of widespread agreement on the need for action. The pressure to come to an agreement among state leaders who had gathered at the INC meeting prior to the Rio Summit, some authors argued,[9] led to a tentative closure under which political leaders undertook responsibility to commit to cutting back on GHG emissions in the future. The reason why the Framework Convention on Climate Change signalled a political closure was because, in the words of some commentators, science was no longer relevant in the post-Rio negotiations,[10] signalling that the process of persuasion and argumentation on the need for a new norm was complete.

These findings have broadly confirmed the hypothesis on the existence of a causal link between political closure and norm strength, but what they have also outlined is the need for further research in this field and the need to work out a more objective test to show when closure has been reached. The relationship between closure and the future of the emerging norm needs to be examined in further depth.

The processes of legalisation and operationalisation have taken the form proposed in the theoretical model in only one of the three cases. The development of the norm prohibiting the use of torture is the only example of clear-cut legalisation followed by attempts at operationalisation. In this case study nongovernmental actors were particularly active and involved in close cooperation with national governments in working out the technical sides of the new norm. The norm prohibiting torture materialised in the Convention against Torture (1984). Non-state actors, however, did not feel that the convention had enough impetus to ensure compliance and the Swiss Committee against Torture called for the creation of an optional protocol, containing provisions for prison inspections and further instruments for the implementation of the new norm. The Optional Protocol was signed in 2002 and took a further four years to be ratified and enter into force.

Chapter 5 demonstrated that legalisation and operationalisation can take place simultaneously and yet manage to have limited success. The success and effectiveness of legalisation is partly dependent on the stability of political closure. In the case of the norm for the protection of the environment a limited political closure was based on contested scientific knowledge, which was supplemented by the unwillingness of states to take determined action to deal with this problem. States with conflicting interests continued to pull in different directions, resulting in the creation of an increasing number of institutions, which were supposed to foster consensus. Consensus, however, was evasive, as the issue of atmosphere protection needed widespread political agreement. It was not until 1997 that such consensus emerged in a very watered-down form – the Kyoto Protocol, which some argue was outdated even at the time of its completion. It took a further seven years for the required number of states to ratify the protocol, which finally entered into force in 2004. This rather disappointing development has been weakened significantly by the sustained opposition of the United States, which is one of the main producers of greenhouse gases. The analysis of the norm for the protection of the atmosphere presented an example of how a 'good norm' can be badly implemented and rendered almost powerless by political considerations.

The study of the development of the norm for the protection of intellectual property seemed as if it afforded a clear example of norm development and knowledge creation by the overpowering muscle of international corporations working closely with the industrialised North. Legalisation advanced in the context of the Uruguay Round of trade negotiations under GATT, with the help of informal meetings among small working groups made up of experts from interested parties. Even though the power of the developed states was by far overwhelming, political and economic might alone proved insufficient to complete these negotiations. The conclusion of the TRIPs agreement was almost entirely circumstantial, fostered by the leadership role of the Director General of GATT. Political analysts have tried to make sense of this unexpected turn in the negotiations, arguing that it was considerations such as the state of the world economy, the expensive nature of the negotiations, fears of protectionism, political events and the emergence of the US as the undisputed hegemon of world politics, that influenced the hasty conclusion of the round of trade negotiations.

This case study also affords an example of the creation of a loop within the model of norm development. The political closure underlying TRIPs came undone when developing states and NGOs began to campaign together for a less rigid approach to the protection of intellectual property rights in the pharmaceutical sector. The network of normative opposition centred attention around the fact that, for centuries, governments had exempted the pharmaceutical industry from the application of intellectual property rights regulations, for reasons of upholding public welfare. Normative issues stemming from the application of IPRs brought together a number of NGOs – the Consumer Project on Technology, Health Action International, Médecins Sans Frontières, Health GAP Coalition, Oxfam UK and others, which campaigned for accessible drugs, for more research and development into neglected diseases and for the establishment of practices that would allow the production and trade of generic drugs in the developing world. The campaign against the pharmacological giants was sustained and hard-hitting and attracted many experts and academics, who exposed some shortcomings of the economic arguments of corporations and presented a strong normative case in favour of more lax legislation in the pharmaceutical sphere.

This normative campaign proceeded in the same sequence as other normative campaigns in this research. The developing states had the support of a variety of NGOs and some UN agencies – the World Health Organisation and the United Nations Development Programme. An extensive number of conferences were held, aiming to attract the attention and support of the wider public for the revision of the initial norm to protect intellectual property rights. A high-profile case by pharmaceutical corporations against the government of South Africa was dropped, as it was generating negative PR for the companies, which signalled that public opinion was successful in exercising pressure in the United States and Great Britain. African states were invited to participate in various workshops on differential pricing and financing of essential drugs, which was another important move in this campaign, as African states had been excluded in the initial negotiations of the TRIPs.

It was a chance happening, however, that allowed the above dynamics to produce the required change. The anthrax attacks that followed the attacks on the World Trade Center in New York acted as a catalyst to the changing position of the US government on issues of IPR protection in the pharmaceutical industry. The Doha Declaration on Public Health (2001) signalled political closure in the debate on the need for special treatment of the pharmaceutical industry. The Doha Declaration was aimed at ameliorating the effects of TRIPs and also at allowing at least partially the limited production of and trade in generic drugs among underdeveloped states. This was a major victory for the normative campaign that sought the revision of the TRIPs agreement, which reflected the power and influence that NGOs can exert together with developing states in the world system. This campaign is not entirely over, as debates on the implementation of TRIPs are likely to continue in future ministerial meetings of the WTO. This case study has yielded abundant material for research and analysis with regards to the normative issues that question international politics today.

Projecting norm development

The comparison between the hypothesis of the theoretical model of norm development and the detailed empirical case studies presented here shows that the model is flexible enough to accommodate differences in the dynamics of the emerging norms, while still reflecting the logically connected stages of norm evolution. The stages of the synthetic model are broadly defined to allow more versatility and to enable it to apply to a variety of fields in global politics. They largely manage to describe and to some degree explain how international norms develop. Findings from the empirical case studies reflect the role of contingencies, chance, the part played by individuals in leadership positions, and call for a reconsideration of the overall perception of policy-making, the roles that different actors play in social, political and economic interactions and the liaisons that they form in their search for political leverage.

It has become apparent that political deadlock is often resolved unexpectedly – under the influence of external events, under political or public pressure, etc. The role of contingencies may hinder the ability of this model to predict the evolution of new norms, but it also opens avenues for further research to counteract uncertainties. Key individuals in leadership positions – like director generals of organisations, secretary generals and chairpeople of meetings – have demonstrated unexpected powers to keep negotiations going and foster agreement and closure. The individual level of analysis, of course, is difficult to accommodate in an overall theory of norm evolution, but it is worth remembering the crucial role that individuals can play.

As outlined on a number of occasions throughout this research, actors form networks of support for various ideas, regardless of their nature. It is not unusual for states to be norm entrepreneurs and for NGOs to seek to stall political negotiations. Since norms are composed of scientific and normative parts, it is not unusual for NGOs to work with scientists, specialists, UN agencies, states and businesses. Normative labels regarding good and bad actors are not relevant and may even hinder political analysis. Further studies into political closure, as well as into the relationship between closure and norm compliance are essential, as these would bear useful answers to the question of why states follow norms and how norms affect state behaviour.

This study has sought to bring theorising of norm development closer to the practical reality of global political processes. It may have raised more questions than it managed to answer, but it also mapped out some of the difficulties and shortcomings of social theories trying to understand the development of non-security norms, which have presented a political conundrum for mainstream IR theories. The aim of this research has been to challenge theorists to think outside of the artificial categories that have been constructed and to appreciate more fully the variety of actors in world politics and the differing and sometimes unconventional methods that they employ in the pursuit of interests and policies.

International behavioural norms are a central element of the analysis of world politics today and understanding how they shape behaviour is rooted in understanding how they come into existence. States alone can validate behavioural norms, but they are also the actors that violate or disregard them, meaning that states are both part of the problem and part of the solution. Reconciling this paradox has presented IR theories with a number of theoretical challenges that have trickled into the greater puzzle of the relationship between international law and international politics. Keeping this in mind, it has been helpful to analyse the roles that other actors play in the process of norm development. The reconstruction of political events has furnished empirical evidence of processes that have often been discounted in the analysis of state behaviour in an increasingly legalised world. Understanding the nature of social processes leading to norm creation might help state and non-state actors alike to moderate or indeed foster the development of better norms, catering for the well-being of people around the world.

Appendix
United Nations General Assembly Resolutions

Resolution 2997   Resolution establishing the United Nations Environmental Programme, December 1972

Resolution 3059   Question of torture and other cruel, inhuman or degrading treatment or punishment, November 1973

Resolution 3218   Torture and other cruel, inhuman or degrading treatment or punishment in relation to detention and imprisonment adopted November 1974

Resolution 3219   *Protection and Human Rights in Chile*, November 1974

Resolution 3452   *Declaration on the Protection of All Persons from Being Subjected to Torture and Other Cruel, Inhuman or Degrading Treatment or Punishment*, December 1975

Resolution 3453   Resolution to consider issues of torture, cruel, inhuman and degrading treatment or punishment in relation to detention and imprisonment

Resolution 34/169   Resolution, containing an Annex, which spelled out the Code of Conduct for Law Enforcement Officials

A/RES/32/62   Resolution requesting the Commission on Human Rights to prepare a draft convention against torture and other cruel, inhuman or degrading treatment or punishment, December 1977

A/RES/39/46   Resolution adopting the Convention against Torture, December 1984

A/RES/43/53   Resolution to further examine issues of the protection of global climate for present and future generations of mankind, adopted without vote, December 1988

A/RES/45/212   Resolution establishing the Intergovernmental Negotiating Committee on Climate Change

A/RES/57/199   Resolution adopting the Optional Protocol to the Convention against Torture, December 2002

Notes

1 Introduction

1 M. Finnemore and K. Sikkink, 'International Norm Dynamics and Political Change', *International Organisation*, Vol. 52, No. 4, 1998, 887–917.
2 Ibid., 888.
3 M. Hoffman, 'Critical Theory and the Inter-Paradigm Debate', *Millennium: Journal of International Studies*, Vol. 16, No. 2, 1987, 233–236. The term 'conventional constructivism' has been used by Ted Hopf to distinguish it from critical constructivism, which offers a different approach to the study of IR – see T. Hopf, 'The Promise of Constructivism in International Relations Theory, *International Security*, Vol. 23, No. 1, 1998, 171–200. This research has been conducted from the theoretical vantage point of conventional constructivism, to which I will refer as constructivism.
4 H. Collins, 'The Sociology of Scientific Knowledge: Studies of Contemporary Science', *Annual Review of Sociology*, No. 9, 1983, 267.
5 F. Kratochwil and J. Ruggie, 'International Organization: A State of the Art on an Art of the State', *International Organisation*, Vol. 40, No. 4, 1986, 773.
6 J. Lezaun, 'Limiting the Social: Constructivism and Social Knowledge in International Relations', *International Studies Review*, Vol. 4, No. 3, 2002, 233.
7 J. Checkel, 'It's the Process Stupid! Process Tracing in the Study of European and International Politics', Working Paper No. 26, Arena Centre for European Studies, University of Oslo, October 2005. Online. Available at: www.arena.uio.no/publications/working-papers2005/papers/wp05_26.pdf (accessed 5 January 2009), 6.
8 D. MacKenzie, *Inventing Accuracy – A Historical Sociology of Nuclear Missile Guidance*, Cambridge, MA: MIT Press, 1990, p. 9, citing D. MacKenzie and J. Wajcman (eds) *The Social Shaping of Technology*, Milton Keynes: Open University Press, 1985.
9 H. Engelhardt and A. Caplan (eds) *Scientific Controversies – Case Studies in the Resolution and Closure of Disputes in Science and Technology*, New York: Cambridge UP, 1987.
10 Finnemore and Sikkink, 'International Norm Dynamics and Political Change', 901–903.
11 A. George, 'Case Studies and Theory Development: The Method of Structured, Focused Comparison' in P. Lauren (ed.) *Diplomacy: New Approaches to History, Theory and Policy*, New York: Free Press, 1979, pp. 43–68.

12 MacKenzie, *Inventing Accuracy*, p. 3.
13 M. Finnemore, 'Constructing Norms of Humanitarian Intervention' in P. Katzenstein (ed.) *The Culture of National Security – Norms and Identity in World Politics*, New York: Columbia University Press, 1996, p. 159 and M. Finnemore, *National Interests in International Society*, University Press 1996a, Ithaca, NY: Cornell – Chapter 1.
14 N. Crawford, *Argument and Change in World Politics – Ethics, Decolonization, and Humanitarian Intervention*, Cambridge: Cambridge University Press, 2002, p. 88.
15 A. Cortell and J. Davis, 'How Do International Institutions Matter? The Domestic Impact of International Rules and Norms', *European Journal of International Relations*, Vol. 7, No. 1, 2001, 456; M. Finnemore, *The Purpose of Intervention – Changing Beliefs about the Use of Force*, p. 12.
16 Finnemore, *National Interests in International Society* , p. 22.
17 T. Farrell, 'Transnational Norms and Military Development: Constructing Ireland's Professional Army', p. 71.
18 M. Shaw, *International Law*, 4th edn, Cambridge: Cambridge University Press, 1997, p. 63 – although Malcolm Shaw uses this criteria to distinguish customary international law from general state practice, the involvement of the major powers in the field is crucial for the development of an effective norm.
19 M. Finnemore, *The Purpose of Intervention*, p. 2.

2 Theorising norm development

1 J. Checkel, 'It's the Process Stupid!', 5.
2 For a discussion of norms as **expectations** – R. Jepperson, A. Wendt and P. Katzenstein, 'Norms, Identity and Culture in National Security' in Katzenstein (ed.) *The Culture of National Security – Norms and Identity in World Politics*, New York: Columbia University Press, 1996, University Press, 1996a, p. 54; M. Finnemore, *National Interests in International Society*, Ithaca, NY: Cornell, p. 22; T. Risse, S. Ropp and K. Sikkink (eds) *The Power of Human Rights – International Norms and Domestic Change*, Cambridge: Cambridge University Press, 1999, p. 7. Norms are perceived as **standards** of behaviour by Finnemore and Sikkink, 'International Norm Dynamics and Political Change', 891; A. Klotz, *Norms in International Relations – The Struggle against Apartheid*, Ithaca, NY: Cornell University Press, 1995, p. 14; J. Checkel, 'The Constructivist Turn in International Relations Theory', *World Politics*, Vol. 50, 1998, pp. 327–328; S. Krasner, *International Regimes*, Ithaca, NY: Cornell University Press, 1983, p. 2.
3 Krasner, *International Regimes*, p. 2.
4 N. Tannenwald, 'The Nuclear Taboo: The United States and the Normative Basis of Nuclear Non-use', *International Organisation*, Vol. 53, No. 3, 1999, 436.
5 Farrell, 'Transnational Norms and Military Development', 71.
6 Crawford, *Argument and Change in World Politics*, p. 86.
7 G. Drori, J. Meyer, F. Ramirez and E. Schofer, *Science in the Modern World Polity – Institutionalization and Globalization*, Stanford, CA: Stanford University Press, 2003, pp. 23, 25, 40–41.
8 Finnemore, *National Interests in International Society*, p. 37; MacKenzie, *Inventing Accuracy*, pp. 1–4, G. Spinardi, *From Polaris to Trident: The Devel-*

opment of US Fleet Ballistic Missile Technology, Cambridge: Cambridge University Press, 1994.

9 J. Ruggie, 'What Makes the World Hang Together? Neo-utilitarianism and the Social Constructivist Challenge', *International Organisation*, Vol. 52, No. 4, 1998, 879.

10 S. Guzzini, 'A Reconstruction of Constructivism in International Relations', *European Journal of International Relations*, Vol. 6, No. 3, 2000, 160.

11 A. Wendt, 'Constructing International Politics', *International Security*, Vol. 20, No. 1, 1995, 71–72.

12 Guzzini, 'A Reconstruction of Constructivism in International Relations', 163.

13 Katzenstein, *The Culture of National Security*; Ruggie, 'What Makes the World Hang Together?', p. 883; M. Zehfuss, *Constructivism in International Relations – The Politics of Reality*, Cambridge: Cambridge University Press, 2002; Checkel, 'The Constructivist Turn in International Relations Theory'.

14 E. Adler, 'Seizing the Middle Ground: Constructivism in World Politics', *European Journal of International Relations*, Vol. 3, No. 3, 1997, 327; Farrell, 'Transnational Norms and Military Development', 71.

15 Finnemore, 'Constructing Norms of Humanitarian Intervention', pp. 153–185.

16 Hopf, 'The Promise of Constructivism in International Relations Theory', 180–181.

17 Crawford, *Argument and Change in World Politics*.

18 Constructivist articles (in IR) from the early 1990s tended to focus their inquiry on the identities and interests of states as a source of understanding of state actions.

19 Tannenwald, 'The Nuclear Taboo', 433–468; C. Rudolph, 'Constructing an Atrocities Regime: The Politics of War Crimes Tribunals', *International Organisation*, Vol. 55, No. 3, 2001, 655–691; E. Nadelmann, 'Global Prohibition Regimes: The Evolution of Norms in International Society', *International Organisation*, Vol. 44, No. 4, 1990, 479–526.

20 Authors include Martha Finnemore, Kathryn Sikkink, Margaret Keck, Emanuel Adler, Audie Klotz, Thomas Risse-Kappen to name but a few.

21 M. Keck and K. Sikkink, *Activists beyond Borders, Advocacy Networks in International Relations*, Ithaca, NY: Cornell University Press, 1998, p. 30; Sikkink briefly introduces this idea in an earlier article – K. Sikkink, 'Human Rights, Principled Issue-Networks, and Sovereignty in Latin America', *International Organisation*, Vol. 47, No. 3, 1993, 412.

22 A. Klotz, 'Transnational Activism and Global Transformations: Anti-Apartheid and Abolitionist Experiences', *European Journal of International Relations*, Vol. 8, No. 1, 2002, 52.

23 P. Haas, 'Introduction: Epistemic Communities and International Policy Coordination', *International Organisation*, Vol. 46, No. 1, 1992, 3.

24 Ibid., 17; see also P. Haas, 'Do Regimes Matter? Epistemic Communities and Mediterranean Pollution Control', *International Organisation*, Vol. 43, No. 3, 1989, 380; W. Drake and K. Nicolaidis, 'Ideas, Interests and Institutionalisation: "Trade in Services" and the Uruguay Round', *International Organisation*, Vol. 46, No. 1, 1992, 39.

25 E. Adler, 'The Emergence of Cooperation: National Epistemic Communities and the International Evolution of the Idea of Nuclear Arms Control', *International Organisation*, Vol. 46, No. 1, 1992, 140–141.

26 'Normatively, elite policy-makers are portrayed as bad; empirically, they are

viewed as passive and reactive; ontologically, they are too often viewed solely as calculating agents' – J. Checkel, 'Why Comply? Constructivism, Social Norms and the Study of International Institutions', ARENA Working Papers, WP 99/24, 1999. Online. Available at: www.arena.uio.no/publications/wp99_24. htm (accessed 15 January 2009).

27 Klotz, 'Transnational Activism and Global Transformations', 51–52; Keck and Sikkink, *Activists beyond Borders*, p. 30.

28 J. March and J. Olsen, 'The Institutional Dynamics of International Political Orders', *International Organisation*, Vol. 52, No. 4, 1998, 943–969, especially 950–951.

29 Ibid., 949.

30 Ibid., 951.

31 T. Risse, '"Let's argue!": Communicative Action in World Politics', *International Organisation*, Vol. 54, No. 1, 2000, 7; for an overall discussion of the logic of argumentation see pp. 6–11.

32 T. Farrell, 'World Culture and Military Power', *Security Studies*, Vol. 14, No. 3, 2005, 448–488; Tannenwald, 'The Nuclear Taboo', 433–468; Rudolph, 'Constructing an Atrocities Regime'; Nadelmann, 'Global Prohibition Regimes'.

33 Finnemore and Sikkink, 'International Norm Dynamics and Political Change', 896.

34 T. Risse and K. Sikkink, 'The Socialization of International Human Rights Norms into Domestic Practices: Introduction', in Risse, Ropp and Sikkink (eds) *The Power of Human Rights*, pp. 17–35.

35 Haas, 'Do Regimes Matter?'

36 R. Hopkins, 'Reform in the International Food Regime: The Role of Consensual Knowledge', *International Organisation*, Vol. 46, No. 1, 1992, 225–264.

37 Drake and Nicolaidis, 'Ideas, Interests and Institutionalisation', 37–100.

38 Adler, 'The Emergence of Cooperation'.

39 R. Lidskog and G. Sundqvist, 'The Role of Science in Environmental Regimes: The Case of LRTAP', *European Journal of International Relations*, Vol. 8, No. 1, 2002, 77–101.

40 Haas, 'Do Regimes Matter?', 384; Drake and Nicolaidis, 'Ideas, Interests and Institutionalisation', 39; P. Haas, 'Banning Chlorofluorocarbons: Epistemic Community Efforts to Protect Stratospheric Ozone', *International Organisation*, Vol. 46, No. 1, 187–224, 197; Adler, 'The Emergence of Cooperation', 104.

41 Haas, 'Do Regimes Matter?', 385 and Haas, 'Banning Chlorofluorocarbons', 190.

42 Adler, 'The Emergence of Cooperation', 104 and 111–124.

43 E. Adler and P. Haas, 'Conclusion: Epistemic Communities, World Order, and the Creation of a Reflective Research Program', *International Organisation*, Vol. 46, No. 1, 1992, 367–390, especially 375–378.

44 Ibid., 378–379.

45 Ibid., 381.

46 Haas, 'Do Regimes Matter?', 397–398.

47 S. Shapin, 'Here and Everywhere: Sociology of Scientific Knowledge', *Annual Review of Sociology*, Vol. 21, 1995, 290; MacKenzie, *Inventing Accuracy*, p. 9; Collins, 'The Sociology of Scientific Knowledge', 266.

48 Collins, 'The Sociology of Scientific Knowledge', 267.

49 L. Fleck, *Genesis and Development of a Scientific Fact*, Chicago: University of Chicago Press, 1935/1979, p. 22.

50 MacKenzie, *Inventing Accuracy*; G. Spinardi, *From Polaris to Trident*; B. Barnes, D. Bloor and J. Henry, *Scientific Knowledge – A Sociological Analysis*, London: Athlone, 1996 – the authors presented a study of the controversy surrounding the issue of the charge of tiny particles of metal and wax; Collins, 'The Sociology of Scientific Knowledge; B. Latour and S. Woolgar, *Laboratory Life – The Construction of Scientific Facts*, Princeton, NJ: Princeton University Press, 1979.

51 Collins, 'The Sociology of Scientific Knowledge', 281; similar arguments have been made by J. Golinski, *Making Natural Knowledge – Constructivism and the History of Science*, New York: Cambridge University Press, 1998, pp. 2, 6; Spinardi, *From Polaris to Trident*, 193; Adler, 'The Emergence of Cooperation', 124; MacKenzie, *Inventing Accuracy*, p. 10.

52 T. Pinch and W. Bijker, 'The Social Construction of Facts and Artefacts: Or How the Sociology of Science and the Sociology of Technology Might Benefit Each Other', *Social Studies of Science*, Vol. 14, No. 3, 1984, 401.

53 Collins, 'The Sociology of Scientific Knowledge', 267.

54 W. Bijker, T. Hughes and T. Pinch (eds) *The Social Construction of Technological Systems – New Directions in the Sociology and the History of Technology*, Cambridge, MA: MIT Press, 1989, p. 18.

55 Golinski, *Making Natural Knowledge*, p. 7.

56 Fleck, *Genesis and Development of a Scientific Fact*, p. 20.

57 B. Barnes and D. Edge (eds) *Science in Context – Readings in the Sociology of Science*, Milton Keynes: Open University Press, p. 278.

58 Good illustration of this point is provided by Bruner and Posman's experiment with playing cards (cited in Kuhn's *Structure of Scientific Knowledge*). In the former, individuals were requested to identify anomalous cards (such as the black four of diamonds) in a colonnade of cards. According to the results of the experiment, 'individuals' expectations, attuned to the conventional format of the cards, appeared to have structured what individuals can and do see' – in Barnes, Bloor and Henry, *Scientific Knowledge*, p. 5.

59 Barnes, Bloor and Henry, *Scientific Knowledge*; Barnes and Edge (eds) *Science in Context*; MacKenzie, *Inventing Accuracy*; Spinardi, *From Polaris to Trident*; Golinski, *Making Natural Knowledge*; Collins, 'The Sociology of Scientific Knowledge'.

60 Latour and Woolgar, *Laboratory Life*, p. 106.

61 Latour and Woolgar discuss an example where the standards of proof had changed pushing one of the researchers out of the field because he could not afford the expenses of investing in new equipment that would guarantee the precision of results (Ibid., pp. 119–124); Adler, 'The Emergence of Cooperation' – members of the epistemic community working to enhance nuclear arms control 'knew each other well ... they learned from one another and together generated the standards by which they verified the validity of their ideas' (p. 112, see also p. 115).

62 Ibid., p. 164.

63 Ibid., p. 121.

64 Engelhardt and Caplan (eds) *Scientific Controversies*, p. 2.

65 Ibid., p. 3.

66 Latour and Woolgar, *Laboratory Life*, p. 176.

67 Engelhardt and Caplan (eds) *Scientific Controversies*, p. 1.

68 Ibid., p. 163.

69 Ibid., pp. 14–15.
70 Ibid., p. 13.
71 Ibid., p. 6.
72 Ibid., p. 14.
73 Ibid., p. 15.
74 As demonstrated earlier, NGOs and advocacy networks are often perceived to resort to moral persuasion: see Klotz, *Norms in International Relations*; Keck and Sikkink, *Activists beyond Borders*; Finnemore, *National Interests in International Society*; whereas epistemic communities and networks of scientists are portrayed as relying on impartial scientific knowledge: see Haas, 'Introduction'; P. Haas, 'Banning Chlorofluorocarbons'; Adler, 'The Emergence of Cooperation' and many others; and TNCs, banks and other economic actors relying primarily on their material resources and capabilities to effectively lobby nation-state governments to adopt policies to the formers' convenience.
75 Anticipated disaster was the reason for the formulation of norms in the case of the use of CFCs – Haas, 'Banning Chlorofluorocarbons', 187–224 and the alert of an environmental crisis brought states around the table to discuss the Med Plan – P. Haas, 'Do Regimes Matter?', 377–403; Farrell, 'Transnational Norms and Military Development', argues that external shock is one of the necessary conditions for radical change in the norms of war (20–21).
76 Examples here come from different fields – the campaign to ban the use of land mines – Price, 'Reversing the Gun Sights'; the idea for the creation of ad hoc war crime tribunals – Rudolph, 'Constructing an Atrocities Regime'; campaigns for woman suffrage, campaigns against foot binding in China, human rights campaigns in Latin America, campaigns drawing attention to violence against women – Keck and Sikkink, *Activists beyond Borders*; movements for the protection of the rights of women – N. Berkovitch, 'The Emergence and Transformation of the International Women's Movement', in J. Boli and G. Thomas, *Constructing World Culture – International Nongovernmental Organisations since 1875*, Stanford, CA: Stanford University Press, 1999.
77 M. Finnemore, 'Rules of War and Wars of Rules: The International Red Cross and the Restraint of State Violence' in Boli and Thomas, *Constructing World Culture*.
78 Finnemore and Sikkink, 'International Norm Dynamics and Political Change', 897 discuss the case of the creation of the ICRC, the campaign for women's suffrage.
79 Haas, 'Do Regimes Matter?', 380; the issue of banning landmine use was also initiated by congresses of experts – Price, 'Reversing the Gun Sights', 617–623.
80 Tannenwald, 'The Nuclear Taboo', Rudolph, 'Constructing an Atrocities Regime', Nadelmann, 'Global Prohibition Regimes', W. Thomas, *The Ethics of Destruction – Norms and Force in International Relations*, Ithaca, NY: Cornell University Press, 2001.
81 Drake and Nicolaidis, 'Ideas, Interests and Institutionalisation', 37–100.
82 This hypothesis is proposed by the studies on military innovation, suggesting that ' "entrepreneurs" proximity to the leadership of the target community is critical to success' – Farrell, 'Transnational Norms and Military Development'. The article has taken into account S. Rosen, *Winning the Next War*, Ithaca, NY: Cornell University Press, 1991; B. Posen, *The Sources of Military Doctrine*, Ithaca, NY: Cornell University Press, 1984 and M. Evangelista, *Unarmed Forces*, Ithaca, NY: Cornell University Press, 1999, p. 83.

83 For an in-depth discussion see F. Frey, *Survey Research on Comparative Social Change*, Boston, MA: MIT Press, 1969.

84 Farrell, 'Transnational Norms and Military Development', 83.

85 Rudolph, 'Constructing an Atrocities Regime' discusses how public pressure and public memory prompted action in Bosnia and Rwanda (ICTY and ICTR), 661.

86 In the case of the construction of atrocities regime, examined by Rudolph in 'Constructing an Atrocities Regime', the above-mentioned factors were not at play in Cambodia, Indonesia and East Timor, and although various crimes against humanity were committed, an ad hoc criminal court was never set up (675–678).

87 Price, 'Reversing the Gun Sights', 620. Price presents evidence of a series of conferences being held between NGOs, advocacy networks and experts of many spheres concerned with the production, trade, use of landmines, as well as the effects of landmines on individuals and communities.

88 Tannenwald, 'The Nuclear Taboo'; W. Thomas, *The Ethics of Destruction*.

89 The issue of landmines, for example, had to be redefined as being not an issue of disarmament, but an international humanitarian disaster, in order for states to agree to participate in negotiations – Price, 'Reversing the Gun Sights', 639.

90 Klotz, 'Transnational Activism and Global Transformations'; Haas, 'Banning Chlorofluorocarbons'; Nadelmann, 'Global Prohibition Regimes'.

91 Kratochwil and Ruggie, 'International Organization', 773.

92 Price, 'Reversing the Gun Sights', 639.

93 Haas, 'Banning Chlorofluorocarbons' – Haas outlines an interesting turn in the position of DuPont, the company, which was at the time the world leader in the production of CFCs, towards the support of CFC limitation, which speeded up the process of the rule formation (205).

94 The United Nations has created a mechanism via which NGOs can gain con-sultative status with some of its agencies. In 1996, the UN Committee of Non-governmental Organisations was created (CONGO) to facilitate relationships with NGOs – www.ngocongo.org/ngopart/index.htm.

95 Latour and Woolgar, *Laboratory Life*, p. 176.

96 C. Sunstein, *Free Markets and Social Justice*, New York: Oxford University Press, 1997, p. 38.

97 Engelhardt and Caplan (eds) *Scientific Controversies*.

98 Ibid., p. 615.

99 *International Organisation* – Special Issue 'Legalisation of World Politics' – Vol. 54, No. 3, 2000.

3 Protecting individuals from torture

1 J. Keane, *Violence and Democracy*, Cambridge: Cambridge University Press, 2004.

2 J. Glover, *Humanity – A Moral History of the Twentieth Century*, London: Pimlico, 2001.

3 'By the 1920s a European scholar could write that torture was a distant relic of a barbarous past, a practice forever left behind on man's journey to progress' – Amnesty International, *Report on Torture*, London: Duckworth in Association with Amnesty International Publications, 1973b, p. 25; '[i]n 1874, Victor Hugo proclaimed "torture has ceased to exist"... [i]n 1929, the

Encyclopaedia Britannica proclaimed that torture was "only of historical interest as far as Europe is concerned" ' – J. Conroy, *Unspeakable Acts, Ordinary People – The Dynamics of Torture*, London: Vision Paperbacks, 2001, p. 30; 'Nineteenth century historians of torture could write with a sense of freedom from institutions and culture of the past ... [h]aving identified once and for all the enemies of reason and humanity ... [that they] were at last free of them' – E. Peters, *Torture*, London: Basil Blackwell, 1985, p. 77.

4 *Danish Medical Bulletin*, Vol. 27, No. 5, 1980 – this issue of the journal included a number of papers on the issue of torture from a medical seminar held in Copenhagen, 1979, under the auspices of Amnesty International.

5 Amnesty International, *Report on Torture*, p. 31.

6 Ibid., p. 23; J. Langbein, *Torture and the Law of Proof – Europe and England in the Ancien Regime*, Chicago: University of Chicago Press, 1976, pp. 3–4; Conroy, *Unspeakable Acts, Ordinary People*, pp. 26–28.

7 G. R. Scott, *A History of Torture*, London: T. Werner Laurie, 1940, p. 35.

8 Ibid., p. 36.

9 Peters, *Torture*, p. 12.

10 Amnesty International, *Report on Torture*, p. 23; G. R. Scott, *A History of Torture*, p. 44; Peters, *Torture*, p. 16.

11 G. R. Scott, *A History of Torture*, p. 44, citing E. Gibbon, *History of the Decline and Fall of the Roman Empire*, London, 1776–1788.

12 Peters, *Torture*, p. 32.

13 Scott, *A History of Torture*, p. 53.

14 Scott cites St Augustine in denouncing the use of torture from the view that 'should the accused individual be innocent, he will undergo for an uncertain crime a certain punishment and that not for having committed a crime, but because it is unknown whether he committed it'; Scott further cites H. C. Lea (*Superstition and Force*, Philadelphia, 1878) that 'In 384 a synod at Roma denounced the use of torture by civil courts' – Scott, *A History of Torture*, p. 56.

15 Ibid., pp. 53–85; Peters, *Torture*, pp. 40–73.

16 Scott, *A History of Torture*, pp. 64–85.

17 Peters, *Torture*, p. 54.

18 Ibid.

19 Langbein, *Torture and the Law of Proof*, p. 5.

20 Ibid.

21 Ibid.

22 Scott, *A History of Torture*, pp. 102–133.

23 Ibid., pp. 135–136.

24 'The efforts of Beccaria in Italy, leading to the abolition of torture in 1786, and of Voltaire in France ... had influence in other countries' who later also abolished the use of judicial torture – Scott, *A History of Torture*, p. 136.

25 Ibid., pp. 135–136.

26 Langbein, *Torture and the Law of Proof*, pp. 55–65.

27 Ibid., p. 66.

28 Ibid., Chapter 3, 'The Revolution in the Law of Proof', pp. 45–69.

29 Ibid., Chapter 2, 'The Transformation of Criminal Sanctions', pp. 27–44.

30 Ibid., p. 56.

31 S. Ratner and J. Abrams, *Accountability for Human Rights Atrocities in International Law – Beyond the Nuremburg Legacy*, Oxford: Clarendon Press, 1997, p. 6.

32 P. Thygesen, 'The Concentration Camp Syndrome', *Danish Medical Bulletin*, Vol. 27, No. 5, 1980, 224, referring to a study of concentration camp survivors in Copenhagen 1947–1948, citing K. Hermann and P. Thygesen, *KZ-syndromet*, Ugeskr, 1954.

33 *The Times Digital* archive shows that between 1970 and 1985 almost 3,000 articles were published on the issue of torture. The archives of medical specialist journal *The Lancet* show that between 1970 and 1990, there were 22 articles, on the issue, while 26 articles were published between 1990 and 2003. The issue of torture hit the headlines in the 1970s partly as a result of the information that surfaced on the torture campaigns in Latin America and the Soviet Union.

34 Thygesen, 'The Concentration Camp Syndrome', 224–228; L. Eitinger, 'Jewish Concentration Camp Survivors in the Postwar World', *Danish Medical Bulletin*, Vol. 27, 1980, 232–235.

35 Thygesen, 'The Concentration Camp Syndrome', 225–226.

36 Ibid., 226.

37 Risse, Ropp and Sikkink (eds) *The Power of Human Rights*, p. 21; according to these authors, the increase in volume of behavioural norms helps the evolution and success of new norms and new norms would 'cascade' more quickly in a rapidly expanding normative context.

38 H. Bull, *The Anarchical Society – A Study of Order in World Politics*, 2nd edn, London: Macmillan Press Ltd, 1977, pp. 85–86.

39 Amnesty International, *Report on Torture*, pp. 26.

40 There had been a series of articles in *The Times* regarding the ICRC report, which found that torture was a common practice among French soldiers who were trying to deal with Algerian rebels – 'Torture Still Used on Captured Rebels – Red Cross Report on Algeria Prison Camp', *The Times*, 5 January, 1960; 'French Paper seized in Algiers – Issue Containing Torture Report', *The Times*, 6 January, 1960; R. Maran, *Torture: The Role of Ideology in the French–Algerian War*, London: Praeger, 1989.

41 The case of South Africa is examined by Peters, *Torture*, pp. 157–158; United Nations General Assembly: Special Committee on Apartheid, *Maltreatment and Torture of Prisoners in South Africa: Report of the Special Committee on Apartheid*, Rapporteur – Barakat Ahmad, New York: United Nations, 1973; Catholic Institute for International Relations, Human Rights Forum (British Council of Churches) and the International Commission of Jurists, *Torture in South Africa*, London: Catholic Institute for International Relations and the International Commission of Jurists, 1982.

42 W. Keylor, *The Twentieth Century World – An International History*, 4th edn, Oxford: Oxford University Press, 2001, p. 403.

43 Keylor, *The Twentieth Century World*, pp. 398–402.

44 Keylor, *The Twentieth Century World*, p. 401; see also 'Chilean Church Leaders Accuse Junta of Torture', *The Times*, 26 April 1974; 'Jurists Condemn Torture in Uruguay', *The Times*, 17 June 1974; 'Torture in Brazil', *The Times*, 28 May 1970; 'Report on Brazil Tortures', *The Times*, 23 July 1970.

45 Amnesty International, *Torture in Greece: The First Torturers' Trial 1975*, London: Amnesty International, 1977; Amnesty International, *Torture in the Eighties*, London: Amnesty International Publications, 1984.

46 N. Belton, *The Good Listener – Helen Bamber Life against Cruelty*, London:

Weidenfeld and Nicolson, 1998, pp. 270–271; M. Knipe, 'Soviet Camp Tortures Alleged', *The Times*, 29 July 1970.

47 Amnesty International, *Report on Torture*, p. 26.

48 S. Ratner and J. Abrams, *Accountability for Human Rights Atrocities in International Law*, p. 6.

49 Ibid., p. 7 citing United Nations War Crimes Commission, *History of the United Nations War Crimes Commission and the Development of the Laws of War* (1948), pp. 192–193.

50 Belton, *The Good Listener*, p. 215.

51 Keylor, *The Twentieth Century World*.

52 The delegations of Sweden, the Netherlands, the United Kingdom, France, Austria, Belgium at the United Nations were some of the strongest supporters and most active actors in the creation of the Convention against Torture – J. Burgers and H. Danelius, *The UN Convention against Torture – A Handbook on the Convention against Torture and Other Cruel, Inhuman and Degrading Treatment or Punishment*, Norwell, MA: Martin Hijhoff Publishers, 1988, pp. 31–113.

53 Amnesty International, *Annual Report*, London: British Section, 1973–1974, p. 8.

54 'Human Rights in the World – Torture Continues', *The Review – International Commission of Jurists*, No. 10, June 1973 – the article cites an ICJ report on the use of torture in Brazil, *ICJ Review*, No. 5, 1970, allegations of torture in Iran – *ICJ Bulletin*, No. 26, 1966 and *ICJ Review*, No. 8, 1972; Indonesia, *ICJ Review*, No. 4, 1969 and further allegations of torture in Turkey, Uruguay, South and North Vietnam, Spain, Greece, South Africa.

55 See 'Study of Reported Violations of Human Rights in Chile, with Particular Reference to Torture and Other Cruel, Inhuman or Degrading Treatment or Punishment' in Commission on Human Rights, Report of the 32nd Session, 2 Febuary–5 March 1976; ECOSOC, Official Records 60th Session, Supplement 3, UN Doc. Index: E/5768, E/CN.4/1213, 16–19; 'Telegram to the Government of Chile', in Commission on Human Rights, Report of the 32nd Session, p. 71; Summary Records of the 2065th meeting of the 29th Session of the Third Committee of the UNGA held on 15 October 1974, UN Doc. Index: A/C.3/SR.2065, p. 79; Summary Records of the 2066th meeting of the 29th Session of the Third Committee of the UNGA held on 15 October 1974, UN Doc. Index: A/C.3/SR.2066, pp. 81–83.

56 Amnesty International addressed separate aspects of torture – the legal, the medical, the political and the socio-economic. See Amnesty International, *Report on Torture*; Amnesty International, *Conference for the Abolition of Torture – Final Report*, Paris, 10–11 December 1973; Report of the 'International Seminar on Torture and Human Rights', Palais de l'Europe, Strasbourg, 3–5 October 1977, London: Amnesty International; Amnesty International, 'Violations of Human Rights: Torture and the Medical Profession', *Report on an Amnesty International Medical Seminar*, Athens, 10–11 March 1978; N. Rodley, *The Treatment of Prisoners under International Law*, 2nd edn, Oxford: Oxford University Press, 1999, pp. 20–21.

57 Amnesty International, *Iran*, London: Amnesty International Publications, 1976; Amnesty International, *Prisoners of Conscience in the USSR: Their Treatment and Conditions*, London: Amnesty International Publications,

1976; Amnesty International, *Report of an Enquiry into Allegations of Ill-treatment Made against the Security Forces in Northern Ireland by Persons Arrested on 9 August 1971*, London: Amnesty International Publications, 1972; Amnesty International, *Report on Allegations of Torture in Brazil*, London: Amnesty International Publications, 1974; Amnesty International, *Tortured to Death in Uruguay: 22 Known Cases*, London: Amnesty International Publications, 1976.

58 Amnesty International, *Report on Torture*, p. 18.
59 E. Prokosch, 'Amnesty International's Anti-torture Campaign' in D. Forrest (ed.) *A Glimpse of Hell – Reports on Torture Worldwide*, London: Cassell, 1996, p. 26.
60 Scott, *A History of Torture*, pp. 44–46 – the author discusses the limitations placed on the use of torture as judicial procedure and juxtaposes that to the lack of such restrictions on the use of torture as punishment.
61 Amnesty International, *Report on Torture*, 'World Survey of Torture', pp. 109–218.
62 Prokosch, 'Amnesty International's Anti-torture Campaign', 27.
63 See www.bma.org/ap.nsf/Content/About+the+BMA+-+An+outline+history+of+the+BMA (accessed 19 June 2004).
64 See www.icj.org/article.php3?id_article=2957&id_rubrique=11&lang=en; and Tolley, *The International Commission of Jurists*, pp. 31–45 and 79–113.
65 See www.cioms.ch/what_is_cioms.htm (accessed 19 June 2004).
66 'It was not until after the end of World War II that general opinion and the medical world became interested in the suffering by those maltreated by torture and their chronic pathological reactions – or rather, their normal reactions to pathological treatment' – Eitinger, 'Torture', p. 9 and it was certainly not until the mid-1970s that knowledge began to amass on the physical and psychological sequelae of torture victims. See *Danish Medical Journal*, Vol. 27, No. 5, November 1980.
67 Belton, *The Good Listener*, p. 275.
68 Online. Available at: www.torturecare.org.uk/about/aboutHistory.htm (accessed 19 June 2004).
69 O. V. Rasmussen and I. Lunde, 'Evaluation of Investigation of 200 Torture Victims', *Danish Medical Bulletin*, Vol. 27, No. 5, 1980, 241; A. Gellhorn, 'Violations of Human Rights: Torture and the Medical Profession', *New England Journal of Medicine*, Vol. 299, No. 7, 1978, 358; O. V. Rasmussen, 'Medical Aspects of Torture', *Danish Medical Bulletin*, Supplement 1, January 1990, 2.
70 U. Abildgaard, G. Daugaard, H. Marcussen, P. Jess, H. Draminsky Petersen and M. Wallach, 'Chronic Organic Psycho-syndrome in Greek Torture Victims', *Danish Medical Bulletin*, Vol. 31, No. 3, 1984, 239.
71 Rasmussen, 'Medical Aspects of Torture', 3.
72 Online. Available at: www.rct.dk/usr/rct/webuk.nsf/fWEB?ReadForm&Load=RTIG-4L5JTU (accessed 28 June 2004).
73 Belton, *The Good Listener*, pp. 204–206.
74 Ibid., p. 206.
75 Online. Available at: www.wma.net/e/history/tokio.htm (accessed 25 June 2004).
76 Online. Available at: www.wma.net/e/history/golden_years.htm (accessed 25 June 2004).

77 Online. Available at: www.wma.net/e/history/tokio.htm (accessed 25 June 2004).
78 Ibid.
79 Burgers and Danelius, *The UN Convention against Torture*, p. 21; Amnesty International, *Annual Report 1974–1975*, London: Amnesty International Publications, 1975, p. 21.
80 The Draft Code of Medical Ethics was the result of the joint efforts of the World Health Organisation and the Council for International Organisations of the Medical Sciences (CIOMS), in consultation with the World Medical Association and other non-state epistemic communities – A. Gellhorn, 'Medicine, Torture and the United Nations', *The Lancet*, Vol. 315, issue 8165, 1980, 428.
81 Amnesty International Health Professional Network. Online. Available at: www.web.amnesty.org/web/web.nsf/print/health-index-eng (accessed 25 June 2004); Amnesty International, the French Medical Commission and Valery Marange, *Doctors and Torture – Collaboration or Resistance?*, London: Bellew Publishing, 1989, pp. 73–80.
82 Tolley, *The International Commission of Jurists*, p. 38.
83 The ICJ had consultative status with UNESCO, and maintained close cooperation with ECOSOC, the ILO, the UN Human Rights Commission, the Organisation of American States, the Organisation of African Unity, the Arab League, the ICRC, Amnesty International, the World Council of Churches, etc. – S. MacBride, 'Meeting of the International Commission of Jurists', *Bulletin of the International Commission of Jurists*, Vol. 28, 1966, p. 27.
84 MacBride had an impressive political career – he was the Minister for External Affairs for Ireland between 1948 and 1951, President of the Committee of Ministers of the Council of Europe in 1950, one of the co-founders of Amnesty International and was also elected a Chairman of the Executive Committee of Amnesty between 1961 and 1975, Secretary General of the ICJ (1963–1970), Chairman of the International Peace Bureau (1968–1974), Assistant Secretary General of the UN (1973–1977), Nobel Peace Prize winner in 1974 – www.nobel.se/peace/laureates/1974/macbride-cv.html.
85 Tolley, *The International Commission of Jurists*, p. 98.
86 Ibid., 106.
87 Ibid., 165.
88 F. De Vargas, 'History of a Campaign' in International Commission of Jurists and Swiss Committee against Torture (eds) *Torture: How to Make the International Convention Effective – A Draft Optional Protocol*, Geneva: International Commission of Jurists, 1979, pp. 41–43.
89 Ibid., pp. 42–43.
90 Personal correspondence with Françoise De Vargas, Secretary General of the CSCT during the years preceding the adoption of the Convention against Torture in 1984.
91 H. Hunke and J. Ellis, *Torture – A Cancer of Our Society*, London: Catholic Institute of International Relations, 1980, pp. 11, 13–16.
92 'Human Rights in the World – Torture Continues', *The Review – International Commission of Jurists*, June 1973, 11.
93 International Commission of Jurists and Swiss Committee against Torture, *Torture*, p. 49.
94 H. Thoolen, *Thirty Years after the Universal Declaration of Human Rights –*

the Need for an International Convention against Torture, Geneva: Commission of the Churches on International Affairs, 1978, pp. 1–2.

95 Burgers and Danelius, *The UN Convention against Torture*, p. 26; Thoolen, *Thirty Years after the Universal Declaration of Human Rights*, p. 14.

96 Report of the 'International Seminar on Torture and Human Rights', Palais de l'Europe, Strasbourg, 3–5 October 1977, published by Amnesty International, London.

97 Report on the 23rd International Red Cross Conference 'Action of the Red Cross against Torture', held in Manila, November 1981 – pp. 5.

98 Amnesty International, *Report on Torture*, citing First Geneva Convention 1949, Art. 12 (2) – p. 31.

99 Lord Gardiner's Report, 'Interrogation Procedures – Minor Report of the Committee of Privy Counsellors', *The Review – International Commission of Jurists*, Vol. 8, June 1972, 17–22.

100 Amnesty International, *Report on Torture*, citing Council of Europe, European Commission of Human Rights, *The Greek Case: Report of the Commission*, Vol. 2, part 1, page 1, p. 31.

101 Ibid., pp. 21–22.

102 Amnesty International, *Report on Torture* , p. 31.

103 Thygesen, 'The Concentration Camp Syndrome', 224–227 provides details of a study of concentration camp survivors conducted as early as 1946–1947.

104 Thygesen, 'The Concentration Camp Syndrome'; R. Daly, 'Compensation and Rehabilitation of Victims of Torture', *Danish Medical Journal*, Vol. 27, No. 5, 245–248.

105 Amnesty International, *Conference for the Abolition of Torture – Final Report*, Paris, 10–11 December 1973, London: Amnesty International Publications, 1973 – pp. 35–65; Amnesty International, *Evidence of Torture: Studies by the Amnesty International Danish Medical Group*, London: Amnesty International Publications, 1977; Amnesty International, *Amnesty International Report*, London: Amnesty International Publications, 1977, pp. 34–39; Report of an Amnesty International Medical Seminar, 'Violations of Human Rights: Torture and the Medical Profession', Athens, 10–11 March 1978, AI Index: CAT 02/03/78 – Report of Working Party III – pp. 22–23; Rasmussen, 'Medical Aspects of Torture'; *Danish Medical Bulletin* – Vol. 27, No. 5, 1980 – containing a report of the seminar 'Sequelae and Rehabilitation of Concentration Camp Victims, Sailors from the Second World War, Hostages and Torture Victims' held in Copenhagen, 8–9 December 1979.

106 Report of an Amnesty International Medical Seminar 'Violations of Human Rights', p. 18.

107 Rasmussen, 'Medical Aspects of Torture'.

108 Amnesty International, *Report of an Enquiry into Allegations of Ill-treatment Made against the Security Forces in Northern Ireland by Persons Arrested on 9 August 1971*, p. 38.

109 Amnesty International, *Conference for the Abolition of Torture*, p. 15.

110 Appendix B – Codes of Medical Ethics Concerning Torture – Declaration of Tokyo in N. Gordon and R. Marton (eds) *Torture – Human Rights, Medical Ethics and the Case of Israel*, London: Zed Books in association with the Association of Israeli–Palestinian Physicians for Human Rights, 1995.

111 'Law and the Prevention of Torture', *The Review – International Commission of Jurists*, Vol. 11, December 1973, p. 23.

112 Rodley, *The Treatment of Prisoners under International Law*, pp. 76–77; *European Court of Human Rights Yearbook: The Greek Case* 72 (1969).
113 The only term omitted in the European Convention is the term 'cruel', referring to treatment or punishment – M. O'Boyle 'Torture and Emergency Powers under the European Convention on Human Rights: Ireland v. United Kingdom', *American Journal of International Law*, No. 71, 1977, 685.
114 *Yearbook of the European Convention on Human Rights* – the Greek Case (1969) cited in O'Boyle, 'Torture and Emergency Powers under the European Convention on Human Rights, 685.
115 Lord Gardiner's Report, 'Interrogation Procedures', 17–22.
116 Ibid., 22.
117 Rodley, *The Treatment of Prisoners under International Law*, p. 78.
118 Ibid., p. 79 citing *Ireland* v. *United Kingdom*, 19 *Yearbook* 512, 750 (1976).
119 Burgers and Danelius, *The UN Convention against Torture*; C. Ingelse, *The UN Committee against Torture – An Assessment*, The Hague: Kluwer Law International, 2001 consider primarily the work of states on CAT and give only marginal attention to the work and influence of non-state actors.
120 Amnesty International, *Conference for the Abolition of Torture*; Resolution adopted by the Inter-Parliamentary Union 'Amnesty International Campaign against Torture – The Problem of Torture in the World', 11 October 1974, Tokyo; Report of the 'International Seminar on Torture and Human Rights'.
121 Verbatim Records of the 2065th Meeting of the Third Committee of the UNGA, 29th Session, 15 October 1974, paragraphs 20, 22, 29; Verbatim Records of the 2066th Meeting of the Third Committee of the UNGA, 29th Session, 15 October 1974, paragraphs 1, 3, 28; Verbatim Records of the 2067th Meeting of the Third Committee of the UNGA, 29th Session, 16 October 1974 – paragraphs 18, 31.
122 Burgers and Danelius, *The UN Convention against Torture*, p. 13; Rodley, *The Treatment of Prisoners under International Law*, pp. 20–21.
123 Ibid., p. 13; Resolution 3059 'Question of Torture and Other Cruel, Inhuman or Degrading Treatment or Punishment', GA 28th Session, 2163rd plenary meeting, 2 November 1973. Online. Available at: www.un.org/documents/resga.htm (accessed 23 September 2004).
124 Verbatim Records of the 2066th Meeting of the Third Committee of the UNGA – 29th Session, 15 October 1974, paragraph 25; Summary Records No. 35 from the 32nd Session of the Third Committee of the UNGA held on 1 November 1977 (UN Doc. Index A/C.3/32/SR/35), paragraphs 14, 17; Summary Records No. 38 from the 32nd Session of the Third Committee of the UNGA held on 3 November 1977 (UN Doc. Index A/C.3/32/SR/38), paragraph 20.
125 Burgers and Danelius, *UN Convention against Torture*, pp. 13, 19–20; Rodley, *The Treatment of Prisoners under International Law*, pp. 21, 23–24; Ingelse, *The UN Committee against Torture*, pp. 67–68.
126 General Assembly 28th Session, 2163rd plenary meeting, 2 November 1973.
127 Verbatim Records of the 2065th Meeting of the Third Committee of the UNGA, 29th Session, 15 October 1974; Verbatim Records of the 2066th Meeting of the Third Committee of the UNGA, 29th Session, 15 October 1974; Verbatim Records of the 2067th Meeting of the Third Committee of the UNGA, 29th Session, 16 October 1974; Verbatim Records of the 2068th Meeting of the Third Committee of the UNGA, 29th Session, 18 October 1974.

128 Verbatim Records of the 2067th Meeting of the Third Committee of the UNGA, 29th Session, 16 October 1974, pp. 86–87, 92.

129 Verbatim Records of the Plenary Meeting of the UNGA, 29th Session, 2244 Meeting, 26 September 1974, pp. 193–197.

130 Rodley, *The Treatment of Prisoners under International Law*, pp. 28–29 – The Netherlands prepared the draft of what became UNGA Resolution 3218 (pp. 25–26); at the 5th UN Congress on the prevention of crime and the treatment of offenders, the Swedish and Dutch delegations submitted a draft declaration for the protection of all persons from being subjected to torture and other cruel, inhuman or degrading treatment or punishment.

131 Verbatim Records of the 2066th Meeting of the Third Committee of the UNGA, 29th Session, 15 October 1974, paragraph 10.

132 Ibid., paragraphs 15, 16, 17.

133 Ibid., paragraph 18.

134 Verbatim Records of the 2067th Meeting of the Third Committee of the UNGA, 29th Session, 16 October 1974, paragraph 4.

135 Ibid., paragraph 48.

136 Resolution 3218 – Torture and other cruel, inhuman or degrading treatment or punishment in relation to detention and imprisonment, GA 29th Session, 2278th plenary meeting, 6 November 1974.

137 Summary Records No. 62 from the 31st Session of the Third Committee of the UNGA held in 1976, UN Doc. Index: A/C.3/31/SR.62, paragraph 38.

138 Rodley, *The Treatment of Prisoners under International Law*, p. 34, citing Fifth UN Crime Congress Report – paragraph 379.

139 Summary Records No. 62 from the 31st Session of the Third Committee of the UNGA held in 1976, UN Doc. Index: A/C.3/31/SR.62, paragraph 38.

140 Resolution 3453, GA 30th Session, 2433 plenary meeting, 9 December 1975.

141 Some such states were Portugal, Mexico, USSR, Greece, Australia, Belgium, Sweden, even Saudi Arabia – Summary Records No. 63 from the 31st Session of the Third Committee of the UNGA held in 1976, UN Doc. Index: A/C.3/31/SR.63; Summary Records No. 64 from the 31st Session of the Third Committee of the UNGA held in 1976, UN Doc. Index: A/C.3/31/SR.64.

142 Summary Records No. 65 from the 31st Session of the Third Committee of the UNGA held in 1976, UN Doc. Index: A/C.3/31/SR.65, Chile, paragraphs 36–41; 43–45; Summary Records No. 66 from the 31st Session of the Third Committee of the UNGA held in 1976, UN Doc. Index: A/C.3/31/SR.66, Chile, paragraphs 92–94.

143 Strategic negotiations particularly in the realm of demilitarisation – landmines, nuclear weapons, chemical and biological weapons – often hit deadlock because of the high stakes in national security that some states find unsurpassable.

144 Resolution 32/62, A/RES/32/62 adopted on the reports of the Third Committee, in the 98th plenary meeting of the UNGA, 8 December 1977.

145 Ibid.

146 Ibid., p. 34.

147 Summary Records No. 34 from the 32nd Session of the Third Committee of the UNGA held on 31 October 1977, UN Doc. Index A/C.3/32/SR.34; Summary Records No. 35 from the 32nd Session of the Third Committee of the UNGA held on 1 November 1977, UN Doc. Index A/C.3/32/SR.35;

184 *Notes*

Summary Records No. 36 from the 32nd Session of the Third Committee of the UNGA held on 1 November 1977, UN Doc. Index A/C.3/32/SR/36; Summary Records No. 38 from the 32nd Session of the Third Committee of the UNGA held on 3 November 1977, UN Doc. Index A/C.3/32/SR/38.

148 Burgers and Danelius, *The UN Convention against Torture*, p. 3.

149 Summary Records No. 35 from the 32nd Session of the Third Committee of the UNGA held on 1 November 1977, UN Doc. Index A/C.3/32/SR/35, Sweden (paragraphs 22–24); the Netherlands (paragraphs 25–32).

150 Ibid; Summary Records No. 36 from the 32nd Session of the Third Committee of the UNGA held on 1 November 1977, UN Doc. Index A/C.3/32/SR/36.

151 N. Chandrahasan, 'Freedom from Torture and the Jurisdiction of Municipal Courts: Sri Lanka and United States Perspective', *Human Rights Quarterly*, Vol. 5, No. 1, 1983, 65.

152 Ibid., citing Filartiga, 630 F.2d at 890, 67.

153 International Commission of Jurists and Swiss Committee against Torture, private communications with Francoise de Vargas.

154 International Commission of Jurists and Swiss Committee against Torture, *Torture*, pp. 44–45.

155 Commission on Human Rights, Report of the 34th Session, 6 February–10 March 1978, ECOSOC, Official Records 1978, Supplement 4, UN Doc. Index: E/1978/34 E/CN.4/1292, p. 29.

156 Burgers and Danelius, *The UN Convention against Torture*, pp. 26 and 36.

157 International Commission of Jurists and Swiss Committee against Torture, *Torture* – the book contains both drafts, which can be further compared – pp. 50–60; Burgers and Danelius, *The UN Convention against Torture*, p. 26.

158 Ibid., pp. 34–113.

159 Commission on Human Rights, Report of the 34th Session, 6 February–10 March 1978, ECOSOC, Official Records 1978, Supplement 4, UN Doc. Index: E/1978/34 E/CN.4/1292, pp. 29–35.

160 Resolution 3452, 'Declaration on the Protection of All Persons from Being subjected to Torture and other Cruel, Inhuman, or Degrading Treatment or Punishment', adopted by UNGA, 9 December 1975. Online. Available at: www.unhchr.ch/html/menu3/b/h_comp38.htm (accessed 30 January 2009).

161 Burgers and Danelius, *The UN Convention against Torture*, pp. 41–47.

162 Ibid., p. 42.

163 'Human Rights in the World – Torture Continues', *The Review – International Commission of Jurists*, No. 10, June 1973 – 'USSR – Repression of Dissidents', pp. 30–33; C. Yeo, 'Psychiatry, the Law and Dissent in the Soviet Union', *The Review – International Commission of Jurists*, Vol. 14, June 1975, 34–41.

164 See the report of Working Group III at the AI Medical Seminar held in Athens (1978); British Medical Association, *The Handbook of Medical Ethics*, London: BMA, 1982, pp. 59–62; P. McNeill, *The Ethics and Politics of Human Experimentation*, Cambridge: Cambridge University Press, 1993.

165 See Amnesty International, *Report of an Enquiry into Allegations of Ill-treatment made against the Security Forces in Northern Ireland by Persons arrested on 9 August 1971*. See also *The Recommendations of the AI Conference in Paris* (1973); M. Jempson, 'The Agencies Involved' in D. Forrest (ed.) *A Glimpse of Hell*, pp. 122–136.

166 Commission on Human Rights, Report of the 35th Session, 12 February–16

March 1979, ECOSOC, Official Records 1979, Supplement 6, UN Doc. Index: E/1979/36, E/CN.4/1347, paragraph 24.

167 Ibid., paragraph 30.

168 Ibid., paragraph 36.

169 Article 2, paragraph 2 states: 'no exceptional circumstances whatsoever, whether a state of war or a threat of war, internal political instability or any other public emergency, may be invoked as a justification for torture' (Ibid.).

170 Burgers and Danelius, *The UN Convention against Torture*, pp. 49–52 and 54–56; Commission on Human Rights, Report of the 36th Session, 4 February–14 March 1980, ECOSOC, Official Records 1980, Supplement 3, UN Doc. Index: E/1980/13 E/CN.4/1408, paragraphs 13–32.

171 Burgers and Danelius, *The UN Convention against Torture*, pp. 56–57; Commission on Human Rights, Report of the 36th Session, 4 February–14 March 1980, ECOSOC, Official Records 1980, Supplement 3, UN Doc. Index: E/1980/13 E/CN.4/1408, paragraphs 33–37.

172 Burgers and Danelius, *The UN Convention against Torture*, pp. 57–60; Commission on Human Rights, Report of the 36th Session, 4 February–14 March 1980, ECOSOC, Official Records 1980, Supplement 3, UN Doc. Index: E/1980/13 E/CN.4/1408, paragraphs 38–53.

173 Burgers and Danelius, *The UN Convention against Torture*, pp. 74–77, 80–84, 96–98.

174 Ibid., pp. 78–80.

175 See Commission on Human Rights, Report of the 37th Session, 2 February–13 March 1981, ECOSOC, Official Records 1981, UN Doc. Index: E/1981/25, E/CN.4/1475, pp. 50–70, 226–227.

176 Commission on Human Rights, Report of the 38th Session, 1 February–12 March 1982, ECOSOC, Official Records 1982, Supplement 2, UN Doc. Index: E/1982/12, E/CN.4/1982/30, pp. 45–49, 139; Commission on Human Rights, Report of the 39th Session, 31 January–11 March 1983, ECOSOC, Official Records 1983, Supplement 3, UN Doc. Index: E/1983/13 E/CN.4/1983/60, pp. 51–53.

177 International Commission of Jurists and Swiss Committee against Torture, *Torture*, p. 42.

178 Ibid., p. 43; Inter-American Institute of Human Rights and the Association for the Prevention of Torture, *Optional Protocol to the United Nations Convention against Torture and Other Cruel, Inhuman or Degrading Treatment or Punishment*, p. 34.

179 The first proposal for such an optional protocol was submitted by the delegation of Costa Rica to the UN Commission on Human Rights on 3 March 1992 (Ibid., p. 39).

180 Amnesty International, *Torture in the Eighties* – the report contains information about the use of torture in 98 countries around the world, and 'about the lack of any will to stop it by many others' – p. 2.

181 Personal correspondence with Françoise de Vargas, former Secretary General of the APT, Lausanne.

182 Inter-American Institute of Human Rights and the Association for the Prevention of Torture, *Optional Protocol to the United Nations Convention against Torture and Other Cruel, Inhuman or Degrading Treatment or Punishment*, p. 47.

183 See CINAT's press release statement from 22 June 2006. Online. Available

at: www.apt.ch/cinat/CINAT_Statement_22.06.06.pdf (accessed 17 September 2006).

184 Optional Protocol to the Convention against Torture, and other Cruel, Inhuman and Degrading Treatment or Punishment, adopted 18 December 2002, UNGA, by resolution A/RES/57/199. Online. Available at: http://www2.ohchr.org/english/law/cat-one.htm (accessed 30 January 2009).

185 J. Mayer, 'Outsourcing Torture – The Secret History of America's "Extraordinary Rendition" Programme', *New Yorker*, 14 February 2005. Online. Available at: www.newyorker.com/archive/2005/02/14/050214fa_fact6 (accessed 19 January 2009).

186 Amnesty International, AI Public Statement, 'Commission on Human Rights, 60th Session, 15 March–23 April 2004 – The Human Rights Scandal of Guantanamo Bay', AI Index IOR 41/024/2004, April 2004; Amnesty International, AI Press Release, 'End Human Rights Scandal in Guantanamo Bay', AI Index POL 30/017/2004, 11 April 2004; Amnesty International, AI Press Release, 'USA: Pattern of Brutality and Cruelty – War Crimes and Abu Ghraib', AI Index AMR 51/077/2004, 7 May 2004; Amnesty International, AI Press Release, 'USA/Iraq: Abuses without accountability a Year after Abu Ghraib', AI Index AMR 51/064/2005, 28 April 2005; Human Rights First, HRF Press Release: 'Human Rights First Condemns Use of Torture Tactics at Guantanamo Bay', 30 November 2005; Human Rights First, 'One Year after the Abu Ghraib Torture Photos: US Government Response "Grossly Inadequate"', 26 April 2005.

187 'US "Shifts" Position on Torture', *BBC News*, 7 December 2005.

188 P. Naughton, 'Rice Signals Shift on US Torture Policy', *Times Online*, 7 December 2005. Online. Available at: www.timesonline.co.uk/article/0,, 11069–1914318,00.html (accessed 14 May 2006).

189 'Congress Presses for Torture Ban', *BBC News*, 15 December 2005; 'House Supports Ban on Torture – Measure Would Limit Interrogation Tactics', *Washington Post*, 15 December 2005; Human Rights First, HRF Press Release, 'Human Rights First Applauds Agreement Banning Abuse of Detainees – Urges Congress to Secure Victory by Keeping Torture Evidence Out of Court', 15 December 2005.

190 'Law Lords Rule against Use of Torture Evidence', *The Times*, 8 December 2005.

191 'Lords Reject Torture Evidence Use', *BBC News*, 8 December 2005.

192 V. Buschschluter, 'The Obama Approach to Interrogation', *BBC News*, 29 January 2009. Online. Available at: http://news.bbc.co.uk/1/hi/world/americas/7847405.stm (accessed 31 January 2009).

4 Protecting intellectual property rights in the pharmaceutical industry

1 UNCTAD–ICTSD Project on IPRs and Sustainable Development, *Intellectual Property Rights: Implications for Development*, Policy Discussion Paper, published by UNCTAD and ICTSD, 2003, p. 28.

2 E. Mansfield, 'Intellectual Property, Technology and Economic Growth' in F. Rushing and C. Brown (eds) *Intellectual Property Rights in Science, Technology and Economic Performance – International Comparison*, London: Westview Press, 1990, p. 23; K. Maskus *Intellectual Property Rights in the Global*

Economy, Washington, DC: Institute for International Economics, 2000, pp. 28–29.
3 V. Shiva, *Protect or Plunder? Understanding Intellectual Property Rights*, London: Zed Books, 2001 – the author argues that knowledge is a collective, cumulative enterprise rather than capital or commodity (p. 21).
4 L. Gillespie-White, *Health and Patents: The Rights Issue*, Presentation to an Audience Convened by the World Intellectual Property Organisation, International Intellectual Property Institute, 11 June 2002. Online. Available at: www.iipi.org/speeches/NewYork061102.pdf (accessed 17 January 2009), pp. 3; B. Lehman, *Patents and Health*, Presentation to the Policy Advisory Commission of the World Intellectual Property Organisation, International Intellectual Property Institute, 22 May 2002. Online. Available at: www.iipi.org/speeches/Beijing_Health_052202.pdf (accessed 17 January 2009), pp. 4–9.
5 Shiva, *Protect or Plunder?*, p. 23.
6 C. Vaitsos, 'Patents Revisited: Their Function in Developing Countries', *Journal of Development*, Vol. 9, No. 1, 1972, 72; Shiva, *Protect or Plunder?*, p. 21.
7 Online. Available at: www.economist.com/research/economics – *The Economist*'s A–Z of economic terms.
8 C. May, *A Global Political Economy of Intellectual Property Rights – the New Enclosures?*, London: Routledge, 2000, p. 49.
9 The Preamble to the WHO Constitution states that: 'The enjoyment of the highest attainable standard of health is one of the fundamental rights of every human being without distinction of race, religion, political belief, economic or social condition' – World Health Organisation, *Constitution of the World Health Organization*, 1946. Online. Available at: www.who.int/about/en/ (accessed 17 January 2009); see also, World Health Organisation, *25 Questions and Answers on Health and Human Rights*, Geneva: WHO, 2002.
10 The TRIPS agreement requires member countries to make patents cover both products and processes, which means that generic producers would be banned from inventing other methods of reproducing medical substances, and generic competition is excluded – 'Overview: the TRIPs Agreement', World Trade Organisation. Online. Available at: www.wto.org/english/tratop_e/trips_e/intel2_e.htm (accessed 31 January 2009).
11 Shiva, *Protect or Plunder?*, p. 14; R. Sherwood, *Intellectual Property and Economic Development*, Oxford: Westview Press, 1990, p. 17; S. Sell and C. May, 'Moments in Law: Contestation and Settlement in the History of Intellectual Property', *Review of International Political Economy*, Vol. 8, No. 3, 2001, 477.
12 Ibid., 482.
13 J. Watal (ed.) *Intellectual Property Rights in the WTO and Developing Countries*, The Hague: Kluwer Law International, 2001, pp. 15–17.
14 C. Bellmann, G. Dutfield and R. Melendez-Ortiz (eds) *Trading in Knowledge – Development Perspectives on TRIPs, Trade and Sustainability*, London: Earthscan Publications, International Centre for Trade and Sustainable Development, 2003, p. 6.
15 UNCTAD–ICTSD, *Intellectual Property Rights: Implications for Development*, p. 34.
16 France introduced pharmaceutical patents in 1960, Ireland in 1964, Switzerland

in 1977, Italy and Sweden in 1978, Spain in 1992 – Bellmann, Dutfield and Melendez-Ortiz (eds) *Trading in Knowledge*, p. 6.

17 P. Drahos, *Developing Countries and International Intellectual Property Standard-Setting*, Study Paper 8 Commissioned by the Commission on Intellectual Property Rights, 2002. Online. Available at: www.iprcommission.org/papers/pdfs/study_papers/sp8_drahos_study.pdf (accessed 17 January 2009), p. 9, citing WIPO, 'Existence, Scope and Form of Generally Internationally Accepted and Applied Standards/Norms for the Protection of Intellectual Property', WO/INF/29 September 1988.

18 Shiva, *Protect or Plunder?*, p. 14.

19 UNCTAD–ICTSD, *Intellectual Property Rights*, p. 33.

20 Shiva, *Protect or Plunder?*, p. 17; UNCTAD–ICTSD, *Intellectual Property Rights*, p. 33.

21 Shiva, *Protect or Plunder?*, p. 12; P. Drahos and J. Braithwaite, *Information Feudalism – Who Owns the Knowledge Economy?*, London: Earthscan Publications Ltd, 2002, pp. 29–35.

22 Ibid.

23 Ibid., pp. 33–34; S. Sell, *Private Power, Public Law – The Globalisation of Intellectual Property Rights*, Cambridge: Cambridge University Press, 2003, p. 11.

24 Sherwood, *Intellectual Property and Economic Development*, pp. 17–18 and 24–26; Drahos and Braithwaite, *Information Feudalism*, pp. 35.

25 Sherwood, *Intellectual Property and Economic Development*, pp. 22–24.

26 Drahos and Braithwaite, *Information Feudalism*, p. 57.

27 S. Sell, *Power and Ideas – North–South Politics of Intellectual Property and Antitrust*, New York: State University of New York Press, 1998, p. 50.

28 Ibid., pp. 51–52.

29 J. McIntyre and D. Papp, *The Political Economy of International Technology Transfer*, New York: Quorum, 1986, pp. 86–88, cited in Sell, *Power and Ideas*, p. 56.

30 Sell, *Power and Ideas*, pp. 107–141; M. Ryan, *Knowledge Diplomacy: Global Competition and the Politics of Intellectual Property*, Washington, DC: Brookings Institution Press, 1998, p. 68.

31 The Andean Group comprised Chile, Colombia, Bolivia, Ecuador and Peru. The countries united in 1969 'in a common front to minimise the negative effects of foreign investment and technology transfer' – Sell, *Power and Ideas*, p. 112.

32 Ibid., p. 117.

33 The Intellectual Property Committee (IPC) in the US began a campaign to mobilise industry representatives in Europe and Japan in order to gain support for the IPC initiative to present IP issues as issues of international trade – Sell, *Private Power, Public Law*, pp. 104–105.

34 Ibid., pp. 131–139.

35 Drahos and Braithwaite, *Information Feudalism*, p. 63.

36 Ibid., p. 61.

37 G. Dutfield, *Intellectual Property Rights and the Life Science Industries*, p. 197; Watal (ed.) *Intellectual Property Rights in the WTO and Developing Countries*, p. 15; A. O. Adede, 'Origins and History of the TRIPS Negotiations' in Bellmann, Dutfield and Melendez-Ortiz (eds) *Trading in Knowledge*, p. 25.

38 Drahos and Braithwaite, *Information Feudalism*, p. 61.

39 J. Goldstein, M. Kahler, R. Keohane and A.-M. Slaughter, 'Introduction: Legalisation of World Politics', *International Organisation*, Vol. 54, No. 3, Summer 2000, 385–399.

40 Ryan, *Knowledge Diplomacy*, p. 69.

41 Mergers indicate that in the early part of the nineteenth century in the US, a decision was taken that in view of the 'stage of economic development, the best policy for the US was lax enforcement of foreign intellectual property'. See Sell, *Private Power, Public Law*, p. 64.

42 Dutfield, *Intellectual Property Rights and the Life Science Industries*, p. 113.

43 In *Henry* v. *A. B. Dick Co.* (224 US 1, 1912) the Supreme Court of the United States indicated that if conditions imposed by a patent holder upon a patent buyer are too limiting, then the patented article will not find a market (p. 34); and further that

> [a]n attack upon the rights under a patent because it secures a monopoly to make, to sell, and to use, is an attack upon the whole patent system. We (the SC) are not at liberty to say that the Constitution has unwisely provided for granting a monopolistic right to inventors, or that Congress has unwisely failed to impose limitations upon the inventor's exclusive right to use.
>
> (p. 35)

44 See US Supreme Court, *Motion Picture Patents Co.* v. *Universal Film Mfg Co.* (243 US 502, 1917) and *Morton Salt Co.* v. *G. S. Suppiger Co.* (314 US 488, 1942). In both cases the Supreme Court upheld the opinion that patent holders may not use their patent rights to impose conditions of use of patented articles that include non-patented consumables (243 US 502, pp. 512 and 518; 314 US 488, p. 494).

45 D. O'Brien, *Storm Center – The Supreme Court in American Politics*, New York: W. W. Norton and Co., p. 228.

46 Ibid., p. 232.

47 See US Supreme Court, *Dawson Chemical Co.* v. *Rohm & Haas Co.* (448 US 176, 1980), p. 223.

48 Sell, *Private Power, Public Law*, p. 60.

49 Drahos and Braithwaite, *Information Feudalism*, p. 63; Dutfield, *Intellectual Property Rights and the Life Science Industries*, p. 199.

50 Sell, *Private Power, Public Law*, pp. 78–79.

51 F. Weiss, 'TRIPS in Search of an Itinerary: Trade Related Intellectual Property Rights and the Uruguay Round Negotiations' in G. Sacerdoti (ed.) *Liberalisation of Services and Intellectual Property in the Uruguay Round of GATT*, Fribourg: University Press, 1990, p. 89; Drahos and Braithwaite, *Information Feudalism*, p. 63.

52 Weiss, 'TRIPS in Search of an Itinerary', p. 89.

53 Sell, *Private Power, Public Law*, p. 79.

54 J. MacLaughlin, T. Richards and L. Kenny, 'The Economic Significance of Piracy', in R. Gadbaw and T. Richards (eds) *Intellectual Property Rights: Global Consensus, Global Conflict?*, Boulder, CO: Westview Press, 1988, p. 94.

55 Drahos and Braithwaite, *Information Feudalism*, p. 63.

56 P. Almeida, 'The "New" Intellectual Property Regime and its Economic

Impact on Developing Countries' in Sacerdoti, *Liberalisation of Services and Intellectual Property in the Uruguay Round of GATT*, p. 74.

57 C. Correa and A. Yusuf (eds) *Intellectual Property and International Trade – The TRIPs Agreement*, London: Kluwer Law International, 1998, p. 23; B. Doern, *Global Change and Intellectual Property Agencies*, London: Pinter, 1999, p. 1.

58 M. Wallerstein, M. Mogee and R. Schoen (eds) *Global Dimensions of Intellectual Property Rights in Science and Technology*, Washington, DC: National Academy Press, 1993, p. 6.

59 Drahos and Braithwaite, *Information Feudalism*, pp. 90–99 and 114–119.

60 Sell, *Private Power, Public Law*, pp. 78–86; Drahos and Braithwaite, *Information Feudalism*, pp. 61–73; Gadbaw and Richards (eds) *Intellectual Property Rights*, pp. 39–40; Watal (ed.) *Intellectual Property Rights in the WTO and Developing Countries*, p. 17; G. Dutfield, 'Introduction' in Bellmann, Dutfield and Melendez-Ortiz (eds) *Trading in Knowledge*, p. 2.

61 T. P. Stewart (ed.) *The GATT Uruguay Round – A Negotiating History (1986–1992)*, Vol. 2 – Commentary, Deventer: Kluwer Law and Taxation Publishers, 1993, citing James Bikoff, President, International Anticounterfeiting Coalition, *Possible Renewal of the Generalised System of Preferences – Part 1: Hearing before the Subcommission on Trade of the U.S. House of Rep. Comm. on Ways and Means*, 98th Congress, 1st Session (1983), p. 2259.

62 Watal, *Intellectual Property Rights in the WTO and Developing Countries*, p. 15; Stewart, *The GATT Uruguay Round*, p. 2260.

63 The international negotiations to revise the Paris Convention began in 1980 and ended in 1984 without any decision being reached – see 'International Negotiations to Revise the Paris Convention on the Protection of Intellectual Property' in Sell, *Power and Ideas*.

64 Drahos and Braithwaite, *Information Feudalism*, p. 81.

65 Ryan, *Knowledge Diplomacy*, p. 68; Sell, *Power and Ideas*, pp. 132–133.

66 The Advisory Committee on Trade Policy and Negotiation (ACTPN) was created by the Trade Act of 1974 to provide the USTR and the US President with policy advice on trade issues. The ACTPN comprises representatives of various companies and industries. The committee is 'a pipeline for US business to the US executive on trade issues. Its function was to advise the USTR on where, in the eyes of the private sector, US economic interests really lay' – Drahos and Braithwaite, *Information Feudalism*, p. 72.

67 Pharmaceutical Research and Manufacturers of America (PhRMA) is one of the biggest, most influential lobbying organisations in Washington, DC. PhRMA represents 48 pharmaceutical companies and is notorious for hiding its lobbying and PR activities behind PhRMA-funded nonprofit groups – in *Pharmaceutical Research and Manufacturers of America*, Centre for Media and Democracy. Online. Available at: http://prwatch.org/node/308/trackback (accessed on 8 January 2005); J. Borger, 'USA: The Pharmaceutical Industry Stalks the Corridors of Power', *Guardian Unlimited*, 13 February 2001. Online. Available at: www.corpwatch.org/article.php?id=178 (accessed on 8 January 2005).

68 Ryan, *Knowledge Diplomacy*, p. 69.

69 Sell, *Power and Ideas*, p. 79.

70 Ibid.

71 See www.iipa.com/aboutiipa.html.

72 Ryan, *Knowledge Diplomacy*, p. 70.

73 US International Trade Commission, *The Effects of Foreign Product Counterfeiting on US Industry*, Washington, DC: USITC, 1984; International Intellectual Property Alliance, *Piracy of U.S. Copyrighted Works in Ten Selected Countries*, Washington, DC: IIPA, 1985; J. Gorlin, 'A Trade-based Approach for the International Copyright Protection for Computer Software'; *Unfair Foreign Trade Practices, Stealing American Intellectual Property: Imitation Is Not Flattery*, 98th Congress, 2nd Session 1–3 (1984).

74 The Intellectual Property Committee was created by Pratt (Pfizer) and Opel (IBM). The initial members of the committee were Pfizer, IBM, Merck, General Electric, DuPont, Warner Communications, Hewlett-Packard, Bristol-Myers, FMC Corporation, General Motors, Johnson & Johnson, Monsanto and Rockwell International – Ryan, *Knowledge Diplomacy*, p. 69.

75 Sell, *Private Power, Public Law*, p. 96.

76 Drahos and Braithwaite, *Information Feudalism*, p. 118.

77 Ibid., p. 117.

78 The lack of implementation procedures of the Paris Convention was a case in point.

79 Sell, *Private Power, Public Law*, p. 99.

80 The choice of technical and normative context is crucial as Price's study of the creation of the Convention Banning the Use of Landmines demonstrates. See Price, 'Reversing the Gun Sights', 613–644.

81 Ryan, *Knowledge Diplomacy*, p. 9, citing John Kingdon, *Agendas, Alternatives and Public Policies*, Boston, MA: Little Brown, 1984, p. 54.

82 S. Mathur, 'Trade-related Aspects of Intellectual Property Rights and Copyright Provisions – Some Issues with Special Reference to Developing Countries', *Journal of World Intellectual Property – Law, Economics, Politics*, Vol. 6, No. 1, 2003, 69.

83 Drahos and Braithwaite, *Information Feudalism*, p. 61.

84 Ryan, *Knowledge Diplomacy*, p. 27.

85 The appropriability problem was a major concern for industries whose R&D required a lot of investment – such as the pharmaceutical industry, the chemical industry and agriculture, to name but a few, where costs of copying are relatively low as well – Ryan, *Knowledge Diplomacy*, p. 27.

86 Stewart, *The GATT Uruguay Round*, p. 2254 and M. Blakeney, *Trade Related Aspects of Intellectual Property Rights: A Concise Guide to the TRIPs Agreement*, London: Sweet and Maxwell, 1996, p. 2. Both citing *Unfair Foreign Trade Practices, Stealing American Intellectual Property*.

87 The study was conducted with regards to only ten countries – Brazil, Egypt, Indonesia, Korea, Malaysia, Nigeria, Philippines, Singapore, Taiwan and Thailand (Stewart, *The GATT Uruguay Round*, p. 2254), citing International Intellectual Property Alliance (1985) *Piracy of U.S. Counterfeited Works in Ten Countries*.

88 The US International Trade Commission is an independent quasi-legal federal agency, established by Congress in 1916. The organisation provides trade expertise to the legislative and executive branches of government; determines the impact of imports on US industries; and directs actions against certain unfair practices such as patent, trademark and copyright infringement – see www.usitc.gov/ext_relations/about_its/index.htm.

89 Sell, *Private Power, Public Law*, p. 105; Wallerstein, Mogee and Schoen (eds) *Global Dimensions of Intellectual Property Rights in Science and Technology*, p. 4; similar figures were cited by E. Finn, Jr, 'That's the $60 Billion Question', *Forbes*, 7 November 1986, 40.

90 See Wallerstein, Mogee and Schoen (eds) *Global Dimensions of Intellectual Property Rights in Science and Technology*.

91 According to Hughes, the US trade deficit grew from $36.3 to $148.5 billion – D. Hughes, 'Opening up Trade Barriers with Section 301 – A Critical Assessment', *Wisconsin International Law Journal*, Vol. 17, 1991, 393–410, and Sell, *Private Power, Public Law*, p. 80.

92 Critical analysis of this seemingly solid causal relationship later proved that such correlation between trade deficit and global trade in pirated and counterfeit goods is not as strong as authors argue. The analysts who conducted these studies were individuals with a strong bias in favour of US industries and vested interests in the advance of IP protection – the authors of *Intellectual Property Rights: Global Consensus, Global Conflict?* Gadbaw and Richards are both economists for Dewey Ballantine. Gadbaw has also served as a Deputy General Counsel for the USTR.

93 Stewart, *The GATT Uruguay Round*, p. 2249, citing H. Kunz-Hallstein, 'The United States Proposal for a GATT Agreement on Intellectual Property and the Paris Convention for the Protection of Industrial Property', *Vanderbilt Journal of Transnational Law*, Vol. 22, 1989, 265.

94 Drahos and Braithwaite, *Information Feudalism*, p. 111.

95 Ryan, *Knowledge Diplomacy*, p. 68; Stewart, *The GATT Uruguay Round*, p. 2253.

96 Changes included the amendments of the 1974 Trade Act (Section 301), which empowered the president to initiate sanctions to protect US industries.

97 The inclusion of the issue of intellectual property protection on the agenda of the Uruguay Round was a last-minute political compromise; the TRIPs item figured almost like a footnote on the crowded agenda of the next round of trade talks – Adede, 'Origins and History of the TRIPS Negotiations', p. 25.

98 '[L]inkage bargaining diplomacy can be exploited to achieve treaties in diplomatically and politically difficult areas in which agreement would otherwise be elusive' – M. Ryan, *Knowledge Diplomacy*, p. 92.

99 The EU and the US opinions clashed over issues related to the protection of geographical indicators and appellations of origin, while Japan and the US disagreed over borrowing rights related to copyright – Drahos and Braithwaite, *Information Feudalism*, pp. 144–145.

100 The developing countries had varying expectations of possible gains in other areas of the Uruguay Round – mainly agriculture and textiles; their level of expertise on these highly technical issues was also diverse, and last but not least, developing countries suffered to a different degree from the effective use of Section 301 of US intellectual property legislation – Watal (ed.) *Intellectual Property Rights in the WTO and Developing Countries*, pp. 43–44 and 19–35.

101 Stewart (ed.) *The GATT Uruguay Round*, p. 2260.

102 See Drahos, *Developing Countries and International Intellectual Property Standard-Setting*, p. 9.

103 Stewart, *The GATT Uruguay Round*, pp. 2260–2261.

104 Ibid., citing US General Accounting Office, *Strengthening Worldwide Protec-*

tion of Intellectual Property Rights, GAO Doc. No. GAO/NSIAD-87-65, 1987.

105 Stewart, *The GATT Uruguay Round*, p. 2262, citing GATT, *GATT Activities in 1985*.

106 Ibid.

107 Drahos, *Developing Countries and International Intellectual Property Standard-Setting*, p. 13.

108 Stewart, *The GATT Uruguay Round*, p. 2256, citing Trade and Tariff Act of 1984, Pub. L. No. 98–573, 304 (f) (2).

109 Sell, *Private Power, Public Law*, pp. 85–86; Ryan, *Knowledge Diplomacy*, pp. 72–79; Drahos and Braithwaite, *Information Feudalism*, pp. 93–99.

110 South Korea was selected for action under Section 301 following continuous complaints from American pharmaceutical and chemical companies, as well as from the IIPA. This action was strategically placed to begin isolating developing countries and targeting them with stringent bilateral action, which affected local developing economies and their resolve to put together a united front of opposition – Ryan, *Knowledge Diplomacy*, pp. 73–79; Sell, *Private Power, Public Law*, p. 90; Stewart, *The GATT Uruguay Round*, p. 2256; Drahos and Braithwaite, *Information Feudalism*, pp. 102–104.

111 Procedures against Brazil were initiated primarily on the grounds of complaints by the US pharmaceutical industry and computer software companies – Ryan, *Knowledge Diplomacy*, p. 79; Sell, *Private Power, Public Law*, p. 90; Stewart, *The GATT Uruguay Round*, p. 2256; Drahos and Braithwaite, *Information Feudalism*, pp. 104–105.

112 Stewart, *The GATT Uruguay Round*, p. 2262, citing GATT Doc. No. L/5925 *Decision of 28 November 1985 on Establishment of the Preparatory Committee*.

113 Ibid., pp. 2262–2263.

114 This became known as the Group of Ten, including Argentina, Brazil, Cuba, Egypt, India, Nicaragua, Nigeria, Peru, Tanzania and Yugoslavia. See Ryan, *Knowledge Diplomacy*, p. 108; Watal (ed.) *Intellectual Property Rights in the WTO and Developing Countries*, p. 19. According to the author, the group of hard-line opposition had shrunk from 25 countries – named as Argentina, Bangladesh, Brazil, Burma, Cameroon, Colombia, Cuba, Cyprus, Egypt, Ghana, India, Ivory Coast, Jamaica, Nicaragua, Nigeria, Pakistan, Peru, Romania, Sri Lanka, Tanzania, Trinidad and Tobago, Uruguay, Yugoslavia, Zaire.

115 Stewart, *The GATT Uruguay Round*, pp. 2264–2265.

116 D. Gervais, *The TRIPS Agreement: Drafting History and Analysis*, 2nd edn, London: Sweet and Maxwell, 2003, p. 11.

117 Adede, 'Origins and History of the TRIPS Negotiations', p. 26.

118 Ryan, *Knowledge Diplomacy*, p. 109; C. A. P. Braga, 'The Economics of Intellectual Property Rights and the GATT: A View from the South', Symposium: Trade Related Aspects of Intellectual Property, Part 1, *Vanderbilt Journal of Transnational Law*, Vol. 22, 1989, 249–250.

119 Watal, *Intellectual Property Rights in the WTO and Developing Countries*, p. 23.

120 Stewart, *The GATT Uruguay Round*, p. 2267. Although the World Trade Organisation de-restricted many documents from the Uruguay Round negotiations on TRIPs, see: www.wto.org/english/traptop_e/trips_e/trips_e.htm

(accessed 20 February 2009), these documents exclude any specific discussions that indicate the positions of different states, as well as any particular proposals made by states.

121 Gervais, *The TRIPS Agreement*, p. 14, citing documents MTN.GNG/ NG11/W/27; MTN.GNG/NG/11/W/28; MTN.GNG/NG11/W/30.

122 Ryan, *Knowledge Diplomacy*, p. 110.

123 Communications culminated in the industry position paper on IPRs – 'Basic Framework of GATT Provisions on Intellectual Property, Statement of Views of the European, Japanese and United States Business Communities'; Watal, *Intellectual Property Rights in the WTO and Developing Countries*, p. 23; Ryan, *Knowledge Diplomacy*, p. 109.

124 Watal, *Intellectual Property Rights in the WTO and Developing Countries*, pp. 23–24; Stewart, *The GATT Uruguay Round*, pp. 2257–2258; Sell, *Public Power, Private Law*, pp. 91–95; Drahos and Braithwaite, *Information Feudalism*, pp. 89–90.

125 Special 301 proceedings were initiated against Argentina, China, Chile, India, Mexico, Thailand – see S. Sell, 'Intellectual Property Protection and Antitrust in the Developing World: Crisis, Coercion and Choice', *International Organisation*, Vol. 49, No. 2, 1995, 327–332.

126 Stewart, *The GATT Uruguay Round*, p. 2269, citing *Mid-Term Meeting*, GATT Doc. No. MTN.TNC/11, 21 April 1989.

127 Stewart, *The GATT Uruguay Round*, pp. 2270–2272 – drafts regarding the scope and application of intellectual property rights were submitted by Australia, Austria, Bangladesh, Brazil, Canada, Hong Kong, India, Korea, New Zealand, the Nordic countries, Peru, Switzerland.

128 See *GATT Summary of TRIPs Talks*, reprinted in 7 Inside U.S. Trade, 22 December, 1989, pp. 10–11.

129 Adede, 'Origins and History of the TRIPS Negotiations', p. 31.

130 Sell, *Private Power, Public Law*, p. 109.

131 G. Evans, 'Intellectual Property Rights as a Trade Issue – The Making of the Agreement on Trade-related Aspects of Intellectual Property Rights', *World Competition: Law and Economics Review*, Vol. 18, No. 2, 1994, 170, citing 3WIPR 1989, 244–245.

132 Ibid. – Argentina, Brazil, Chile, Colombia, Indonesia, Malaysia, Mexico, Peru, Thailand and Uruguay.

133 Sell, *Private Power, Public Law*, p. 110, citing M. Ryan, 'The Function Specific and Linkage Bargain Diplomacy of International Intellectual Property Lawmaking', *University of Pennsylvania Journal of International Economic Law*, Summer, 1998, 553–586.

134 Sell, *Private Power, Public Law*, pp. 110, citing J. Whalley, 'Developing Countries and System Strengthening in the Uruguay Round', in W. Martin and L. A. Winters (eds) *The Uruguay Round and Developing Economies*, Washington, DC: World Bank, 1995.

135 See the Intellectual Property Committee, Keidanren, UNICE, *Basic Framework of GATT Provisions on Intellectual Property: Statement of Views of the European, Japanese and United States Business Communities*, June 1998.

136 Sell, *Private Power, Public Law* – pp. 109–110.

137 Sell, 'Intellectual Property Protection and Antitrust in the Developing World' – the author provides evidence that the sanctions against Brazil, India, Mexico and Thailand still failed to ensure compliance with domestic legislation, as

the profits from piracy and free-riding outweigh the costs (pp. 332, 348); G. Dutfield, *Trade, Intellectual Property and Biogenetic Resources: A Guide to the International Regulatory Landscape*, 19–21 April 2002, pp. 201–204.

138 Drahos and Braithwaite, *Information Feudalism*, pp. 192–194.

139 Ibid., p. 193; Adede, 'Origins and History of the TRIPS Negotiations', p. 30.

140 GATT (1990) MTN.GNG/NG11/W/68, cited in Stewart, *The GATT Uruguay Round*, p. 2273; Evans, 'Intellectual Property Rights as a Trade Issue', p. 171.

141 Watal, *Intellectual Property Rights in the WTO and Developing Countries*, p. 29; Gervais, *The TRIPS Agreement*, p. 16.

142 Stewart, *The GATT Uruguay Round*, p. 2273; Evans, 'Intellectual Property Rights as a Trade Issue', p. 171.

143 Ibid., citing GATT (1990): MTN.GNG/NG11/W/71.

144 Stewart, *The GATT Uruguay Round*, p. 2274, citing *Meeting of Negotiating Group of 20th July 1990, Note by the Secretariat*, GATT Doc. No. MTN. GNG/NG11/24; Evans 'Intellectual Property Rights as a Trade Issue', p. 171.

145 Gervais, *The TRIPS Agreement*, pp. 17–18; Watal, *Intellectual Property Rights in the WTO and Developing Countries*, pp. 31–32; Blakeney, *Trade Related Aspects of Intellectual Property Rights*, p. 6.

146 Jayashree Watal was a trade negotiator for India in the TRIPs negotiating group and is currently an intellectual property expert at the WTO – 'The Right to Good Ideas', *The Economist*, 21 June 2001.

147 Drahos and Braithwaite, *Information Feudalism*, p. 142 – the authors conducted a series of interviews at the GATT Secretariat in 1993, which revealed the careful selection of the states that were appropriate to attend the small group sessions.

148 South Centre, *The TRIPs Agreement – A Guide for the South. The Uruguay Round Agreement on Trade-related Intellectual Property Rights*, Geneva: South Centre, 1997, p. 9.

149 The Cairns Group represented agricultural exporters from developed and developing countries alike and comprised Argentina, Australia, Brazil, Canada, Chile, Colombia, Fiji, Hungary, Indonesia, Malaysia, the Philippines, New Zealand, Thailand and Uruguay – J. Ford, 'A Social Theory of Trade Regime Change: GATT to WTO', *International Studies Review*, 127.

150 Evans, 'Intellectual Property Rights as a Trade Issue', p. 173, citing 4 WIPR, 1990.

151 Ford, 'A Social Theory of Trade Regime Change'.

152 Stewart, *The GATT Uruguay Round*, p. 2276.

153 Ibid., p. 2277, citing GATT, *Uruguay Round Poised to Enter Decisive Phase, Focus*, 1, 11, August 1991.

154 Ibid., p. 2280, citing *Progress of Work in Negotiating Groups: Stock Taking*, GATT Doc. No. MTN.TNC/W/89/Add.1, November 1991.

155 Ibid., p. 2282.

156 Ibid., pp. 2284–2285; and Sell, *Private Power, Public Law*, pp. 114–120.

157 The final form of the Agreement on TRIPs does not differ substantially from the Dunkel Draft – very few changes were implemented, leaving out demands made by developed and developing countries alike. See Evans, 'Intellectual Property Rights as a Trade Issue', p. 175, citing Agreement on Trade-related Aspects of Intellectual Property Rights, Final Act Embodying the Results of the Uruguay Round of Multilateral Trade Negotiations, 15 April 1994, Annex 1C; Ryan, *Knowledge Diplomacy*, p. 112; Drahos and

Braithwaite, *Information Feudalism*, pp. 145–146; Gervais, *The TRIPS Agreement*, p. 26; Blakeney, *Trade Related Aspects of Intellectual Property Rights*, p. 7.

158 Evans, 'Intellectual Property Rights as a Trade Issue', – pp. 174–175.

159 Watal, *Intellectual Property Rights in the WTO and Developing Countries*, p. 41.

160 Drahos, *Developing Countries and Intellectual Property Standard-setting*, pp. 13–14.

161 Ryan cites a GATT Secretariat official, who pointed out to developing states that they were acting as if they had a choice of forum between GATT and WIPO, while their real choice was between GATT and the USTR – Ryan, *Knowledge Diplomacy*, p. 110.

162 Ibid., p. 112.

163 Drahos, *Developing Countries and Intellectual Property Standard-setting*, p. 14.

164 Ibid., p. 26.

165 Online. Available at: www.sunsonline.org/trade/areas/environm/02230294. htm (accessed 25 May 2004).

166 *Declaration on TRIPs Agreement and Public Health*, World Trade Organisation, Ministerial Conference, 4th Session, Doha, 9–14 November 2001. Doc. No. WT/MN(01)/DEC/2.

167 P. Drahos, 'BITs and BIPs – Bilateralism in Intellectual Property', *Journal of World Intellectual Property – Law, Economics, Politics*, Vol. 4, No. 6, 2001, 791.

168 Drahos, 'BITs and BIPs', p. 793, citing F. Abbott, 'Protecting First World Assets in the Third World: Intellectual Property Negotiations in the GATT Multilateral Framework, Symposium: Trade-related Aspects of Intellectual Property', *Vanderbilt Journal of Transnational Law*, Vol. 22, 1989.

169 Ibid., pp. 794–796.

170 Sell, *Private Power, Public Law*, pp. 129–132.

171 Susan Sell argues that the HIV/AIDS pandemic was 'a contingency that sped up the revelation of the negative consequences of TRIPs' – Sell, *Private Power, Public Law*, p. 181.

172 Online. Available at: www.actupny.org/documents/firstworkingdoc.html – Original Working Document (1987).

173 R. Nader and J. Love, 'Federally Funded Pharmaceutical Inventions', *Testimony before the Special Committee on the Aging of the US Senate*, 24 February 1993. Online. Available at: www.cptech.org/pharm/pryor.html (accessed 25 May 2004).

174 Ibid.

175 S. Kahn, 'The Whole World Is Watching – US AIDS Activists Go Global', *HIV Plus*, No. 5, September 1999.

176 Some of the neglected diseases are tuberculosis, sleeping sickness, leishmaniasis, malaria and AIDS. Most neglected diseases are found in the developing countries – some are climate-specific, while others have been eradicated in the industrialised countries. Part of the problem of neglected diseases is the evolution of drug-resistant strands, which may threaten the health and life of many.

177 Sell, *Private Power, Public Law*, pp. 146–147.

178 Health Action International is a coalition of NGOs in 70 countries. HAI is

supported by powerful NGOs, consumer, health and development groups, as well as by isolated health workers and concerned individuals.

179 Sell, *Private Power, Public Law*, pp. 147–148.
180 Ibid., p. 149.
181 'Modification of WTO Rules on Protection of Pharmaceuticals', *American Journal of International Law*, Vol. 97, No. 4, October 2003, 981.
182 The Trade Law Centre for South Africa provides an in-depth legal brief on the development of this case together with a legal discussion of the underlying South African legislation. See also Drahos and Braithwaite, *Information Feudalism*, p. 7.
183 Online. Available at: http://news.bbc.co.uk/1/hi/world/africa/1285097.stm (accessed 30 May 2004).
184 D. Berman and N. Ford, *AIDS and Essential Medicines and Compulsory Licensing*, Summary of the 25–27 March 1999 Geneva Meeting.
185 Ibid.
186 See P. R. Vagelos, 'Are Prescription Drug Prices High?' *Science*, Vol. 252, No. 5009, 1991, 1080–1084. The author P. Roy Vagelos is the Chairman and Chief Executive Officer at Merck & Co., Inc. This message was echoed in later articles as well – A. Attaran and L. Gillespie-White, 'Do Patents for Antiretroviral Drugs Constrain Access to AIDS Treatment in Africa?' *Journal of the American Medical Association*, Vol. 286, No. 15, 17 October 2001, 1886–1892; Gillespie-White, *Health and Patents*.
187 J. Orbinski, 'Challenges to the Health of Children in the 21st Century', 14 June 2000. Online. Available at: www.doctorswithoutborders.org/publications/article.cfm?id=1350&cat=speech (accessed 1 March 2009).
188 The information is cited in Berman and Ford, *AIDS and Essential Medicines and Compulsory Licensing*; and J. Sachs, 'Helping the World's Poorest', *The Economist*, 12 August 1999.
189 Berman and N. Ford, *AIDS and Essential Medicines and Compulsory Licensing*.
190 *Fatal Imbalance – The Crisis in Research and Development for Neglected Diseases*, DND Working Group, Médecins Sans Frontières – 'Campaign for Access to Essential Medicines', September 2001, p. 10, citing World Health Organisation, *The World Health Report 2000*, Geneva: World Health Organisation, 2000.
191 *Amsterdam Statement to WTO Member States on Access to Medicines*, 25–26 November 1999. Online. Available at: www.haiweb.org/campaign/novseminar/amsterdam_statement.html (accessed 1 March 2009).
192 World Health Organisation, *World Health Report 1996 – Fighting Disease, Fostering Development*, 49th World Health Assembly, Provisional Agenda Item 10, Doc. No. A49/3, 1996.
193 Oxfam, *World Trade Rules and Poor People's Access to Essential Drugs*, 1999. Online. Available at: www.oxfam.org.uk/what_we_do/issues/health/worldtrade_drugs.htm (accessed 1 November 2004).
194 World Health Organisation, *World Health Report 1996*.
195 A Free Trade Agreement signed with Jordan in 2000 contains a TRIPs-Plus feature, narrowing grounds for exclusion from patentability, introducing conditions on compulsory licensing and requiring Jordan to implement the TRIPs agreement before it is required to do so by the WTO. Similar agreements are said to have been negotiated with Chile and Singapore – Drahos, 'BITs and BIPs', pp. 797–798.

196 Ibid., p. 803.
197 Orbinski, 'Challenges to the Health of Children in the 21st Century'.
198 'A War over Drugs and Patents – Johannesburg', *The Economist*, 8 March 2001.
199 Vagelos, 'Are Prescription Drug Prices High?', 1083.
200 Gillespie-White, *Health and Patents*. This view is further supported by PhRMA – its opinion is quoted in S. Kahn, 'The Whole World Is Watching'.
201 Ibid.
202 Vagelos, 'Are Prescription Drug Prices High?', p. 1080; Dutfield, *Intellectual Property Rights and the Life Science Industries*, p. 106.
203 L. Gillespie-White, *Patent Protection and Patients' Access to HIV/AIDS Drugs in Sub-Saharan Africa*, Washington, DC: International Intellectual Property Institute, 2001, p. 7.
204 Kahn, 'The Whole World Is Watching'; a similar point was made by Lehman, *Patents and Health*, pp. 12–13.
205 Oxfam, *Cutting the Cost of Global Health*, Oxfam Parliamentary Briefing 16, Oxfam GB, 2001, p. 3; Oxfam, *Implausible Denial: Why the Drug Giants' Arguments on Patents Do Not Stack Up*, 2001. Online. Available at: www.oxfam.org.uk/what_we_do/issues/health/implausible_denial.htm (accessed 14 April 2005) – the article quotes profit margins for Pfizer in the year 2000 at 30 per cent, Glaxo-Smith-Kline at 28 per cent, where R&D costs amount to around 15 per cent of the production costs.
206 Oxfam, *Implausible Denial*.
207 United Nations Development Programme, *Human Development Report*, 1999. Online. Available at: http://hdr.undp.org/en/media/HDR_1999_EN.pdf (accessed 17 January 2009), p. 73.
208 Mathur, 'Trade-related Aspects of Intellectual Property Rights and Copyright Provisions – the author quotes econometric analysis of US and Japanese firms, conducted in 2000, which concluded that there was no evidence of an increase in R&D spending or innovative output that could plausibly be attributed to patent reform' (p. 93).
209 R. Mayne, 'The TRIPs Agreement and Access to Medicines: An NGO Perspective' in H. Katrak and R. Strange (eds) *The WTO and Developing Countries*, New York: Palgrave Macmillan, 2004, p. 155, citing Commission on Intellectual Property Rights, *Integrating Intellectual Property Rights and Development Policy*, London: Commission on Intellectual Property, 2002.
210 J. Sachs, 'Helping the World's Poorest', *The Economist*, 12 August 1999.
211 Ibid.
212 *Fatal Imbalance*, p. 9.
213 Ibid., p. 10.
214 Oxfam, *Implausible Denial*.
215 Oxfam, *Patent Injustice: How World Trade Rules Threaten the Health of Poor People*, Oxfam GB. Online. Available at: www.oxfam.org.uk/resources/policy/health/downloads/patentinjustice.pdf (accessed 14 April 2005), 2001, p. 12.
216 M. Ainsworth, 'AIDS, Development, and the East Asian Crisis', Plenary Address to the 5th International Conference on AIDS in Asia and the Pacific, 25 October 1999, Development Research Group, World Bank, p. 3.
217 A. Attaran and J. Sachs, 'Defining and Refining International Donor Support for Combating the AIDS Pandemic', *The Lancet*, Vol. 357, 2001, 57, citing

World Bank, *Intensifying Action against HIV/AIDS in Africa: Responding to a Development Crisis*, Washington, DC: World Bank, 1999.
218 Sachs, 'Helping the World's Poorest'.
219 P. Piot, 'Human Rights and HIV/AIDS', Statement by the Executive Director of the Joint United Nations Programme on HIV/AIDS (UNAIDS), April 1996. Online: Available at: www.unaids.og/EN/other/functionalities/search.asp (accessed 18 March 2005).
220 Sell, *Private Power, Public Law*, p. 154.
221 Médecins Sans Frontières, *MSF Summary of the 53rd World Health Assembly*, 15–21 May 2000. Online. Available at: www.msfaccess.org/resources/key-publications/key-publication-detail/?tx_ttnews[tt_news]=1430&cHash=5bcbbd6392 (accessed 17 January 2009).
222 Ibid.
223 N. Lewis, 'Clinton Issues Order to Ease Availability of AIDS Drugs in Africa', *New York Times*, 11 May 2000; see also Sell, *Private Power, Public Law*, p. 154.
224 Ibid., pp. 154–156.
225 Oxfam calls these corporate moves 'islands of philanthropy' amidst industry's continued efforts to 'promote a global patent system which would enhance profitability, but which could also consign millions to unnecessary suffering' – Oxfam, *Cutting the Cost of Global Health*, p. 3.
226 Sell, *Private Power, Public Law*, p. 157.
227 According to a 1998 estimate of the UNDP, the top ten pharmaceutical corporations controlled 35 per cent of a $297 billion market – United Nations Development Programme, *Human Development Report*, 1999, p. 67.
228 See Report of the Workshop on 'Differential Pricing and Financing of Essential Drugs' – World Health Organisation and World Trade Organisation Secretariats, Norwegian Foreign Affairs Ministry, Global Health Council, 8–11 April 2001.
229 Drahos, *Developing Countries and International Intellectual Property Standard-Setting*, p. 26.
230 See for example C. Correa, *Some Assumptions on Patent Law and Pharmaceutical R&D*, Quaker United Nations Office, Occasional Paper 6, Geneva: 2001; Drahos, 'BITs and BIPs'; Oxfam, *Patent Injustice*; Oxfam, *Cutting the Cost of Global Health*; Oxfam, *Implausible Denial*; A. Guilloux and S. Moon, *Hidden Price Tags: Disease-specific Drug Donations: Costs and Alternatives*, Geneva: Access to Essential Medicines Campaign, Médecins Sans Frontières, 2001.
231 See Attaran and Gillespie-White, 'Do Patents for Antiretroviral Drugs Constrain Access to AIDS Treatment in Africa?', 1886–1892.
232 Sell, *Private Power, Public Law*, p. 159.
233 Ibid., p. 160.
234 The change of attitude among developed countries towards the possibility of granting more rights to the governments of developing countries was signalled when the US and EU withdrew their initial support for the 39 pharmaceutical companies in their lawsuit against the SA government.
235 'Governments Share Interpretations on TRIPS and Public Health', WTO News, TRIPS Council, 20 June 2001. Online. Available at: www.wto.org/english/news_e/news01_e/trips_drugs_010620_e.htm (accessed 17 January 2009).
236 Doc. No. WT/MIN(01)/DEC/2.

237 Paragraph 1 of the Doha Declaration reads 'We recognise the gravity of the public health problems afflicting many developing and least-developed countries, especially those resulting from HIV/AIDS, tuberculosis, malaria and other epidemics'. See Doc. No. WT/MIN(01)/DEC/2.

238 Paragraph 6 of the Doha Declaration. See Doc. No. WT/MIN(01)/DEC/2.

239 Paragraph 7 of the Doha Declaration. See Doc. No. WT/MIN(01)/DEC/2.

240 P. Trouiller, P. Olliaro, E. Torreele, J. Orbinski, R. Laing and N. Ford, 'Drug Development for Neglected Diseases: A Deficient Market and a Public-Health Policy Failure', *The Lancet*, Vol. 359, 2002, 2188–2194; C. M. Correa, 'Public Health and Intellectual Property Rights', *Global Social Policy*, Vol. 2, No. 3, 2002, 261–278; T. Kongolo, 'Towards a New Fashion of Protecting Pharmaceutical Patents in Africa – Legal Approach', *International Review of Industrial Property and Copyright Law*, Vol. 33, No. 2, 2002, 185–211; T. Kongolo, 'TRIPs, the Doha Declaration and Public Health', *Journal of World Intellectual Property – Law, Economics, Politics*, Vol. 6, No. 2, 2003, 373–388; D. Henry and J. Lexchin, 'The Pharmaceutical Industry as a Medicines Provider', *The Lancet*, Vol. 360, 2002, 1590–1595.

241 *The Crisis of Neglected Diseases: Developing Treatments and Ensuring Access*, Workshop and Conference, New York, 12–14 March 2002, organised by MSF; A. Berkman, *The Global AIDS Crisis: Human Rights, International Pharmaceutical Markets and Intellectual Property Symposium*, 2002. Online. Available at: www.healthgap.org/press_releases/02/031402_HGAP_ALAN_PP_IPR.pdf; *Conference Report – Implementation of the Doha Declaration on the TRIPS Agreement and Public Health: Technical Assistance – How to Get it Right?*, 28 March 2002. International Conference Centre of Geneva.

242 Oxfam, *US Bullying on Drug Patents: One Year after Doha*, Oxfam Briefing Paper 33, Oxfam GB: 2002; Oxfam, *TRIPS and Public Health – The Next Battle*, Oxfam Briefing Paper 15, Oxfam GB: 2002; K. Bluestone (VSO), A. Heaton (Save the Children UK) and C. Lewis (Oxfam GB), *Beyond Philanthropy: The Pharmaceutical Industry, Corporate Social Responsibility and the Developing World – Joint Report*, Oxford: Oxfam, 2002.

243 *Decision Removes Final Patent Obstacle to Cheap Drug Imports* (2003) WTO News Press Release Doc. Press/350/Rev.1. Online. Available at: www.wto.org/english/news_e/pres03_e/pr350_e.htm (accessed 15 January 2009).

5 Protecting the atmosphere to avoid climate change

1 Report of the World Commission on Environment and Development, *Our Common Future*, 42nd Session of the UN General Assembly, 4 August 1987, Doc. No. A/42/427, p. 24.

2 Ibid., p. 21.

3 S. Boehmer-Christiansen, 'Global Climate Protection Policy: The Limits of Scientific Advice – Part 1', *Global Environmental Change*, Vol. 4, No. 2, 1994, 141; I. Rowlands, *The Politics of Global Atmospheric Change*, Manchester: Manchester University Press, 1995, p. 92.

4 P. Damon and S. Kunen, 'Global Cooling? No, Southern Hemisphere Warming Trends May Indicate the Onset of the CO_2 "Greenhouse" Effect', *Science*, Vol. 193, No. 4252, August 1976, 451–452; M. Walton, 'Changes in Gulf Stream Could Chill Europe', 10 May 2005. Online. Available at: www.cnn.com/2005/TECH/science/05/10/gulfstream/index.html (accessed 23 February 2005).

5 P. Newell, *Climate for Change – Non-state Actors and the Global Politics of the Greenhouse*, Cambridge: Cambridge University Press, 2000, p. 135.

6 L. Elliot, *The Global Politics of the Environment*, Basingstoke: Palgrave Macmillan, 2004, p. 117; S. Boehmer-Christiansen, 'Uncertainty in the Service of Science: Between Science Policy and the Politics of Power' in G. Fermann (ed.) *International Politics of Climate Change – Key Issues and Critical Actors*, Oslo: Scandinavian University Press, 1997, pp. 138–140.

7 F. Yamin and J. Depledge, *The International Climate Change Regime – A Guide to Rules, Institutions and Procedures*, Cambridge University Press: Cambridge, 2004, p. 35.

8 J. Gupta and R. Tol, 'Why Reduce Greenhouse Gas Emissions? Reasons, Issue-Linkages and Dilemmas' in E. Ierland, J. Gupta and M. Kok (eds) *Issues in International Climate Policy: Theory and Policy*, Cheltenham: Edward Elgar, p. 33.

9 'The Economics of Climate Change', *OECD Economic Outlook*, No. 63, 1998, available from www.oecd.org, p. 197.

10 A. Najam, 'The Case against a New International Environmental Organisation', in P. Diehl (ed.) *The Politics of Global Governance – International Organisations in an Interdependent World*, 3rd edn, London: Lynne Rienner, 2005, pp. 398–415.

11 Boehmer-Christiansen, 'Global Climate Protection Policy', pp. 142–143; C. Boettcher, 'The Use and Misuse of Science in Policy Making', in T. Gerholm (ed.) *Climate Policy after Kyoto*, Brentwood: Multiscience Publishing Co. Ltd, 1999, pp. 40–49.

12 J. Houghton, 'The Case for the Greenhouse Effect', in P. Thompson (ed.) *Global Warming – The Debate*, Chichester: John Wiley and Sons, 1991, p. 8.

13 Examples of natural sinks are clouds, increased plant growth and resulting organic matter in the soil produces sulphur gases, which also have a cooling effect; the world ocean also absorbs carbon dioxide from the atmosphere – S. Idso, 'Real-world Constraints on Global Warming' in L. Jones (ed.) *Global Warming – The Science and the Politics*, Vancouver: Fraser Institute, 1997, pp. 92–97; S. Schneider, 'The Greenhouse Effect: Science and Policy', *Science*, Vol. 243, No. 4892, 1989, 773–774.

14 House of Lords, Select Committee on Economic Affairs, *The Economics of Climate Change*, Vol. 1: Report, 2nd Report of Session 2005–6, London: Stationery Office, 2005, p. 12.

15 T. Wigley, 'The Science of Climate Change' in E. Claussen, V. Cochran and D. Davies (eds) *Climate Change – Science Strategies and Solutions*, Arlington, VA: Pew Center on Global Climate Change, 2001, pp. 12–22.

16 C. Thomas, *The Environment in International Relations*, London: Royal Institute of International Affairs, 1992, p. 125.

17 Ibid., pp. 115–153.

18 S. Weart, *The Discovery of Global Warming*, Cambridge, MA: Harvard University Press, 2003, pp. 11–12.

19 J. R. Fleming, *Historical Perspectives on Climate Change*, Oxford: Oxford University Press, 1998, pp. 34–43.

20 Ibid., pp. 42 and 53.

21 W. Karlen, 'Is the Temperature Increase of the Last 100 Years Unique?' in Gerholm (ed.) *Climate Policy After Kyoto*, p. 52.

22 Fleming, *Historical Perspectives on Climate Change*, p. 56; Christianson, *Greenhouse – The 200-year Story of Global Warming*, London: Constable and Company Ltd, 1999, p. 33.

23 Weart, *The Discovery of Global Warming*, p. 3; Fleming, *Historical Perspectives on Climate Change*, p. 65.

24 Christianson, *Greenhouse*, p. 110; Fleming, *Historical Perspectives on Climate Change*, p. 67.

25 J. Tyndall, 'Note on the Transition of Heat through Gaseous Bodies', *Proc. Roy. Inst. Gt. Br.*, Vol. 10, No. 37, 1859.

26 Christianson, *Greenhouse*, pp. 111–113.

27 S. Arrhenius 'On the Influence of Carbonic Acid in the Air upon the Temperature of the Ground', *The London, Edinburgh and Dublin Philosophical Magazine and Journal of Science*, 5th Series, April 1896.

28 Weart, *The Discovery of Global Warming*, pp. 15–18.

29 Fleming, *Historical Perspectives on Climate Change*, p. 108.

30 Houghton, 'The Case for the Greenhouse Effect', p. 11.

31 G. C. Callendar, 'The Artificial Production of Carbon Dioxide and Its Influence on Temperature', *Quarterly Journal of the Royal Meteorological Society*, Vol. 64, 1938, 223–240.

32 Christianson, *Greenhouse*, p. 141.

33 Fleming, *Historical Perspectives on Climate Change*, p. 82.

34 D. Demeritt, 'The Construction of Global Warming and the Politics of Science', *Annals of the Association of American Geographers*, Vol. 91, No. 2, 2001, 315, citing the work of D. Kleinman, *Politics on the Endless Frontier: Postwar Research Policy in the United States*, Durham, NC: Duke University Press, 1995 and C. Kwa, 'Modelling Technologies of Control', *Science as Culture*, Vol. 4, 1994, 363–391. Demeritt reminds us that much of the postwar science in the United States and elsewhere was justified for the needs of the military.

35 A. Jamison, *The Making of Green Knowledge – Environmental Politics and Cultural Transformation*, Cambridge: Cambridge University Press, 2001, pp. 65–66.

36 Weart, *The Discovery of Global Warming*, p. 40.

37 Fleming, *Historical Perspectives on Climate Change*, p. 119.

38 In 1956, Gilbert Plass, an infrared physicist, proposed that

> if at the end of this century, measurements show that carbon dioxide content of the atmosphere has risen appreciably, and at the same time temperature has continued to rise throughout the world, it will be firmly established that carbon dioxide is an important factor in causing climate change.
>
> (M. Nye, D. Lindberg and R. Numbers, *The Cambridge History of Science – The Modern Physical and Mathematical Sciences*, Vol. 5, Cambridge: Cambridge University Press, 2003, pp. 647–648)

39 Thomas, *The Environment in International Relations*, p. 23; Jamison, *The Making of Green Knowledge*, pp. 71–72.

40 Weart, *The Discovery of Global Warming*, p. 91.

41 J. Connelly and G. Smith, *Politics and the Environment – From Theory to Practice*, 2nd edn, London: Routledge, 2003, p. 97.

42 Ibid., p. 86.

43 Examples include World Resource Institute, Washington, DC, US; the Centre for Science and Environment, India; Pembina Institute, Canada; Institute for International and European Environmental Policy, Germany and so on.
44 Jamison, *The Making of Green Knowledge*, p. 91; Weart, *The Discovery of Global Warming*, pp. 142–146.
45 I. Rowlands, *The Politics of Global Atmospheric Change*, Manchester: Manchester University Press, 1995, p. 67, citing the Conservation Foundation Report, *Implications of Rising Carbon Dioxide Content of the Atmosphere*, New York, 1963.
46 Weart, *The Discovery of Global Warming*, p. 44; Rowlands, *The Politics of Global Atmospheric Change*, p. 67.
47 Weart, *The Discovery of Global Warming*, pp. 39–40.
48 D. Bodansky, 'Prologue to the Climate Change Convention' in I. Mintzer and J. Leonard (eds) *Negotiating Climate Change – The Inside Story of the Rio Convention*, Cambridge: Cambridge University Press and Stockholm Environmental Institute, 1994, pp. 46–47, citing National Research Council, *Carbon Dioxide and Climate: A Scientific Assessment*, Washington, DC: NRC, 1979, p. viii.
49 Ibid., p. 47.
50 Jamison, *The Making of Green Knowledge*, pp. 87–88.
51 G. Borsting and G. Fermann, 'Climate Change Turning Political: Conference Diplomacy and Institution-building to Rio and Beyond' in Fermann (ed.) *International Politics of Climate Change*, p. 53.
52 Examples include the first World Climate Conference called by the World Meteorological Organisation in 1979. An investigation to study explicitly the causes and consequences of carbon dioxide accumulation was also launched by the US National Academy of Sciences (NAS) in 1975.
53 Jamison, *The Making of Green Knowledge*, pp. 90–93.
54 Ibid., p. 91.
55 Fleming, *Historical Perspectives on Climate Change*, citing *Saturday Evening Post* of 1950, p. 119.
56 R. Revelle and H. Suess, 'Carbon Dioxide Exchange between Atmosphere and Ocean and the Question of an Increase of Atmospheric CO_2 during the Past Decades', *Tellus*, Vol. 9, No. 18, 1957.
57 J. Lanchbery and D. Victor, 'The Role of Science in the Global Climate Negotiations' in H. Bergesen, G. Parmann and O. Themmessen (eds) *Green Globe Yearbook of International Co-operation on Environment and Development 1995*, Oxford: Oxford University Press, 1995, p. 30.
58 Ibid., p. 31.
59 Weart, *The Discovery of Global Warming*, pp. 63–64.
60 Revelle and Suess, 'Carbon Dioxide Exchange between Atmosphere and Ocean and the Question of an Increase of Atmospheric CO_2 during the Past Decades'.
61 Rowlands, *The Politics of Global Atmospheric Change*, p. 68.
62 Demeritt, 'The Construction of Global Warming and the Politics of Science', 315; J. Morris (ed.) *Climate Change – Challenging Conventional Wisdom*, IEA Studies of the Environment No. 10, London: Harlington Fine Arts Ltd, 1997, p. 18.
63 C. Dasgupta, 'The Climate Change Negotiations' in I. Mintzer and J. Leonard (eds) *Negotiating Climate Change – The Inside Story of the Rio Convention*,

pp. 129–130, citing WMO, *World Climate Conference Declaration and Supporting Documents*, Geneva: WMO, 1979.

64 At least 4,000 NGOs are listed as engaged with the issue of climate change in the database of one environmental organisation – G. Porter and J. Brown, *Global Environmental Politics*, Oxford: Westview Press, 1996, p. 50.

65 Ibid., pp. 41–65; C. Gough and S. Shackley, 'The Respectable Politics of Climate Change: The Epistemic Communities and NGOs', *International Affairs*, Vol. 77, No. 2, 2001, 331–336; J. E. Smith, 'The Role of Special Purpose and Non-governmental Organisations in the Environmental Crisis', *International Organisation*, Vol. 26, No. 2, 1972, 302–326; D. A. Davies, 'The Role of the WMO in Environmental Issues', *International Organisation*, Vol. 26, No. 2, 1972, 327–336; R. Gardner, 'The Role of the UN in Environmental Problems', *International Organisation*, Vol. 26, No. 2, 1972, 237–254.

66 Massachusetts Institute of Technology, *Man's Impact on the Global Environment – Report of the Study of Critical Environmental Problems*, Cambridge, MA: MIT Press, 1970; Massachusetts Institute of Technology, *Inadvertent Climate Modification – Report of the Study of Man's Impact on Climate*, Cambridge, MA: MIT Press, 1971.

67 M. Gemmell and J. Lehr, 'Ecology's Ancestry' in J. Lehr (ed.) *Rational Readings on Environmental Concerns* (John Wiley and Sons: 1992) – p. 14.

68 S. Oberthuer and H. Ott, *The Kyoto Protocol – International Climate Policy for the 21st Century*, Berlin: Springer, 1999, p. 31.

69 R. Schmalensee, 'Symposium on Global Climate Change', *Journal of Economic Perspectives*, Vol. 7, No. 3, 1993, 3–10.

70 The Global Climate Coalition was established in 1989 to look after the interests of industries concerned with the global climate change issue.

71 B. Arts and J. Cozijnsen, 'Between "Curbing the Trends" and "Business-as-Usual": NGOs in International Climate Change Policy' in Ierland, Gupta and Kok (eds) *Issues in International Climate Policy – Theory and Policy*, pp. 248–249.

72 Rowlands, *The Politics of Global Atmospheric Change*, p. 71.

73 D. A. Davies, 'The Role of the WMO in Environmental Issues', *International Organisation*, Vol. 26, No. 2, 1972, 329.

74 Elliott, *The Global Politics of the Environment*, p. 123.

75 Weart, *The Discovery of Global Warming*, p. 174; L. Susskind, *Environmental Diplomacy – Negotiating More Effective Global Agreements*, New York: Oxford University Press, 1994, pp. 63–66.

76 The International Geophysical Year was organised by the International Council of Scientific Unions (ICSU) and stretched between 1 January 1957 and 31 December 1958 – Smith, 'The Role of Special Purpose and Non-governmental Organisations in the Environmental Crisis', p. 308.

77 W. J. Maunder, *The Human Impact of Climate Uncertainty – Weather Information, Economic Planning and Business Management*, London: Routledge, 1989, p. 15.

78 J. Walter and A. Simms, *The End of Development? – Global Warming, Disasters and the Great Reversal of Human Progress*, London: New Economic Foundation (NEF) and Bangladesh Centre for Advanced Studies (BCAS); R. Roach, *Dried Up, Drowned Out – Voices from the Developing World on a Changing Climate*, Teddington: Tearfund Publications, 2005.

79 Porter and Brown, *Global Environmental Politics*, pp. 52–53.

80 Connelly and Smith, *Politics and the Environment*, p. 237.

81 Report of the World Commission on Environment and Development, *Our Common Future*, 42nd Session of the UN General Assembly, 4 August 1987, Doc. No. A/42/427, paragraph 30.

82 Ibid., paragraph 29.

83 An earlier report entitled *Limits to Growth*, published in the United States in 1972, suggested that continued economic growth would have devastating environmental consequences for three main reasons – humanity will run out of resources, it will be unable to come up with a concerted effort to fix resource shortages, and the only way for this disaster to be avoided is through population control – Rowlands, *The Politics of Global Atmospheric Change*, p. 127, citing D. Meadows, D. Meadows, J. Randers and W. Behrens, *The Limits to Growth*, New York: Universe Books, 1972.

84 Rowlands, *The Politics of Global Atmospheric Change*, p. 128.

85 Statement by the UNEP/WMO/ICSU, *The Greenhouse Effect, Climate Change, and Ecosystems*, Villach, Austria, 9–15 October 1985. Online. Available at: www.icsu-scope.org/downloadpubs/scope29/statement.html (accessed 14 March 2005).

86 Ibid.

87 Borsting and Fermann, 'Climate Change Turning Political', p. 55.

88 Ibid., pp. 19–25.

89 The Toronto Conference issued a 'call for action' to (i) reduce CO_2 emissions by 20 per cent of the 1988 levels by the year 2000; (ii) improve energy efficiency by as much as 10 per cent by the year 2005; (iii) initiate the necessary technological changes to reach these goals; (iv) prepare principles and components of a framework treaty for the protection of the atmosphere in time for the 1992 UNCED – Borsting and Fermann, 'Climate Change Turning Political', pp. 56–57, citing Toronto Conference Statement, *American Journal of International Law and Policy*, Vol. 5, No. 15, 1988.

90 *Developing Policies for Responding to Climate Change*, a Summary of the discussions and recommendations of the workshop held in Villach (28 September–2 October 1987) and Bellagio (9–13 November 1987) – pp. 6–7; Houghton, 'The Case for the Greenhouse Effect', p. 11.

91 P. Fras, 'Does CO_2 Respond to Global Temperature Changes rather than Cause Them? – Counter Evidence from Greenhouse Assumptions from Ice Core Data and Volcanoes', in R. Bate, F. Boettcher and J. Emsley (eds) *The Global Warming Debate*, Report of the European Science and Environment Forum, Bournemouth: Bourne Press Limited, 1996, pp. 74–75; T. Segalstad, 'The Distribution of CO_2 between Atmosphere, Hydrosphere, and Lithosphere; Minimal Influence from Anthropogenic CO_2 on the Global Greenhouse Effect', in Bate, Boettcher and Emsley (eds) *The Global Warming Debate*, pp. 41–48; Idso, 'Real-world Constraints on Global Warming', pp. 92–97.

92 W. Nitze, *The Greenhouse Effect: Formulating a Convention*, London: The Royal Institute of International Affairs, 1990, p. 13.

93 Gupta and Tol, 'Why Reduce Greenhouse Gas Emissions?', p. 26.

94 Schmalensee, 'Symposium on Global Climate Change'; Porter and Brown, *Global Environmental Politics*, pp. 59–65; Oberthuer and Ott, *The Kyoto Protocol*, pp. 72–73.

95 J. Morris, 'Introduction: Climate Change – Prevention or Adaptation?' in J. Morris (ed.) *Climate Change – Challenging Conventional Wisdom*, IEA Studies of the Environment No. 10, London: Harlington Fine Arts Ltd, 1997, p. 21.

96 W. Franz, *The Development of an International Agenda for Climate Change: Connecting Science to Policy*, ENRP Discussion Paper E-97-07, Kennedy School of Government, Harvard University, August 1997, p. 11.

97 Report of the Intergovernmental Negotiating Committee for a Framework Convention on Climate Change on the work of its first session, Washington, DC, 4–11 February 1991, UNGA Doc. No. A/AC.237/6, p. 37.

98 P. Bunyard, *The Breakdown of Climate – Human Choices or Global Disaster?*, Edinburgh: Floris Books, 1999, p. 201.

99 E. Skolnikoff, 'The Policy Gridlock on Global Warming', *Foreign Policy*, Vol. 79, 1990, p. 84.

100 Newell, *Climate for Change*, p. 16.

101 Yamin and Depledge, *The International Climate Change Regime*, pp. 40–41.

102 The OPEC countries were regularly briefed by business lobbyists from the Global Climate Coalition and the Climate Council – see Oberthuer and Ott, *The Kyoto Protocol*, p. 45; Porter and Brown, *Global Environmental Politics*, pp. 62–64.

103 D. Runnalls, 'The International Politics of Climate Change' in J. Parikh, R. Culpeper, D. Runnalls and J. Painuly (eds) *Climate Change and North–South Cooperation – Indo-Canadian Cooperation in Joint Implementation*, New Delhi Tata, McGraw-Hill Publishing Co. Ltd, p. 36.

104 Newell, *Climate for Change*, p. 17.

105 Gupta and Tol, 'Why Reduce Greenhouse Gas Emissions?', p. 23.

106 Runnalls, 'The International Politics of Climate Change', pp. 35–36.

107 Newell, *Climate for Change*, p. 17.

108 Ibid., p. 18.

109 Runnalls, 'The International Politics of Climate Change', p. 29.

110 The US uses more energy per capita than any other OECD Country –Nitze, *The Greenhouse Effect: Formulating a Convention*, p. 5.

111 Ibid., p. 14.

112 Dasgupta, 'The Climate Change Negotiations', p. 130.

113 Lanchbery and Victor, 'The Role of Science in the Global Climate Negotiations', p. 33.

114 Rapporteur's Report of the Executive Session: 'Negotiating a Global Climate Change Agreement', 14–15 March 1991, *CSIA Discussion Paper*, 91–10, Kennedy School of Government, Harvard University, November 1991, 3.

115 The US delegation explained this position as a desire to afford 'flexibility in nations' choices of their own measures' – Dasgupta, 'The Climate Change Negotiations', pp. 134–135.

116 Runnalls, 'The International Politics of Climate Change', pp. 28–30.

117 Ibid., p. 27; Dasgupta, 'The Climate Change Negotiations', p. 135.

118 See Report of the Intergovernmental Negotiating Committee for a Framework Convention on Climate Change on the work of its first session, Washington, DC, 4–11 February 1991, UNGA Doc. No. A/AC.237/6; Report of the Intergovernmental Negotiating Committee for a Framework Convention on Climate Change on the work of its second session, Geneva, 19–28 June 1991, UNGA Doc. No. A/AC.237/9; Report of the Intergovernmental Negotiating Committee for a Framework Convention on Climate Change on the work of its third session, Nairobi, 9–20 September 1991, UNGA Doc. No. A/AC.237/12.

119 Dasgupta, 'The Climate Change Negotiations', pp. 136–137.
120 Yamin and Depledge, *The International Climate Change Regime*, p. 35.
121 Runnalls, 'The International Politics of Climate Change', p. 37.
122 Dasgupta, 'The Climate Change Negotiations', pp. 144–145.
123 Elliot, *The Global Politics of the Environment*, p. 85.
124 W. Morrissey, *Global Climate Change: A Survey of Scientific Research and Policy Reports*, CRS Report for Congress, 2000. Online. Available at: www. ncseonline.org/NLE/CRSreports/Climate/clim-24.cfm (accessed 15 March 2005), p. 3.
125 Lanchbery and Victor, 'The Role of Science in the Global Climate Negotiations', p. 37.
126 United Nations Framework Convention on Climate Change Secretariat, *The United Nations Framework Convention on Climate Change – Essential Background*, 2005. Online. Available at: http://unfccc.int/essential_background/ feeling_the_heat/items/2914.php (accessed 15 March 2005).
127 Borsting and Fermann, 'Climate Change Turning Political', p. 75.
128 Ibid., p. 69.
129 *Earth Negotiations Bulletin – A Reporting Service for Environment and Development Negotiations*, Vol. 12 – United Nations Framework Convention on Climate Change, 11th Session of the INC for the FCCC, No. 4, 9 February 1995. Online. Available at: www.iisd.ca/Vol. 12/1204002e.html (accessed 20 March 2005).
130 Ibid., No. 3, 8 February 1995. Online. Available at: www.iisd.ca/Vol. 12/1204002e.html (accessed 20 March 2005).
131 'Challenges for Berlin', *Earth Negotiations Bulletin – A Reporting Service for Environment and Development Negotiations*, Vol. 12 – United Nations Framework Convention on Climate Change, 11th Session of the INC for the FCCC, No. 11, 17 February 1995. Online. Available at: www.iisd.ca/Vol. 12/1204002e.html.
132 Yamin and Depledge, *The International Climate Change Regime*, p. 399.
133 Borsting and Fermann, 'Climate Change Turning Political', pp. 74, 78.
134 J. Depledge, *The Organisation of Global Negotiations: Constructing the Climate Change Regime*, London: Earthscan, 2005, p. 23.
135 Document: FCCC/CP/1996/15/Add.1.
136 T. Wirth, Under Secretary of State for Global Affairs, reprinted in 'Global Issues – Confronting Climate Change', *Electronic Journal of the US Information Agency*, Vol. 2, No. 2, April 1997.
137 For detailed description and further analysis of events see Oberthuer and Ott, *The Kyoto Protocol*, pp. 77–91.
138 Elliott, *The Global Politics of the Environment*, p. 89.
139 'Putin Clears Way for Kyoto Treaty', *BBC News*, 5 November 2004.
140 'UN Poised for New Climate Talks', *BBC News*, 9 December 2005; M. Milliken and T. Gardner, 'US Isolated at World Climate Talks', *Reuters UK*, 9 December 2005.
141 'Bush "Isolated in US" on Climate', *BBC News*, 9 December 2005.
142 UN FCCC Secretariat, 'Montreal Climate Conference Adopts "Rule Book" of the Kyoto Protocol', Press Release, Montreal, 30 November 2005.
143 'UN Poised for New Climate Talks'.
144 'Last-minute Climate Deals Reached', *BBC News*, 10 December 2005.

6 Conclusions

1 See Keck and Sikkink, *Activists beyond Borders*, p. 30; Sikkink briefly introduces this idea in an earlier article – Sikkink, 'Human Rights, Principled Issue-
   Networks, and Sovereignty in Latin America', 412; and Klotz, 'Transnational
   Activism and Global Transformation, p. 52.
2 Finnemore and Sikkink, 'International Norm Dynamics and Political Change';
   Haas, 'Do Regimes Matter?'; Drake and Nicolaidis, 'Ideas, Interests and Institutionalisation'; Adler, 'The Emergence of Cooperation'.
3 In their article 'International Norm Dynamics and Political Change' Finnemore
   and Sikkink discuss persuasion, but do not examine the process in much detail,
   while constructivists studying the behaviour of epistemic communities seem to
   suggest that the changes in the opinion of states takes place, due to the so-
   called process of 'policy diffusion', i.e., policy change from within – see Adler
   and Haas, 'Conclusion', pp. 375–378.
4 Finnemore and Sikkink, 'International Norm Dynamics and Political Change',
   901.
5 P. Malanczuk, *Akehurst's Modern Introduction to International Law*, 7th edn,
   London: Routledge, 1997, p. 36.
6 Drahos and Braithwaite, *Information Feudalism*, p. 61.
7 Farrell, 'Transnational Norms and Military Development', p. 71.
8 Engelhardt and Caplan (eds) *Scientific Controversies*.
9 Dasgupta, 'The Climate Change Negotiations', pp. 144–145.
10 Lanchbery and Victor, 'The Role of Science in the Global Climate Negotiations', p. 37.

Bibliography

Abbott, F. (2002) *Compulsory Licensing for Public Health Needs: The TRIPs Agenda at the WTO after the Doha Declaration on Public Health*, Quaker United Nations Office, Occasional Paper 9.

Abildgaard, U., Daugaard, G., Marcussen, H., Jess, P., Draminsky Petersen, H. and Wallach, M. (1984) 'Chronic Organic Psycho-Syndrome in Greek Torture Victims', *Danish Medical Bulletin*, Vol. 31, No. 3, 239–242.

Adede, A. O. (2003) 'Origins and History of the TRIPS Negotiations' in C. Bellmann, G. Dutfield and Melendez-Ortiz, R. (ed.) *Trading in Knowledge – Development Perspectives on TRIPS, Trade and Sustainability*, London: Earthscan Publications, International Centre for Trade and Sustainable Development.

Adler, E. (1992) 'The Emergence of Cooperation: National Epistemic Communities and the International Evolution of the Idea of Nuclear Arms Control', *International Organisation*, Vol. 46, No. 1, 101–145.

Adler, E. (1997) 'Seizing the Middle Ground: Constructivism in World Politics', *European Journal of International Relations*, Vol. 3, No. 3.

Adler, E. and Haas, P. (1992) 'Conclusion: Epistemic Communities, World Order, and the Creation of a Reflective Research Program', *International Organisation*, Vol. 46, No. 1, 367–390.

Ainsworth, M. (1999) 'AIDS, Development, and the East Asian Crisis', Plenary Address to the 5th International Conference on AIDS in Asia and the Pacific, 25 October 1999, Development Research Group, World Bank.

Alikhan, S. (2000) *Socio-economic Benefits of Intellectual Property Protection in Developing Countries*, Geneva: WIPO (38).

Amnesty International (1972) *Report of an Enquiry into Allegations of Ill-treatment Made against the Security Forces in Northern Ireland by Persons Arrested on 9 August 1971*, London: Amnesty International Publications.

Amnesty International (1973) *Conference for the Abolition of Torture – Final Report*, Paris, 10–11 December 1973, London: Amnesty International Publications.

Amnesty International (1973) *Report on Torture*, London: Duckworth in Association with Amnesty International Publications.

Amnesty International (1973–1974) *Annual Report*, London: British Section.

Amnesty International (1974) *Report on Allegations of Torture in Brazil*, London: Amnesty International Publications.

Amnesty International (1975) *Annual Report 1974–1975*, London: Amnesty International Publications.

Amnesty International (1976) *Iran*, London: Amnesty International Publications.

Amnesty International (1976) *Prisoners of Conscience in the USSR: Their Treatment and Conditions*, London: Amnesty International Publications.

Amnesty International (1976) *Tortured to Death in Uruguay: 22 Known Cases*, London: Amnesty International Publications.

Amnesty International (1977) *Evidence of Torture: Studies by the Amnesty International Danish Medical Group*, London: Amnesty International Publications.

Amnesty International (1977) *Torture in Greece: The First Torturers' Trial 1975*, London: Amnesty International.

Amnesty International Report (1977) London: Amnesty International Publications.

Amnesty International (1978) *Report on an Amnesty International Medical Seminar 'Violations of Human Rights: Torture and the Medical Profession'*, Athens, 10–11 March, AI Index: CAT 02/03/78.

Amnesty International (1984) *Codes of Professional Ethics*, London: Amnesty International Publications.

Amnesty International (1984) *Torture in the Eighties*, London: Amnesty International Publications.

Amnesty International, the French Medical Commission and V. Marange (1989) *Doctors and Torture – Collaboration or Resistance?*, London: Bellew Publishing.

Amnesty International (2004) AI Public Statement: 'Commission on Human Rights, 60th Session (15 March–23 April 2004) – The Human Rights Scandal of Guantanamo Bay', AI Index IOR 41/024/2004, April.

Amnesty International (2004) AI Press Release: 'End Human Rights Scandal in Guantanamo Bay', AI Index POL 30/017/2004, 11 April.

Amnesty International (2004) AI Press Release: 'USA: Pattern of Brutality and Cruelty – War Crimes and Abu Ghraib', AI Index AMR 51/077/2004, 7 May.

Amnesty International (2005) AI Press Release: 'USA/Iraq: Abuses without Accountability a Year after Abu Ghraib', AI Index AMR 51/064/2005, 28 April.

Amsterdam Statement to WTO Member States on Access to Medicines (1999) 25–26 November. Online. Available at: www.haiweb.org/campaign/novseminar/amsterdam_statement.html.

Amstutz, M. (1999) *International Ethics – Concepts, Theories and Cases in Global Politics*, Lanham, MD: Rowman and Littlefield Publishers.

Anderson, K. (2000) 'The Ottawa Convention Banning Landmines, the Role of International Non-governmental Organisations and the Idea of International Civil Society', *European Journal of International Law*, Vol. 11, No. 1.

Arrhenius, S. (1896) 'On the Influence of Carbonic Acid in the Air upon the Temperature of the Ground', *The London, Edinburgh, and Dublin Philosophical Magazine and Journal of Science*, 5th ser., April, 237–276.

Askevold, F. (1980) 'The War Sailor Syndrome', *Danish Medical Bulletin*, Vol. 27, 220.

Attaran, A. (2004) 'How Do Patents and Economic Policies Affect Access to Essential Medicines in Developing Countries?', *Health Affairs*, Vol. 23, No. 3, 155–166.

Attaran, A. and Gillespie-White, G. (2001) 'Do Patents for Antiretroviral Drugs Constrain Access to AIDS Treatment in Africa?', *Journal of the American Medical Association*, Vol. 286, No. 15, 17 October, 1886–1892.

Attaran, A. and Sachs, J. (2001) 'Defining and Refining International Donor Support for Combating the AIDS Pandemic', *The Lancet*, Vol. 357, 57–61.

Axelrod, R. (1986) 'An Evolutionary Approach to Norms', *American Political Science Review*, Vol. 80, No. 4, 1095–1111.

Bailey, M. (2002) *Conference on Knowledge and Intellectual Property – World Social Forum*, Conference address.

Barnes, B. and Edge, D. (eds) (1982) *Science in Context – Readings in the Sociology of Science*, Milton Keynes: Open University Press.

Barnes, B., Bloor, D. and Henry, J. (1996) *Scientific Knowledge – A Sociological Analysis*, London: Athlone.

Barnett, M. and Finnemore, M. (2004) *Rules for the World – International Organisations in Global Politics*, Ithaca, NY: Cornell University Press.

Bate, R. and Morris, J. (1994) *Global Warming: Apocalypse or Hot Air?*, London: Institute of Economic Affairs, Environment Unit.

Bate, R., Boettcher, F. and Emsley, J. (eds) (1996) *The Global Warming Debate*, Report of the European Science and Environment Forum, Bournemouth: Bourne Press Limited.

Bellmann, C., Dutfield, G. and Melendez-Ortiz, R. (eds) (2003) *Trading in Knowledge – Development Perspectives on TRIPs, Trade and Sustainability*, International Centre for Trade and Sustainable Development, London: Earthscan Publications.

Belton, N. (1998) *The Good Listener – Helen Bamber Life against Cruelty*, London: Weidenfeld and Nicolson.

Benford, R. and Snow, D. (2000) 'Framing Processes and Social Movements – An Overview and Assessment', *Annual Review of Sociology*, Vol. 26, 611–639.

Benko, R. (1987) *Protecting Intellectual Property Rights – Issues and Controversies*, Washington, DC: American Enterprise Institute for Public Policy Research.

Berger, P. (1980) 'Documentation of Physical Sequelae', *Danish Medical Bulletin*, Vol. 27, No. 5, November, 215–216.

Berger, P. and Luckmann, T. (1966) *The Social Construction of Reality*, New York: Anchor.

Bergesen, H. (1995) 'A Global Climate Regime – Mission Impossible?' in H. Bergesen, G. Parmann and O. Themmessen (eds) *Green Globe Yearbook of International Co-operation on Environment and Development 1995*, Oxford: Oxford University Press.

Bergesen, H., Parmann, G. and Themmessen, O. (eds) (1995) *Green Globe Yearbook of International Co-operation on Environment and Development 1995*, Oxford: Oxford University Press.

Berkman, A. (2002) *The Global AIDS Crisis: Human Rights, International Pharmaceutical Markets and Intellectual Property Symposium*. Online. Available at: www.healthgap.org/press_releases/02/031402_HGAP_ALAN_PP_IPR.pdf.

Berman, D. and Ford, N. (1999) *AIDS and Essential Medicines and Compulsory Licensing*, Summary of the 25–27 March Meeting, Geneva.

Bhandari, P. (1998) 'Historical Perspective on Negotiations' in *Climate Change Post-Kyoto Perspectives from the South*, New Delhi: Tata Energy Research Group.

Bijker, W., Hughes, T. and Pinch, T. (eds) (1989) *The Social Construction of Technological Systems – New Directions in the Sociology and the History of Technology*, Cambridge, MA: MIT Press.

Bjorkdahl, A. (2002) 'Norms in International Relations: Some Conceptual and Methodological Reflections', *Cambridge Review of International Affairs*, Vol. 15, No. 1.

Blakeney, M. (1996) *Trade Related Aspects of Intellectual Property Rights: A Concise Guide to the TRIPs Agreement*, London: Sweet and Maxwell.

Bluestone, K. (VSO), Heaton, A. (Save the Children UK) and Lewis, C. (Oxfam GB) (2002) *Beyond Philanthropy: The Pharmaceutical Industry, Corporate Social Responsibility and the Developing World – Joint Report*, Oxford: Oxfam.

Boehmer-Christiansen, S. (1994) 'Global Climate Protection Policy: The Limits of Scientific Advice – Part 1', *Global Environmental Change*, Vol. 4, No. 2, 140–159.

Boehmer-Christiansen, S. (1994) 'Global Climate Protection Policy: The Limits of Scientific Advice – Part 2', *Global Environmental Change*, Vol. 4, No. 3, 185–200.

Boehringer, C., Finns, M. and Vogt, C. (eds) (2002) *Controlling Global Warming – Perspectives from Economics, Game Theory and Public Choice*, Cheltenham: Edward Elgar Publishing Ltd.

Boli, J. and Thomas, G. (eds) (1999) *Constructing World Culture – International Nongovernmental Organisations since 1875*, Stanford, CA: Stanford UP.

Borger, J. (2001) 'USA: The Pharmaceutical Industry Stalks the Corridors of Power', *Guardian Unlimited*, 13 February. Online. Available at: www.corp-watch.org/article.php?id=178 (accessed 15 January 2009).

Bowden, M. (2003) 'Now Let's Talk', *Sunday Telegraph – Review*, 7 December.

Braga, C. (1989) 'The Economics of Intellectual Property Rights and the GATT: A View from the South', Symposium: Trade Related Aspects of Intellectual Property, Part 1, *Vanderbilt Journal of Transnational Law*, Vol. 22, 243–264.

Brecher, B. (2004) 'Torture Is Always an Evil Option', *The Times Higher*, 18 June.

British Medical Association (1982) *The Handbook of Medical Ethics*, London: BMA.

British Medical Association (1986) *The Torture Report – A Report of a Working Party of the British Medical Association Investigating the Involvement of Doctors in Torture*, London: BMA.

British Medical Association (1992) *Medicine Betrayed – The Participation of Doctors in Human Rights Abuses*, London: Zed Books.

Brownlie, I. (1972) 'Interrogation in Depth: The Compton and Parker Reports' *The Modern Law Review*, Vol. 35, No. 5, 501–507.

Brownsey, P. (1980) 'Commentary: On the Permissibility of Torture by Gary Jones', *Journal of Medical Ethics*, Vol. 6, 14–15.

Bull, H. (1977) *The Anarchical Society – A Study of Order in World Politics*, 2nd edn, London: Macmillan Press Ltd.

Bunyard, P. (1999) *The Breakdown of Climate – Human Choices or Global Disaster?*, Edinburgh: Floris Books.

Burgers, J. and Danelius, H. (1988) *The UN Convention against Torture – A Handbook on the Convention against Torture and Other Cruel, Inhuman and Degrading Treatment or Punishment*, Norwell, MA: Martin Hijhoff Publishers.

Burges, S. (1980) 'Doctors and Torture: the Police Surgeon', *Journal of Medical Ethics*, Vol. 6, 120–123.

Buschschluter, V. (2009) 'The Obama Approach to Interrogation', *BBC News*, 29 January. Online. Available at: http://news.bbc.co.uk/1/hi/world/americas/7847405.stm (accessed 31 January 2009).

Bynum, W., Lock, S. and Porter, R. (eds) (1992) *Medical Journals and Medical Knowledge – Historical Essays*. London: Routledge.

Callendar, G. C. (1938) 'The Artificial Production of Carbon Dioxide and Its Influence on Temperature', *Quarterly Journal of the Royal Meteorological Society*, Vol. 64, 223–240.

Carlsnaes, W. (1992) 'The Agency-Structure Problem in Foreign Policy Analysis', *International Studies Quarterly*, Vol. 36, No. 3, 245–270.

Carraro, C. (ed.) (1999) *International Environmental Agreements on Climate Change*, Dordrecht, the Netherlands: Kluwer Academic Publishers.

Cassese, A. (ed.) (1979) *UN Law/Fundamental Rights Two Topics in International Law*, Alphen aan den Rijn, the Netherlands: Sijthoff and Noordhoff.

Cassese, A. (ed.) (1991) *The International Fight against Torture*, Baden-Baden: Nomos Verlagsgesellschaft.

Castro, J. A. A. (1972) 'Environment and Development: The Case of the Developing Countries', *International Organisation*, Vol. 26, No. 2, 401–416.

Catholic Institute for International Relations, Human Rights Forum (British Council of Churches) and the International Commission of Jurists (1982) *Torture in South Africa*, London: Catholic Institute for International Relations and the International Commission of Jurists.

Centre for Global Environmental Research (1998) *Climate Change: Post-Kyoto Perspectives from the South*, New Delhi: Tata Energy Research Institute. Online. Available at: www.teriin.org/climate/cp-4/contents.htm (accessed 14 May 2006).

Chandrahasan, N. (1983) 'Freedom from Torture and the Jurisdiction of Municipal Courts: Sri Lanka and United States Perspective', *Human Rights Quarterly*, Vol. 5, No. 1, 58–67.

Chasek, P. (2001) *Earth Negotiations – Analyzing Thirty Years of Environmental Diplomacy*, New York: United Nations University Press.

Checkel, J. (1998) 'The Constructivist Turn in International Relations Theory', *World Politics*, Vol. 50, 324–348.

Checkel, J. (1999) 'International Institutions and Socialisation', ARENA Working Papers WP 99/5. Online. Available at: www.arena.uio.no/publications/wp99_5.htm (accessed 15 January 2009).

Checkel, J. (1999) 'Norms, Institutions, and National Identity in Contemporary Europe', *International Studies Quarterly*, Vol. 43, 83–114.

Checkel, J. (1999) 'Why Comply? Constructivism, Social Norms and the Study of International Institutions', ARENA Working Papers, WP 99/24. Online. Available at: www.arena.uio.no/publications/wp99_24.htm (accessed 15 January 2009).

Checkel, J. (2005) 'It's the Process Stupid! Process Tracing in the Study of European and International Politics', ARENA Working Paper No. 26, October 2005. Online. Available at: www.arena.uio.no/publications/working-papers2005/papers/wp05_26.pdf (accessed 15 January 2009).

Chen, P., Boulding, E. and Schneider, S. (eds) (1983) *Social Science Research and Climate Change*, Dordrecht, the Netherlands: D. Reidel Publishing Company.

Christianson, G. (1999) *Greenhouse – The 200-year Story of Global Warming*, London: Constable and Company Ltd.

Clark, A. (2001) *Diplomacy of Conscience – Amnesty International and Changing Human Rights Norms*, Princeton, NJ: Princeton University Press.

Claussen, E., Cochran, V. and Davies, D. (eds) (2001) *Climate Change – Science Strategies and Solutions*, Arlington, VA: Pew Center on Global Climate Change.

Coates, K. (2004) 'This Creeping Sickness', *The Guardian*, 23 March 2004.

Colas, A. (2002) *International Civil Society – Social Movements in World Politics*. Oxford: Polity Press.

Collins, H. (1983) 'The Sociology of Scientific Knowledge: Studies of Contemporary Science', *Annual Review of Sociology*, No. 9, 265–285.

Commission on Human Rights, Report of the 32nd Session (2 February–5 March 1976), ECOSOC, Official Records 60th Session, Supplement 3 (UN Doc. Index: E/5768, E/CN.4/1213), pp. 34–35, 67–68.

Commission on Human Rights, Report of the 34th Session (6 February–10 March 1978), ECOSOC, Official Records 1978, Supplement 4 (UN Doc. Index: E/1978/34 E/CN.4/1292), pp. 29–35.

Commission on Human Rights, Report of the 35th Session (12 February–16 March 1979), ECOSOC, Official Records 1979, Supplement 6 (UN Doc. Index: E/1979/36, E/CN.4/1347), pp. 34–44, 124.

Commission on Human Rights, Report of the 36th Session (4 February–14 March 1980), ECOSOC, Official Records 1980, Supplement 3 (UN Doc. Index: E/1980/13 E/CN.4/1408), pp. 51–74, 195–196.

Commission on Human Rights, Report of the 37th Session (2 February–13 March 1981), ECOSOC, Official Records 1981 (UN Doc. Index: E/1981/25, E/CN.4/1475), pp. 50–70, 226–227.

Commission on Human Rights, Report of the 38th Session (1 February–12 March 1982), ECOSOC, Official Records 1982, Supplement 2 (UN Doc. Index: E/1982/12, E/CN.4/1982/30), pp. 45–49, 139.

Commission on Human Rights, Report of the 39th Session (31 January–11 March 1983), ECOSOC, Official Records 1983, Supplement 3 (UN Doc. Index: E/1983/13 E/CN.4/1983/60), pp. 51–53.

Commission on Human Rights, Report of the 40th Session (6 February–16 March

1984), ECOSOC, Official Records 1984, Supplement 4 (UN Doc. Index: E/1984/14, E/CN.4/1984/77), pp. 55–57, 138–142.

Conference Report – Implementation of the Doha Declaration on the TRIPS Agreement and Public Health: Technical Assistance – How to Get it Right? (28 March, 2002), International Conference Centre of Geneva.

Connelly, J. and Smith, G. (2003) *Politics and the Environment – From Theory to Practice*, 2nd edn, London: Routledge.

Conroy, J. (2001) *Unspeakable Acts, Ordinary People – The Dynamics of Torture*, London: Vision Paperbacks.

Correa, C. (2001) *TRIPS Disputes: Implications for the Pharmaceutical Sector*, Quaker United Nations Office, Occasional Paper 5, Geneva.

Correa, C. (2001) *Some Assumptions on Patent Law and Pharmaceutical R&D*, Quaker United Nations Office, Occasional Paper 6, Geneva.

Correa, C. M. (2002) 'Public Health and Intellectual Property Rights', *Global Social Policy*, Vol. 2, No. 3, 261–278.

Correa, C. and Yusuf, A. (eds) (1998) *Intellectual Property and International Trade – The TRIPs Agreement*, London: Kluwer Law International.

Corrilon, C. (1989) 'The Role of Science and Scientists in Human Rights', *The Annals of the American Academy of Political and Social Science*, Vol. 506 – 'Human Rights Around the World', 129–140.

Cortell, A. and Davis, J. (1996) 'How Do International Institutions Matter? The Domestic Impact of International Rules and Norms', *International Studies Quarterly*, Vol. 40, No. 4, 451–478.

Country Report – Malaysia (1979) *The Review – International Commission of Jurists*, No. 22, June, pp. 6–10.

Country Report – Paraguay (1979) *The Review – International Commission of Jurists*, No. 22, June 1979, pp. 11–13.

Coursier, H. (1961) *The International Red Cross*, Geneva: International Committee of the Red Cross.

Cox, R. and Jacobson, H. (1973) *The Anatomy of Influence: Decision Making in International Organisation*, London: Yale University Press.

Crawford, N. (2002) *Argument and Change in World Politics – Ethics, Decolonization, and Humanitarian Intervention*, Cambridge: Cambridge University Press.

Crelinsten, R. and Schmid, A. (eds) (1995) *The Politics of Pain – Torturers and Their Masters*, Boulder, CO: Westview Press.

The Crisis of Neglected Diseases: Developing Treatments and Ensuring Access (2002) Workshop and Conference, New York, 12–14 March 2002.

Daly, R. (1980) 'Compensation and Rehabilitation of Victims of Torture', *Danish Medical Journal*, Vol. 27, No. 5, 245–248.

Damon, P. and Kunen, S. (1976) 'Global Cooling? No, Southern Hemisphere Warming Trends May Indicate the Onset of the CO_2 "Greenhouse" Effect', *Science*, Vol. 193, No. 4252, August, 447–453.

Davies, D. (1972) 'The Role of the WMO in Environmental Issues', *International Organisation*, Vol. 26, No. 2, 327–336.

Davies, D. (2005) 'Torture Inc', *Daily Mail*, 26 February.

Decision Removes Final Patent Obstacle to Cheap Drug Imports (2003) WTO News Press Release Doc. Press/350/Rev.1. Online. Available at: www.wto.org/english/news_e/pres03_e/pr350_e.htm (accessed 15 January 2009).

Declaration of the United Nations Conference on the Human Development, 21st Plenary Meeting, 16 June 1972. Online. Available at: www.unep.org/Documents.Multilingual/Default.asp?DocumentID=97&ArticleID=1503 (accessed 15 January 2009).

Declaration on TRIPs Agreement and Public Health (2001) World Trade Organisation, Ministerial Conference, 4th Session, Doha 9–14 November. Doc. No. WT/MN(01)/DEC/2.

Deeley, P. (1971) *Beyond Breaking Point*, London: Arthur Baker Ltd.

Demeritt, D. (2001) 'The Construction of Global Warming and the Politics of Science', *Annals of the Association of American Geographers*, Vol. 91, No. 2, 307–337.

Depledge, J. (2005) *The Organisation of Global Negotiations: Constructing the Climate Change Regime*, London: Earthscan.

Dershowitz, A. (2004) 'When Torture Is the Least Evil of Terrible Options', *The Times Higher*, 11 June.

Dessler, D. (1989) 'What is at Stake in the Agent-Structure Debate?', *International Organization*, Vol. 43, No. 3, 441–473.

Developing Policies for Responding to Climate Change (1988) A Summary of the Discussions and Recommendations of the Workshop Held in Villach (28 September–2 October 1987) and Bellagio (9–13 November 1987) under the Auspices of the Beijer Institute, Sweden. Doc. No. WMO/TD-No. 225 (April).

Diehl, P. (2005) (ed.) *The Politics of Global Governance – International Organisations in an Interdependent World*, London: Lynne Rienner.

Doern, B. (1999) *Global Change and Intellectual Property Agencies*, London: Pinter.

Donnelly, J. (1986) 'International Human Rights: A Regime Analysis', *International Organisation*, Vol. 40, No. 3.

Drahos, P. (2001) 'BITs and BIPs – Bilateralism in Intellectual Property', *Journal of World Intellectual Property – Law, Economics, Politics*, Vol. 4, No. 6, 791–808.

Drahos, P. (2002) *Developing Countries and International Intellectual Property Standard-Setting*, Study Paper 8 Commissioned by the Commission on Intellectual Property Rights. Online. Available at: www.iprcommission.org/papers/pdfs/study_papers/sp8_drahos_study.pdf (accessed 17 January 2009).

Drahos, P. and Braithwaite, J. (2002) *Information Feudalism – Who Owns the Knowledge Economy?*, London: Earthscan Publications Ltd.

Drahos, P. and Mayne, R. (eds) (2002) *Global Intellectual Property Rights – Knowledge, Access and Development*, Oxfam, London: Palgrave Macmillan.

Drake, W. and Nicolaidis, K. (1992) 'Ideas, Interests and Institutionalisation: "Trade in Services" and the Uruguay Round', *International Organisation*, Vol. 46, No. 1, 37–100.

Drori, G., Meyer, J., Ramirez, F. and Schofer, E. (2003) *Science in the Modern World Polity – Institutionalisation and Globalisation*, Stanford, CA: Stanford University Press.

Dryzek, J., Clark, M. and McKenzie, G. (1989) 'Subject and System in International Relations', *International Organization*, Vol. 43, No. 3, 475–503.

duBois, P. (1991) *Torture and Truth*, New York: Routledge.

Dugger, C. (2001) 'A Catch-22 on Drugs for the World's Poor', *New York Times*, 16 November.

Dutfield, G. (2002) *Trade, Intellectual Property and Biogenetic Resources: A Guide to the International Regulatory Landscape*, Background Paper Prepared for the Multi-Stakeholder Dialogue on Trade, Intellectual Property and Biological and Genetic Resources in Asia, BRAC Centre for Development Management, Rajendrapur, Bangladesh, 19–21 April.

Dutfield, G. (2003) *Intellectual Property Rights and the Life Science Industries – A Twentieth Century History*, Aldershot: Ashgate Publishing.

Earth Negotiations Bulletin – A Reporting Service for Environment and Development Negotiations, Vol. 12 – United Nations Framework Convention on Climate Change, 11th Session of the INC for the FCCC, Nos 3, 4 and 11 – 8 February 1995. Online. Available at: www.iisd.ca/vol. 12/1204002e.html (accessed 17 January 2009).

Edwards, M. and Gaventa, J. (eds) (2001) *Global Citizen Action*, London: Earthscan Publications Ltd.

Eitinger, L. (1980) 'Jewish Concentration Camp Survivors in the Postwar World', *Danish Medical Bulletin*, Vol. 27, 232–235.

Eitinger, L. (1991) 'Torture – A Perspective on the Past', *Journal of Medical Ethics*, Vol. 17, Supplement – Proceedings of the International Symposium on 'Torture and the Medical Profession' – University of Tromso, Norway, 5–7 June 1990.

Elliot, L. (2004) *The Global Politics of the Environment*, Basingstoke: Palgrave Macmillan.

Elliot, R. (2001) *TRIPS and Rights: International Human Rights Laws, Access to Medicines, and the Interpretation of the WTO Agreement on Trade Related Aspects of International Property Rights*, Canadian HIV/AIDS Legal Network and AIDS Law Project, South Africa.

Engelhardt, H. and Caplan, A. (eds) (1987) *Scientific Controversies – Case Studies in the Resolution and Closure of Disputes in Science and Technology*, New York: Cambridge UP.

European Court of Human Rights Yearbook (1969) 'The Greek Case', 72.

Evans, G. (1994) 'Intellectual Property Rights as a Trade Issue – The Making of the Agreement on Trade-related Aspects of Intellectual Property Rights', *World Competition: Law and Economics Review*, Vol. 18, No. 2, 137–180.

Farrell, T. (2001) 'Transnational Norms and Military Development: Constructing Ireland's Professional Army', *European Journal of International Relations*, Vol. 7, No. 1, 63–102.

Farrell, T. (2005) *The Norms of War – Cultural Beliefs and Modern Conflict*, Boulder, CO: Lynne Rienner Publishers.

Farrell, T. (2005) 'World Culture and Military Power', *Security Studies*, Vol. 14, No. 3, 448–488.

Fatal Imbalance – The Crisis in Research and Development for Neglected Diseases

(2001), DND Working Group, Mèdecins Sans Frontières – 'Campaign for Access to Essential Medicines', September.

Fermann, G. (1997) (ed.) *International Politics of Climate Change – Key Issues and Critical Actors*, Oslo: Scandinavian University Press.

Fink, C. (2001) 'Patent Protection, Transnational Corporations, and Market Structure: A Simulation Study of the Indian Pharmaceutical Industry', *Journal of Industry, Competition and Trade*, Vol. 1, No. 1, 101–121.

Finn, E. Jr (1986) 'That's the $60 Billion Question', *Forbes*, 7 November.

Finnemore, M. (1996) *National Interests in International Society*, Ithaca, NY: Cornell University Press.

Finnemore, M. (1996) 'Norms, Culture, and World Politics: Insights from Sociology's Institutionalism', *International Organisation*, Vol. 50, No. 2, 325–347.

Finnemore, M. (2003) *The Purpose of Intervention – Changing Beliefs about the Use of Force*, Ithaca, NY: Cornell University Press.

Finnemore, M. and Sikkink, K. (1998) 'International Norm Dynamics and Political Change', *International Organisation*, Vol. 52, No. 4, 887–917.

Finnemore, M. and Toope, S. (2001) 'Alternatives to "Legalisation": Richer Views of Law and Politics', *International Organisation*, Vol. 55, No. 3, 743–758.

Fleck, L. (1935) *Genesis and Development of a Scientific Fact*, Chicago: University of Chicago Press.

Fleming, J. R. (1998) *Historical Perspectives on Climate Change*, New York: Oxford University Press.

Florini, A. (1996) 'The Evolution of International Norms', *International Studies Quarterly*, Vol. 40, No. 3, 363–389.

Follesdal, A. (1999) 'Global Ethics and Respect for Culture', ARENA Working Papers WP99/20. Online. Available at: www.arena.uio.no/publications/working-papers1999/papers/wp99_20.htm (accessed 17 January 2009).

Ford, J. (2002) 'A Social Theory of Trade Regime Change: GATT to WTO', *International Studies Review*, Vol. 4, No. 3, 115–138.

Ford, N. (2004) 'Patents, Access to Medicines and the Role of Non-governmental Organisations', *Journal of Generic Medicines*, Vol. 1, No. 2, 137–145.

Ford, N. and Berman, D. (1999) 'Essential Medicines and Compulsory Licensing', *HAI-Lights*, Special Issue for the 52nd World Health Assembly, Vol. 3, No. 1. Online. Available at: www.haiweb.org/pubs/hailights/may99.html (accessed 25 March 2005).

Forrest, D. (ed.) (1996) *A Glimpse of Hell – Reports on Torture Worldwide*, London: Cassell.

Franz, W. (1997) *The Development of an International Agenda for Climate Change: Connecting Science to Policy*, ENRP Discussion Paper E-97–07, Kennedy School of Government, Harvard University, August.

Frey, F. (1969) *Survey Research on Comparative Social Change*, Boston, MA: MIT Press.

Gadbaw, R. (1989) 'Intellectual Property and International Trade: Merger or Marriage of Convenience?', Symposium: Trade-related Aspects of Intellectual Property, Part 1, *Vanderbilt Journal of Transnational Law*, Vol. 22, 223–242.

Gadbaw, R. and Gwynn, R. (1988) 'Intellectual Property Rights in the New GATT Round' in R. Gadbaw and T. Richards (eds) *Intellectual Property Rights: Global Consensus, Global Conflict?*, Boulder, CO: Westview Press.

Gadbaw, R. and Richards, T. (eds) (1988) *Intellectual Property Rights: Global Consensus, Global Conflict?*, Boulder, CO: Westview Press.

Gardner, R. (1972) 'The Role of the UN in Environmental Problems', *International Organisation*, Vol. 26, No. 2, 237–254.

GATT Summary of TRIPs Talks (1989) reprinted in 7 Inside US Trade, 22 December.

Gellhorn, A. (1978) 'Violations of Human Rights: Torture and the Medical Profession', *New England Journal of Medicine*, Vol. 299, No. 7, 258–259.

Gellhorn, A. (1980) 'Medicine, Torture and the United Nations', *The Lancet*, Vol. 315, issue 8165, 428–429.

George, A. (1979) 'Case Studies and Theory Development: The Method of Structured, Focused Comparison' in P. Lauren (ed.) *Diplomacy: New Approaches to History, Theory and Policy*, New York: Free Press.

Gereffi, G. (1983) *The Pharmaceutical Industry and Dependency in the Third World*, Princeton, NJ: Princeton University Press.

Gerholm, T. (ed.) (1999) *Climate Policy after Kyoto*, Brentwood: Multiscience Publishing Co Ltd.

Gervais, D. (2003) *The TRIPS Agreement: Drafting History and Analysis*, 2nd edn, London: Sweet and Maxwell.

Gillespie-White, L. (2001) *Patent Protection and Patients' Access to HIV/AIDS Drugs in Sub-Saharan Africa*, Washington, DC: International Intellectual Property Institute.

Gillespie-White, L. (2002) *Health and Patents: The Rights Issue*, Presentation to an Audience Convened by the World Intellectual Property Organisation, International Intellectual Property Institute, 11 June. Online. Available at: www.iipi. org/speeches/NewYork061102.pdf (accessed 17 January 2009).

Gleckman, H. (1995) 'Transnational Corporations' Strategic Responses to "Sustainable Development"' in H. Bergesen, G. Parmann and O. Themmessen (eds) *Green Globe Yearbook of International Co-operation on Environment and Development 1995*, Oxford: Oxford University Press.

Glover, J. (2001) *Humanity – A Moral History of the Twentieth Century*, London: Pimlico.

Goertz, G. and Diehl, P. (1992) 'Toward a Theory of International Norms: Some Conceptual and Measurement Issues', *International Organisation*, Vol. 36, No. 4, 634–664.

Goldberg, D. (2002) 'Global Warming and Sustainable Development', *Centre for International Environmental Law* – Issue Brief for the World Summit on Sustainable Development, 26 August–4 September, Washington, DC.

Goldstein, J. and Keohane, R (eds) (1993) *Ideas and Foreign Policy – Beliefs, Institutions and Political Change*, Ithaca, NY: Cornell UP.

Goldstein, J., Kahler, M., Keohane, R. and Slaughter, A. (2000) 'Introduction: Legalisation of World Politics', *International Organisation*, Vol. 54, No. 3, 385–399.

Golinski, J. (1998) *Making Natural Knowledge – Constructivism and the History of Science*. New York: Cambridge University Press.

Gordon, N. and Marton, R. (eds) (1995) *Torture – Human Rights, Medical Ethics and the Case of Israel*. London: Zed Books in association with the Association of Israeli–Palestinian Physicians for Human Rights, Tel Aviv.

Gough, C. and Shackley, S. (2001) 'The Respectable Politics of Climate Change: The Epistemic Communities and NGOs', *International Affairs*, Vol. 77, No. 2, 329–345.

Griffin, J. (ed.) (2003) *Global Climate Change – The Science, Economics and Politics*, Cheltenham: Edward Elgar Publishing Ltd.

Grubb, M. and Anderson, A. (eds) (1995) *The Emerging International Regime for Climate Change: Structures and Options after Berlin*, Report of a Workshop held at the Royal Institute of International Affairs, June, London: Royal Institute of International Relations.

Guilloux, A. and Moon, S. (2001) *Hidden Price Tags: Disease-specific Drug Donations: Costs and Alternatives*, Access to Essential Medicines Campaign, Geneva: Médecins Sans Frontières.

Gupta, J. (1997) *The Climate Change Convention and Developing Countries: From Conflict to Consensus?*, Dordrecht: Kluwer Academic Publishers.

Gupta, J. (1999/2000) 'Evaluation of the Global Climate Regime and Related Developments', *Yearbook of International Cooperation on Environment and Development*, 19–29.

Gupta, S. and Kumar, K. (1998) 'The Science and Economics of Climate Change' in *Climate Change: Post-Kyoto Perspectives from the South*, Centre for Global Environmental Research, New Delhi: Tata Energy Research Institute.

Guzzini, S. (2000) 'A Reconstruction of Constructivism in International Relations', *European Journal of International Relations*, Vol. 6, No. 3.

Haas, E. (1990) *When Knowledge Is Power: Three Models of Change in International Organizations*, Berkeley: University of California Press.

Haas, P. (1989) 'Do Regimes Matter? Epistemic Communities and Mediterranean Pollution Control', *International Organisation*, Vol. 43, No. 3, 377–403.

Haas, P. (1990) 'Obtaining International Environmental Protection through Epistemic Consensus', *Millennium Journal*, Vol. 19, No. 3, 347–363.

Haas, P. (1992) 'Introduction: Epistemic Communities and International Policy Coordination', *International Organisation*, Vol. 46, No. 1, 1–35.

Haas, P. (1992) 'Banning Chlorofluorocarbons: Epistemic Community Efforts to Protect Stratospheric Ozone', *International Organisation*, Vol. 46, No. 1, 187–224.

Hall, R. (1997) 'Moral Authority as a Power Resource', *International Organisation*, Vol. 51, No. 4, 591–622.

Hansen, J., Sato, M., Glascoe, J. and Ruedy, R. (1998) 'A Common-sense Climate Index: Is Climate Changing Noticeably?', *Proceedings of the National Academy of Sciences of the United States of America*, Vol. 95, 4113–4120.

Hansen, J., Sato, M., Reudy, R., Lacis, A. and Oinas, V. (2000) 'Global Warming in the Twenty-first Century: An Alternative Scenario', *Proceedings of the*

National Academy of Sciences of the United States of America, Vol. 97, No. 18, 9875–9880.

Henry, D. and Lexchin, J. (2002) 'The Pharmaceutical Industry as a Medicines Provider', *The Lancet*, Vol. 360, 1590–1595.

Highleyman, L. (1999) 'Activists Decry Lack of Drug Access: Clinton Hints at Modified Policy', *Bay Area Reporter*, 10 December 1999. Online. Available at: www. aegis.com/news/bar/1999/BR991203.html (accessed 18 January 2009).

Hoffman, M. (1987) 'Critical Theory and the Inter-paradigm Debate', *Millennium: Journal of International Studies*, Vol. 16, No. 2, 233–236.

Hohmeyer, O. and Rennings, K. (eds) (1997) *Man-made Climate Change – Economic Aspects and Policy Options*, Proceedings of an international conference held at Mannheim, Germany, 6–7 March 1997, Heidelberg: Physica-Verlag.

Holdgate, M., Kassas, M. and White, G. (eds) (1982) *The World Environment 1972–1982 – A Report by the United Nations Environment Programme*, Dublin: Tycooly International Publishing Limited.

Hopf, T. (1998) 'The Promise of Constructivism in International Relations Theory', *International Security*, Vol. 23, No. 1, 171–200.

Hopkins, R. (1992) 'Reform in the International Food Regime: The Role of Consensual Knowledge', *International Organisation*, Vol. 46, No. 1, 225–264.

House of Lords, Select Committee on Economic Affairs (2005) *The Economics of Climate Change*, Vol. 1, 2nd Report of Session 2005–2006; London: Stationery Office.

Hoyng, W. and Fink-Hooijer, F. (1990) 'The Patent Term of Pharmaceuticals and the Legal Possibilities of Its Extension', *International Review of Industrial Property and Copyright Law*, Vol. 21, No. 2, 161–182.

Hughes, D. (1991) 'Opening up Trade Barriers with Section 301 – A Critical Assessment', *Wisconsin International Law Journal*, Vol. 17, 393–410

Human Rights First (2004) HRF Press Release: 'Human Rights First Condemns Use of Torture Tactics at Guantanamo Bay', 30 November. Online. Available at: www.humanrightsfirst.org/media/2004_alerts/usls_1130_icrc_gitmo.htm (accessed 17 January 2009).

Human Rights First (2005) 'One Year after the Abu Ghraib Torture Photos: US Government Response "Grossly Inadequate"', 26 April. Online. Available at: www.humanrightsfirst.org/us_law/etn/statements/abu-yr-042605.htm (accessed 17 January 2009).

Human Rights First (2005): 'Human Rights First Applauds Agreement Banning Abuse of Detainees – Urges Congress to Secure Victory by Keeping Torture Evidence Out of Court', 15 December. Online. Available at: www.humanrightsfirst.org/media/2005_statements/etn_1215_mccain.htm (accessed 27 September 2007).

Hunke, H. and Ellis, J. (1980) *Torture – A Cancer of Our Society*, London: Catholic Institute of International Relations. This report on torture in southwest Africa/Namibia was banned prior to publication by the South African authorities on 20 January 1978.

Idris, K. (2000) *Intellectual Property – A Power Tool for Economic Growth*, Geneva: WIPO.

Ierland, E., Gupta, J. and Kok, M. (eds) (2003) *Issues in International Climate Policy – Theory and Policy*, Cheltenham: Edward Elgar.

Ingelse, C. (2001) *The UN Committee against Torture – An Assessment*, The Hague: Kluwer Law International.

The Intellectual Property Committee, Keidanren, UNICE (1988) *Basic Framework of GATT Provisions on Intellectual Property: Statement of Views of the European, Japanese and United States Business Communities*, June.

Inter-American Institute of Human Rights and the Association for the Prevention of Torture (2002) *Optional Protocol to the United Nations Convention against Torture and Other Cruel, Inhuman or Degrading Treatment or Punishment – A Manual for Prevention*, New York: IIHR and APT.

International Commission of Jurists and Swiss Committee against Torture (1979) *Torture: How to Make the International Convention Effective – A Draft Optional Protocol*, Geneva: International Commission of Jurists.

International Intellectual Property Alliance (1985) 'A Trade-based Approach for the International Copyright Protection for Computer Software'; *Unfair Foreign Trade Practices, Stealing American Intellectual Property: Imitation Is Not Flattery*, 98th Congress, 2nd Session, 1–3.

'International Seminar on Torture and Human Rights' (1977) Palais de l'Europe, Strasbourg, 3–5 October, report published by Amnesty International, London.

Jadresic, A. (1980) 'Doctors and Torture: An Experience as a Prisoner', *Journal of Medical Ethics*, Vol. 6, 124–127.

Jamison, A. (2001) *The Making of Green Knowledge – Environmental Politics and Cultural Transformation*, Cambridge: Cambridge University Press.

Jervis, R. (1976) *Perception and Misperception in International Politics*, Princeton, NJ: Princeton University Press.

Johnson, B. (1972) 'The United Nations' Institutional Response to Stockholm: A Case Study in the International Politics of Institutional Change', *International Organisation*, Vol. 26, No. 2, 255–301.

Johnson, F. and Arvidson, A. (1999) 'A Brief History of Renewable Energy for Development', *Renewable Energy for Development*, Vol. 12, No. 2/3.

Jonas, S. (1973) 'Doctors and Torture', *The Lancet*, 24 November, 1212.

Jones, G. (1980) 'On the Permissibility of Torture', *Journal of Medical Ethics*, Vol. 6, 11–13.

Jones, L. (ed.) (1997) *Global Warming – The Science and the Politics*, Vancouver: Fraser Institute.

Kahn, S. (1999) 'The Whole World Is Watching – US AIDS Activists Go Global', *HIV Plus*, No. 5, September.

Katrak, H. and Strange, R. (eds) (2004) *The WTO and Developing Countries*, New York: Palgrave Macmillan.

Katzenstein, P. (ed.) (1996) *The Culture of National Security – Norms and Identity in World Politics*. New York: Columbia University Press.

Keane, J. (2004) *Violence and Democracy*, Cambridge: Cambridge University Press.

Keck, M. and Sikkink, K. (1998) *Activists beyond Borders: Advocacy Networks in International Relations*, Ithaca, NY: Cornell University Press.

Kellogg, W. and Schware, R. (1981) *Climate Change and Society – Consequences of Increasing Atmospheric Carbon Dioxide*, Boulder, CO: Westview Press.

Keohane, R. and Nye, J. (1972) *Transnational Relations and World Politics*, Cambridge, MA: Harvard University Press.

Kerr, R. (1989) 'The Global Warming Is Real', *Science*, Vol. 243, No. 4891, 603.

Keylor, W. (2001) *The Twentieth Century World – An International History*, 4th edn, Oxford: Oxford University Press.

King, G., Keohane, R. and Verba, S. (1994) *Designing Social Inquiry – Scientific Inference and Qualitative Research*, Princeton, NJ: Princeton University Press.

Klare, M. and Chandrani, Y. (1998) *World Security – Challenges for a New Century*, 3rd edn, New York: St Martin's Press.

Klein, N. (2000) *No Logo*. London: HarperCollins.

Klein, N. (2002) *Fences and Windows – Dispatches from the Front Line of the Globalisation Debate*, London: HarperCollins.

Kleinman, D. (1995) *Politics on the Endless Frontier: Postwar Research Policy in the United States*, Durham, NC: Duke University Press.

Klotz, A. (1995) *Norms in International Relations – The Struggle against Apartheid*, Ithaca, NY: Cornell University Press.

Klotz, A. (2002) 'Transnational Activism and Global Transformations: The Anti-Apartheid and Abolitionist Experiences', *European Journal of International Relations*, Vol. 8, No. 1, 49–76.

Knipe, M. (1970) 'Soviet Camp Tortures Alleged', *The Times*, 29 July.

Kongolo, T. (2002) 'Towards a New Fashion of Protecting Pharmaceutical Patents in Africa – Legal Approach', *International Review of Industrial Property and Copyright Law*, Vol. 33, No. 2, 185–211.

Kongolo, T. (2003) 'TRIPs, the Doha Declaration and Public Health', *Journal of World Intellectual Property – Law, Economics, Politics*, Vol. 6, No. 2, 373–388.

Krasner, S. (1983) *International Regimes*, Ithaca, NY: Cornell University Press.

Kratochwil, F. (1989) *Rules, Norms, and Decisions – On the Conditions of Practical and Legal Reasoning in International Relations and Domestic Affairs*, Cambridge: Cambridge University Press.

Kratochwil, F. and Ruggie, J. (1986) 'International Organization: A State of the Art on an Art of the State', *International Organisation*, Vol. 40, No. 4, 753–775.

Krueck, C. and Borchers, J. (1999) 'Science in Politics: A Comparison of Climate Modelling Centres', *Minerva*, Vol. 37, 105–123.

Kunz-Hallstein, H. (1979) 'The Revision of the International System of Patent Protection in the Interest of Developing Countries', *International Review of Industrial Property and Copyright Law*, Vol. 10, No. 6, 649–670.

Kuzma, J. and Dobrovolny, L. (eds) (2004) *The Global Climate and Economic Development*, Centre for Science, Technology and Public Policy, University of Minnesota: Hubert and Humphrey Institute of Public Affairs.

Kwa, C. (1994) 'Modelling Technologies of Control', *Science as Culture*, Vol. 4, 363–391.

Lanchbery, J. and Victor, D. (1995) 'The Role of Science in the Global Climate Negotiations' in H. Bergesen, G. Parmann and O. Themmessen (eds) *Green*

Globe Yearbook of International Co-operation on Environment and Develop-ment 1995, Oxford: Oxford University Press.

Langbein, J. (1976) *Torture and the Law of Proof – Europe and England in the Ancien Regime*, Chicago: University of Chicago Press.

Lange, D. (1998–1999) 'Public–Private Initiatives after TRIPs: Designing a Global Agenda', *Duke Journal of Comparative and International Law*, Vol. 9, No. 1, 1–10.

Latour, B. and Woolgar, S. (1979) *Laboratory Life – The Construction of Scientific Facts*, Princeton, NJ: Princeton University Press.

'Law and the Prevention of Torture' (1973) Report by the Secretary General of the International Commission of Jurists given to the Conference on Torture, con-vened by the British Section of Amnesty International, London, 20 October, *Review International Commission of Jurists*, No. 11, December, 22–27.

Legro, J. (1997) 'Which Norms Matter? Revisiting the "Failure" of International-ism', *International Organisation*, Vol. 51, No. 1, 31–63.

Lehman, B. (2002) *Patents and Health*, Presentation to the Policy Advisory Com-mission of the World Intellectual Property Organisation, International Intellec-tual Property Institute, 22 May. Online. Available at: www.iipi.org/speeches/Beijing_Health_052202.pdf (accessed 17 January 2009).

Lehr, J. (ed.) (1992) *Rational Readings on Environmental Concerns*, New York: John Wiley and Sons.

Levy, M., Young, O. and Zuern, M. (1995) 'The Study of International Regimes', *European Journal of International Relations*, Vol. 1, No. 3.

Lewis, N. (2000) 'Clinton Issues Order to Ease Availability of AIDS Drugs in Africa', *New York Times*, 11 May.

Lezaun, J. (2002) 'Limiting the Social: Constructivism and Social Knowledge in International Relations', *International Studies Review*, Vol. 4, No. 3, 229–234.

Lidskog, R. and Sundqvist, G. (2002) 'The Role of Science in Environmental Regimes: The Case of LRTAP', *European Journal of International Relations*, Vol. 8, No. 1, 77–101.

Lippman, M. (1979) 'The Protection of Universal Human Rights: The Problem of Torture', *Universal Human Rights*, Vol. 1, No. 4, 25–55.

Lord Gardiner's Report (1972) 'Interrogation Procedures – Minor Report of the Committee of Privy Counsellors', *The Review – International Commission of Jurists*, Vol. 8, June, 17–22.

Luckmann, T. and Berger, P. (1967) *The Social Construction of Reality*, London: Allen Lane, Penguin.

MacBride, S. (1966) 'Meeting of the International Commission of Jurists', *Bulletin of the International Commission of Jurists*, Vol. 28, 1–28.

MacKenzie, D. (1990) *Inventing Accuracy – A Historical Sociology of Nuclear Missile Guidance*, Cambridge, MA: MIT Press.

MacLaughlin, J., Richards, T. and Kenny, L. (1988) 'The Economic Significance of Piracy' in R. Gadbaw and T. Richards (eds) *Intellectual Property Rights: Global Consensus, Global Conflict?*, Boulder, CO: Westview Press.

Malanczuk, P. (1997) *Akehurst's Modern Introduction to International Law*, 7th edn, London: Routledge.

Maran, R. (1989) *Torture: The Role of Ideology in the French-Algerian War*, London: Praeger.

March, J. (1994) *A Primer on Decision Making – How Decisions Happen*, New York: Free Press.

March, J. and Olsen, J. (1989) *Rediscovering Institutions – The Organisational Basis of Politics*, New York: Free Press.

March, J. and Olsen, J. (1998) 'The Institutional Dynamics of International Political Orders', *International Organisation*, Vol. 52, No. 4, 943–969.

Martin, W. and Winters, L. A. (eds) (1995) *The Uruguay Round and Developing Economies*, Washington, DC: World Bank.

Maskus, K. (2000) *Intellectual Property Rights in the Global Economy*, Washington, DC: Institute for International Economics.

Massachusetts Institute of Technology (1970) *Man's Impact on the Global Environment – Report of the Study of Critical Environmental Problems*, Cambridge, MA: MIT Press.

Massachusetts Institute of Technology (1971) *Inadvertent Climate Modification – Report of the Study of Man's Impact on Climate*, Cambridge, MA: MIT Press.

Mathur, S. (2003) 'Trade-related Aspects of Intellectual Property Rights and Copyright Provisions – Some Issues with Special Reference to Developing Countries', *Journal of World Intellectual Property – Law, Economics, Politics*, Vol. 6, No. 1, 65–99.

Matscher, F. (ed.) (1990) *The Prohibition of Torture and Freedom of Religion and Conscience, Comparative Aspects*, Kehl am Rhein: N. P. Engel Verlag.

Mattoo, A. and Stern, R. (eds) (2003) *India and the World Trade Organisation*, Washington, DC: World Bank and Oxford University Press.

Maunder, W. J. (1989) *The Human Impact of Climate Uncertainty – Weather Information, Economic Planning and Business Management*, London: Routledge.

May, C. (2000) *A Global Political Economy of Intellectual Property Rights – The New Enclosures?*, London: Routledge.

Mayer, J. (2005) 'Outsourcing Torture – The Secret History of America's "Extraordinary Rendition" Programme', *New Yorker*, 14 February 2005. Online. Available at: www.newyorker.com/archive/2005/02/14/050214fa_fact6 (accessed 19 January 2009).

Mayne, R. and Bailey, M. (2002) *TRIPs and Public Health – The Next Battle*, Oxfam Briefing Paper 15, Oxfam GB – Cut the Cost Campaign.

McIntyre, J. and Papp, D. (1986) *The Political Economy of International Technology Transfer*, New York: Quorum.

McKibbin, W. and Wilcoxen, P. (1995) 'Economic Implications of Greenhouse Gas Policy', Paper prepared for the PAFTAD Conference on 'Environment and Development in the Pacific', Ottawa, 1995. Online. Available at: www.brook.edu/views/papers/bdp/bdp116/bdp116.pdf (accessed 22 March 2004).

McNeill, P. (1993) *The Ethics and Politics of Human Experimentation*, Cambridge: Cambridge University Press.

Médecins Sans Frontières (2000) *MSF Summary of the 53rd World Health Assembly*, 15–21 May. Online. Available at: www.msfaccess.org/resources/key-

publications/key-publication-detail/?tx_ttnews[tt_news]=1430&cHash=
5bcbbd6392 (accessed 17 January 2009).

Meron, T. (1986) *Human Rights Law-making in the United Nations – A Critique of Instruments and Process*, Oxford: Clarendon Press.

Merton, R. (ed.) (1973) *The Sociology of Science – Theoretical and Empirical Investigations*, Chicago: University of Chicago Press.

Meyer, J., Frank, D., Hironaka, A., Schofer, E. and Tuma, N. (1997) 'The Structuring of a World Environmental Regime, 1870–1990', *International Organisation*, Vol. 51, No. 4, 623–651.

Milliken, M. and Gardner, T. (2005) 'US Isolated at World Climate Talks', *Reuters UK*, 9 December 2005.

Mintzer, I. and Leonard, J. (eds) (1994) *Negotiating Climate Change – The Inside Story of the Rio Convention*, Cambridge: Cambridge University Press and Stockholm Environmental Institute.

Mohnen, V., Goldstain, W. and Wang, W. C. (1991) 'The Conflict over Global Warming – The Application of Scientific Research to Policy Choices', *Global Environmental Change*, Vol. 1, No. 2, 109–123.

Morris, J. (ed.) (1997) *Climate Change – Challenging Conventional Wisdom*, IEA Studies of the Environment No. 10, London: Harlington Fine Arts Ltd.

Morrissey, W. (2000) *Global Climate Change: A Survey of Scientific Research and Policy Reports*, CRS Report for Congress. Online. Available at: www.ncseonline.org/NLE/CRSreports/Climate/clim-24.cfm (accessed 18 October 2005).

Morrissey, W. (1998) *Global Climate Change: A Concise History of Negotiations and Chronology of Major Activities Preceding the 1992 UN Framework Convention*, CRS Report for Congress – Guide to Federal Programs in Appropriations Bills – National Library for the Environment. Online. Available at: www.ncseonline.org/nle/crsreports/climate/clim-6.cfm (accessed 18 October 2005).

Mueller, B. (2002/3) 'The Global Climate Change Regime: Taking Stock and Looking Ahead', *Yearbook of International Co-operation on Environment and Development*, 27–39.

Mueller, H. (2004) 'Arguing, Bargaining and All That: Communicative Action, Rationalist Theory and the Logic of Appropriateness in International Relations', *European Journal of International Relations*, Vol. 10, No. 3, 395–435.

Nadelmann, E. (1990) 'Global Prohibition Regimes: The Evolution of Norms in International Society', *International Organisation*, Vol. 44, No. 4, 479–526.

Nader, R. and Love, J. (1993) 'Federally Funded Pharmaceutical Inventions', *Testimony before the Special Committee on the Aging of the US Senate*, 24 February 1993. Online. Available at: www.cptech.org/pharm/pryor.html (accessed 25 May 2004).

Naughton, P. (2005) 'Rice Signals shift on US Torture Policy', *Times Online*, 7 December. Online. Available at: www.timesonline.co.uk/article/0,,11069–1914318,00.html (accessed 4 December 2006).

Newell, P. (2000) *Climate for Change – Non-state Actors and the Global Politics of the Greenhouse*, Cambridge: Cambridge University Press.

Nitze, W. (1990) *The Greenhouse Effect: Formulating a Convention*, London: Royal Institute of International Affairs.

Nye, M., Lindberg, D. and Numbers, R. (2003) *The Cambridge History of Science – the Modern Physical and Mathematical Sciences*, Vol. 5, Cambridge: Cambridge University Press.

Oberthuer, S. and Ott, H. (1999) *The Kyoto Protocol – International Climate Policy for the 21st Century*, Berlin: Springer.

O'Boyle, M. (1977) 'Torture and Emergency Powers under the European Convention on Human Rights: Ireland v. United Kingdom', *American Journal of International Law*, No. 71, 674–706.

O'Brien, D. (2000) *Storm Center – The Supreme Court in American Politics*, New York: W. W. Norton and Co.

Ombaka, E. (1999) 'Trade-related Aspects of Intellectual Property Rights and Pharmaceuticals', *Echoes – Justice, Peace and Creation News*, No. 15.

Orbinski, J. (2000) 'Challenges to the Health of Children in the 21st Century', Speech delivered at the 27th Annual Global Health Forum. Online. Available at: www.doctorswithoutborders.org/publications/article.cfm?id=1350 (accessed 17 January 2009).

Oxfam (1999) *World Trade Rules and Poor People's Access to Essential Drugs*. Online. Available at: www.oxfam.org.uk/what_we_do/issues/health/worldtrade_drugs.htm (accessed 14 April 2005).

Oxfam (2001) *Patent Injustice: How World Trade Rules Threaten the Health of Poor People*, Oxfam GB. Online. Available at: www.oxfam.org.uk/resources/policy/health/downloads/patentinjustice.pdf (accessed 14 April 2005).

Oxfam (2001) *South Africa vs. the Drug Giants*. Online. Available at: www.oxfam.org.uk/resources/policy/health/drugcomp_sa.html (accessed 17 January 2009).

Oxfam (2001) *Cutting the Cost of Global Health*, Oxfam Parliamentary Briefing 16, Oxfam GB.

Oxfam (2001) *Drug Companies vs. Brazil: The Threat to Public Health*. Online. Available at: www.oxfam.org.uk/resources/policy/health/ (accessed 14 April 2005).

Oxfam (2001) *Implausible Denial: Why the Drug Giants' Arguments on Patents Do Not Stack Up*. Online. Available at: www.oxfam.org.uk/what_we_do/issues/health/implausible_denial.htm (accessed 14 April 2005).

Oxfam (2002) *TRIPS and Public Health – The Next Battle*, Oxfam Briefing Paper 15, Oxfam GB.

Oxfam (2002) *US Bullying on Drug Patents: One Year after Doha*, Oxfam Briefing Paper 33, Oxfam GB.

Parikh, J., Culpeper, R., Runnalls, D. and Painuly, J. (eds) (1997) *Climate Change and North–South Cooperation – Indo-Canadian Cooperation in Joint Implementation*, New Delhi: Tata McGraw-Hill Publishing Co. Ltd.

Paskins, B. (1976) 'What's wrong with Torture?', *British Journal of International Studies*, No. 2, 138–148.

Patterson, M. and Grubb, M. (1992) 'The International Politics of Climate Change', *International Affairs*, Vol. 68, No. 2, 293–310.

Pecoul, B., Chirac, P., Troullier, P. and Pinel, J. (1999) 'Access to Essential Drugs in Poor Countries – A Lost Battle?', *Journal of American Medical Association*, Vol. 281, No. 4, 361–367.

Peters, E. (1985) *Torture*, Oxford: Basil Blackwell.

Pharmaceutical Research and Manufacturers of America, Centre for Media and Democracy. Online. Available at: www.prwatch.org/prwissues/2003Q4/phrma. html (accessed 17 January 2009).

Pickering, A. (ed.) (1992) *Science as Practice and Culture*, Chicago: University of Chicago Press.

Pinch, T. and Bijker, W. (1984) 'The Social Construction of Facts and Artefacts: Or How the Sociology of Science and the Sociology of Technology Might Benefit Each Other', *Social Studies of Science*, Vol. 14, No. 3, 399–441.

Piot, P. (1996) 'Human Rights and HIV/AIDS', Statement by the Executive Director of the Joint United Nations Programme on HIV/AIDS (UNAIDS), April 1996. Online: Available at: www.unaids.org/EN/other/functionalities/search.asp (accessed 18 March 2005).

Plant, G. (1990) 'Institutional and Legal Responses to Global Climate Change', *Millennium Journal*, Vol. 19, No. 3, 413–428.

Porpora, D. (1993) 'Cultural Rules and Material Relations', *Sociological Theory*, Vol. 11, No. 2, 212–229.

Porter, G. and Brown, J. (1996) *Global Environmental Politics*, Oxford: Westview Press.

Possible Renewal of the Generalised System of Preferences – Part 1, Hearing before the Subcommittee on Trade of the U.S. House of Rep. Comm. on Ways and Means, 98th Congress, 1st Session (1983).

Power, J. (2002) *Like Water on Stone – The Story of Amnesty International*, London: Penguin Books.

Price, R. (1998) 'Reversing the Gun Sights: Transnational Civil Society Targets Land Mines', *International Organisation*, Vol. 52, No. 3, 613–644.

Proceedings of the International Symposium on 'Torture and the Medical Profession' (1991) University of Tromso, Norway, 5–7 June 1990, *Journal of Medical Ethics*, No. 17, Supplement.

Proposal by the Secretary General of the International Commission of Jurists on Human Rights Day (1965) 'A World Campaign for Human Rights', *Bulletin of ICJ*, December, No. 28, 1–3.

Ramakrishna, K. (1990) 'North–South Issues, Common Heritage of Mankind and Global Climate Change', *Millennium Journal*, Vol. 19, No. 3, 429–445.

Rapporteur's Report of the Executive Session (1991) 'Negotiating a Global Climate Change Agreement', CSIA Discussion Paper 91–10, 14–15 March, Kennedy School of Government, Harvard University.

Rasmussen, O. V. (1990) 'Medical Aspects of Torture', *Danish Medical Bulletin*, Supplement 1, January.

Rasmussen, O. V. and Lunde, I. (1980) 'Evaluation of Investigation of 200 Torture Victims', *Danish Medical Bulletin*, Vol. 27, No. 5, 241–243.

Ratner, S. and Abrams, J. (1997) *Accountability for Human Rights Atrocities in International Law – Beyond the Nuremburg Legacy*, Oxford: Clarendon Press.

Raymond, G. (1997) 'Problems and Prospects in the Study of International Norms', *Mershon International Studies Review*, Vol. 41, No. 2, 205–245.

Renshon, S. and Duckitt, J. (eds) (2000) *Political Psychology – Cultural and Crosscultural Foundations*, Basingstoke: Macmillan Press Ltd.

Report of Secretary General to the International Commission of Jurists Meeting, Geneva (1966) 30 September–2 October, *Bulletin of the International Commission of Jurists*, December 1966, Vol. 28, 1–28.

Report of the Committee of Privy Counsellors Appointed to Consider Authorised Procedures for the Interrogation of Persons Suspected of Terrorism, HMSO – Lord Gardiner (1972) *Review – International Commission of Jurists*, Vol. 8, June.

Report of the Intergovernmental Negotiating Committee for a Framework Convention on Climate Change on the work of its first session, Washington, DC, 4–11 February 1991, UNGA Doc. No. A/AC.237/6.

Report of the Intergovernmental Negotiating Committee for a Framework Convention on Climate Change on the work of its second session, Geneva, 19–28 June 1991, UNGA Doc. No. A/AC.237/9.

Report of the Intergovernmental Negotiating Committee for a Framework Convention on Climate Change on the work of its third session, Nairobi, 9–20 September 1991, UNGA Doc. No. A/AC.237/12.

Report of the Intergovernmental Negotiating Committee for a Framework Convention on Climate Change on the work of its fourth session, Geneva, 9–20 December 1991, UNGA Doc. No. A/AC.237/15.

Report of the Intergovernmental Negotiating Committee for a Framework Convention on Climate Change on the work of its fifth session, New York, 18–28 February 1992, UNGA Doc. No. A/AC.237/18.

Report of the Intergovernmental Negotiating Committee for a Framework Convention on Climate Change on the work of its sixth session (Draft), Geneva, 7–10 December 1992, UNGA Doc. No. A/AC.237/L.16.

Report of the Workshop on 'Differential Pricing and Financing of Essential Drugs' – World Health Organisation and World Trade Organisation Secretariats, Norwegian Foreign Affairs Ministry, Global Health Council, 8–11 April 2001.

Report of the World Commission on Environment and Development, *Our Common Future*, 42nd Session of the UN General Assembly, 4 August 1987, Doc. No. A/42/427.

Report on the International Meeting 'Doctors, Ethics and Torture' (1987) Copenhagen, 23 August 1986, *Danish Medical Bulletin*, Vol. 34, No. 4, August, 185–216.

Report on the 23rd International Red Cross Conference 'Action of the Red Cross Against Torture', held in Manila, November 1981.

Resolution adopted by the Inter-Parliamentary Union 'Amnesty International Campaign against Torture – The Problem of Torture in the World', 11 October 1974, Tokyo.

Revelle, R. and Suess, H. (1957) 'Carbon Dioxide Exchange between Atmosphere and Ocean and the Question of an Increase of Atmospheric CO_2 during the Past Decades', *Tellus*, Vol. 9, No. 18.

Riis, P. (1980) 'The Many Faces of Inhumanity and the Few Faces of its Psychic and Somatic Sequelae', *Danish Medical Bulletin*, Vol. 27, No. 5, 213–214.

Risse, T. (2000) '"Let's Argue!": Communicative Action in World Politics', *International Organisation*, Vol. 54, No. 1, 1–39.

Risse, T. and Sikkink, K. (1999) 'The Socialization of International Human Rights Norms into Domestic Practices: Introduction' in T. Risse, S. Ropp and K. Sikkink, (eds) *The Power of Human Rights – International Norms and Domestic Change*, Cambridge: Cambridge University Press.

Risse, T., Ropp, S. and Sikkink, K. (eds) (1999) *The Power of Human Rights – International Norms and Domestic Change*, Cambridge: Cambridge University Press.

Risse-Kappen, T. (1994) 'Ideas Do Not Float Freely: Transnational Coalitions, Domestic Structures, and the End of the Cold War', *International Organisation*, Vol. 48, No. 2, 185–214.

Risse-Kappen, T. (1995) *Bringing Transnational Relations Back In: Non-state Actors, Domestic Structures and International Institutions*, Cambridge: Cambridge UP.

Roach, R. (2005) *Dried Up, Drowned Out – Voices from the Developing World on a Changing Climate*, Teddington: Tearfund Publications.

Rodley, N. (1999) *The Treatment of Prisoners under International Law*, 2nd edn, Oxford: Oxford University Press.

Rowlands, I. (1995) *The Politics of Global Atmospheric Change*, Manchester: Manchester University Press.

Rowlands, I. and Greene, M. (eds) (1992) *Global Environmental Change and International Relations*, London: Millennium Publishing Group.

Rudolph, C. (2001) 'Constructing an Atrocities Regime: The Politics of War Crimes Tribunals', *International Organisation*, Vol. 55, No. 3, 655–691.

Ruggie, J. (1998) 'What Makes the World Hang Together? Neo-utilitarianism and the Social Constructivist Challenge', *International Organisation*, Vol. 52, No. 4.

Rushing, F. and Brown, C. (eds) (1990) *Intellectual Property Rights in Science, Technology and Economic Performance – International Comparison*, London: Westview Press.

Ruthven, M. (1978) *Torture – The Grand Conspiracy*, London: Weidenfeld and Nicolson.

Ryan, M. (1998) *Knowledge Diplomacy: Global Competition and the Politics of Intellectual Property*, Washington, DC: Brookings Institution Press.

Sacerdoti, G. (1990) *Liberalisation of Services and Intellectual Property in the Uruguay Round of GATT*, Fribourg: University Press Fribourg.

Sachs, J. (1999) 'Helping the World's Poorest', *The Economist*, 12 August.

Sahn, S. (1998) *Technology Transfer, Dependence, and Self-Reliant Development in the Third World – The Pharmaceutical and Machine Tool Industries in India*, Westport, CT: Praeger Publishers.

Sampson, G. (ed.) (2001) *The Role of the World Trade Organisation in Global Governance*, Tokyo: United Nations University Press.

Schmalensee, R. (1993) 'Symposium on Global Climate Change', *Journal of Economic Perspectives*, Vol. 7, No. 3, 3–10.

Schneider, S. (1989) 'The Greenhouse Effect: Science and Policy', *Science*, Vol. 243, No. 4892, 771–781.

Scoble, H. and Wiseberg, L. (1974) 'Human Rights and Amnesty International', *Annals of the American Academy of Political and Social Science*, Vol. 413, Interest Groups in International Perspective, 11–26.

Scotchmer, S. (1991) 'Standing on the Shoulders of Giants: Cumulative Research and the Patent Law', *Journal of Economic Perspectives*, Vol. 5, No. 1, 29–41.

Scott, C. (2001) *Torture as Tort – Comparative Perspectives on the Development of Transnational Human Rights Litigation*, Portland, OR: Hart Publishing.

Scott, G. (1940) *A History of Torture*, London: T. Werner Laurie.

Sebenius, J. (1992) 'Challenging Conventional Explanations of International Cooperation: Negotiation Analysis and the Case of Epistemic Communities', *International Organisation*, Vol. 46, No. 1.

Sell, A. and Mundkowski, M. (1979) 'Patent Protection and Economic Development – Some Results of an Empirical Analysis in the Pharmaceutical Industry in Latin America', *International Review of Industrial Property and Copyright Law*, Vol. 10, No. 5, 565–572.

Sell, S. (1995) 'Intellectual Property Protection and Antitrust in the Developing World: Crisis, Coercion and Choice', *International Organisation*, Vol. 49, No. 2, 315–349.

Sell, S. (1998) *Power and Ideas – North–South Politics of Intellectual Property and Antitrust*, New York: State University of New York Press.

Sell, S. (2003) *Private Power, Public Law – The Globalisation of Intellectual Property Rights*, Cambridge: Cambridge University Press.

Sell, S. and May, C. (2001) 'Moments in Law: Contestation and Settlement in the History of Intellectual Property', *Review of International Political Economy*, Vol. 8, No. 3, 467–500.

Sending, O. (2002) 'Constitution, Choice and Change: Problems with the "Logic of Appropriateness" and Its Use in Constructivist Theory', *European Journal of International Relations*, Vol. 8, No. 4, 443–470.

Shapin, S. (1995) 'Here and Everywhere: Sociology of Scientific Knowledge', *Annual Review of Sociology*, Vol. 21, 289–321.

Shaw, M. (1997) *International Law*, 4th edn, Cambridge: Cambridge University Press.

Sherwood, R. (1990) *Intellectual Property and Economic Development*, Oxford: Westview Press.

Shiva, V. (2001) *Protect or Plunder? Understanding Intellectual Property Rights*, London: Zed Books.

Shokeir, M. (1973) 'Doctors and Torture', *The Lancet*, 22 December, 1439–1440.

Shue, H. (1978) 'Torture', *Philosophy and Public Policy*, Vol. 7, No. 2, 124–143.

Siebeck, W. (1990) 'Strengthening Protection of Intellectual Property in Developing Countries', World Bank Discussion Papers 112, IBRD/WB, Washington, DC.

Sikkink, K. (1993) 'Human Rights, Principled Issue-Networks, and Sovereignty in Latin America', *International Organisation*, Vol. 47, No. 3, 411–441.

Sikkink, K. (1998) 'Transnational Politics, International Relations Theory, and Human Rights', *Political Science and Politics*, Vol. 31, No. 3, 516–523.

Singer, S. F. (2000) *Climate Policy from Rio to Kyoto – A Political Issue for 2000 and Beyond*, Essays in Public Policy, No. 102, Hoover Institution on War, Revolution and Peace, Stanford University Press.

Skolnikoff, E. (1990) 'The Policy Gridlock on Global Warming', *Foreign Policy*, Vol. 79, 77–93.

Smith, A. (1982) 'The Ethics of Society rather than Medical Ethics', *Journal of Medical Ethics*, Vol. 8, 120–121.

Smith, J. E. (1972) 'The Role of Special Purpose and Non-governmental Organisations in the Environmental Crisis', *International Organisation*, Vol. 26, No. 2, 302–326.

Smith, K. and Light, M. (eds) (2001) *Ethics and Foreign Policy*, Cambridge: Cambridge University Press.

Smith, S., Booth, K. and Zalewski, M. (eds) (1996) *International Theory: Positivism and Beyond*, Cambridge: Cambridge University Press.

South Centre (1997) *The TRIPs Agreement – A Guide for the South. The Uruguay Round Agreement on Trade-related Intellectual Property Rights*, Geneva: South Centre.

Spinardi, G. (1994) *From Polaris to Trident: The Development of US Fleet Ballistic Missile Technology*, Cambridge: Cambridge University Press.

Statement by the UNEP/WMO/ICSU (1985) *The Greenhouse Effect, Climate Change, and Ecosystems*, International Conference on the Assessment of the Role of Carbon Dioxide and of Other Greenhouse Gases in Climate Variation and Associated Impacts, Villach, Austria, 9–15 October. Online. Available at: www.icsu-scope.org/downloadpubs/scope29/statement.html (accessed 12 May 2004).

Stewart, T. P. (ed.) (1993) *The GATT Uruguay Round – A Negotiating History (1986–1992), Vol. 2 – Commentary*, Deventer: Kluwer Law and Taxation Publishers.

Summary Records No. 34 from the 32nd Session of the Third Committee of the UNGA held on 31 October 1977 (UN Doc. Index: A/C.3/32/SR/34).

Summary Records No. 35 from the 32nd Session of the Third Committee of the UNGA held on 1 November 1977 (UN Doc. Index: A/C.3/32/SR/35).

Summary Records No. 36 from the 32nd Session of the Third Committee of the UNGA held on 1 November 1977 (UN Doc. Index: A/C.3/32/SR/36).

Summary Records No. 38 from the 32nd Session of the Third Committee of the UNGA held on 3 November 1977 (UN Doc. Index: A/C.3/32/SR/38).

Summary Records No. 62 from the 31st Session of the Third Committee of the UNGA held in 1976 (UN Doc. Index: A/C.3/31/SR.62).

Summary Records No. 63 from the 31st Session of the Third Committee of the UNGA held in 1976 (UN Doc. Index: A/C.3/31/SR.63).

Summary Records No. 64 from the 31st Session of the Third Committee of the UNGA held in 1976 (UN Doc. Index: A/C.3/31/SR.64).

Summary Records No. 65 from the 31st Session of the Third Committee of the UNGA held in 1976 (UN Doc. Index: A/C.3/31/SR.65).

Summary Records No. 66 from the 31st Session of the Third Committee of the UNGA held in 1976 (UN Doc. Index: A/C.3/31/SR.66).

Summary Records No. 67 from the 31st Session of the Third Committee of the UNGA held in 1976 (UN Doc. Index: A/C.3/31/SR.67).

Summary Records of the 2065th meeting of the 29th Session of the Third Committee of the UNGA held on 15 October 1974 (UN Doc. Index: A/C.3/SR.2065).

Summary Records of the 2066th meeting of the 29th Session of the Third Committee of the UNGA held on 15 October 1974 (UN Doc. Index: A/C.3/SR.2066).

Summary Records of the 2067th meeting of the 29th Session of the Third Committee of the UNGA held on 16 October 1974 (UN Doc. Index: A/C.3/SR.2067).

Sunstein, C. (1997) *Free Markets and Social Justice*, New York: Oxford University Press.

Susskind, L. (1994) *Environmental Diplomacy – Negotiating More Effective Global Agreements*, New York: Oxford University Press.

Swales, J. D. (1982) 'Medical Ethics – Some Reservations', *Journal of the Society for the Study of Medical Ethics*, Vol. 8, 117–119.

Tannenwald, N. (1999) 'The Nuclear Taboo: The United States and the Normative Basis of Nuclear Non-use', *International Organisation*, Vol. 53, No. 3, 433–468.

Thomas, C. (1992) *The Environment in International Relations*, London: Royal Institute of International Affairs.

Thomas, W. (2001) *The Ethics of Destruction – Norms and Force in International Relations*, Ithaca, NY: Cornell University Press.

Thompson, P. (ed.) (1991) *Global Warming – The Debate*, Chichester: John Wiley and Sons.

Thoolen, H. (1978) *Thirty Years after the Universal Declaration of Human Rights – The need for an International Convention against Torture*, Geneva: Commission of the Churches on International Affairs.

Thygesen, P. (1980) 'The Concentration Camp Syndrome', *Danish Medical Bulletin*, Vol. 27, No. 5, 224–232.

Thygesen, P., Hermann, K. and Wilanger, R. (1970) 'Concentration Camp Survivors in Denmark – Persecution, Disease, Disability, Compensation', *Danish Medical Bulletin*, Vol. 17, 65–108.

Tolley, H. (1994) *The International Commission of Jurists – Global Advocates for Human Rights*, Philadelphia: University of Pennsylvania Press.

Trouiller, P., Olliaro, P., Torreele, E., Orbinski, J., Laing, R. and Ford, N. (2002) 'Drug Development for Neglected Diseases: A Deficient Market and a Public-health Policy Failure', *The Lancet*, Vol. 359, 2188–2194.

Tyndall, J. (1859) 'Note on the Transition of Heat through Gaseous Bodies', *Proc. Roy. Inst. Gt. Br*, Vol. 10, 37.

UN FCCC – Secretariat (2005) 'Montreal Climate Conference Adopts 'Rule Book' of the Kyoto Protocol', Press Release, Montreal, 30 November.

UNCTAD–ICTSD Project on IPRs and Sustainable Development (2003) *Intellectual Property Rights: Implications for Development*, Policy Discussion Paper, published by UNCTAD and ICTSD.

Unfair Foreign Trade Practices, Stealing American Intellectual Property: Imitation Is Not Flattery (1984) 98th Congress, 2nd Session 1–3.

United Nations Development Programme (1999) *Human Development Report*.

Online. Available at: http://hdr.undp.org/en/media/HDR_1999_EN.pdf (accessed 17 January 2009).

United Nations Environment Programme (2004) *Natural Allies – UNEP and Civil Society*, Stevenage: UNEP.

United Nations Framework Convention on Climate Change Secretariat (2005) *UN Framework Convention on Climate Change – The First Ten Years*, Halesworth: UNFCCC.

United Nations General Assembly: Special Committee on Apartheid (1973) 'Maltreatment and Torture of Prisoners in South Africa', *Report of the Special Committee on Apartheid*, New York.

US International Trade Commission (1984) *The Effects of Foreign Product Counterfeiting on US Industry*, Washington, DC: USITC.

Vagelos, P. R. (1991) 'Are Prescription Drug Prices High?', *Science*, Vol. 252, No. 5009, 1080–1084.

Vaitsos, C. (1972) 'Patents Revisited: Their Function in Developing Countries', *The Journal of Development*, Vol. 9, No. 1, 71–97.

Van Ierland, E., Gupta, J. and Kok, M. (2003) *Issues in International Climate Policy – Theory and Policy*, Cheltenham: Edward Elgar.

van Niekerk, B. (1974) 'Torture – our Last Hurdle toward Civilization: Reflections on a Recent Conference', *South African Law Journal*, Vol. 91, 515–525.

Velasquez, G. and Boulet, P. (1999) *Globalisation and Access to Drugs*, 2nd edn, Geneva: WHO.

Verbatim Records of the Plenary Meeting of the UNGA – 29th Session, 2244th Meeting, 26 September 1974.

Verbatim Records of the 2065th Meeting of the Third Committee of the UNGA – 29th Session, 15 October 1974.

Verbatim Records of the 2066th Meeting of the Third Committee of the UNGA – 29th Session, 15 October 1974.

Verbatim Records of the 2067th Meeting of the Third Committee of the UNGA – 29th Session, 16 October 1974.

Verbatim Records of the 2068th Meeting of the Third Committee of the UNGA – 29th Session, 18 October 1974.

Verbatim Records of the 2069th Meeting of the Third Committee of the UNGA – 29th Session, 21 October 1974.

Verbatim Records of the 2070th Meeting of the Third Committee of the UNGA – 29th Session, 22 October 1974.

Walker, C. and Bloomfield, M. (eds) (1989) *Intellectual Property Rights and Capital Formation in the Next Decade*, Lanham, MD: University Press of America.

Wallerstein, M., Mogee, M. and Schoen, R. (eds) (1993) *Global Dimensions of Intellectual Property Rights in Science and Technology*, Washington, DC: National Academy Press.

Walter, J. and Simms, A. (2002) *The End of Development? – Global Warming, Disasters and the Great Reversal of Human Progress*, London: New Economic Foundation (NEF) and Bangladesh Centre for Advanced Studies (BCAS).

Walton, M. (2005) 'Changes in Gulf Stream Could Chill Europe', 10 May. Online.

Available at: www.cnn.com/2005/TECH/science/05/10/gulfstream/index.html (accessed 23 June 2005).

Watal, J. (ed.) (2001) *Intellectual Property Rights in the WTO and Developing Countries*, The Hague: Kluwer Law International.

Weart, S. (2003) *The Discovery of Global Warming*, Cambridge, MA: Harvard University Press.

Wendt, A. (1992) 'Anarchy Is What States Make of It: The Social Constructions of Power Politics', *International Organisation*, Vol. 46, No. 2, 391–425.

Wendt, A. (1994) 'Collective Identity Formation and the International State', *American Political Science Review*, Vol. 88, No. 2, 384–396.

Wendt, A. (1995) 'Constructing International Politics', *International Security*, Vol. 20, No. 1, 71–81.

Westin, S. (2000) *World Trade Organisation – Seattle Ministerial: Outcomes and Lessons Learned*, Testimony to the Committee on Finance, US Senate, US General Accounting Office, Doc. No. GAO/T-NSIAD-00–86.

WIPO (1988) 'Existence, Scope and Form of Generally Internationally Accepted and Applied Standards/Norms for the Protection of Intellectual Property', WO/INF/29 September.

Wirth, D. (1989) 'Climate Chaos', *Foreign Policy*, No. 74, 3–22.

Wirth, T. (1997) 'Global Issues – Confronting Climate Change', *Electronic Journal in the US Information Agency*, Vol. 2, No. 2.

World Health Organisation (1946) *Constitution of the World Health Organization*. Online. Available at: www.who.int/about/en/ (accessed 17 January 2009).

World Health Organisation (1996) *World Health Report 1996 – Fighting Disease, Fostering Development*, 49th World Health Assembly, Provisional Agenda Item 10, Doc. No. A49/3.

World Health Organisation (2002) 'TRIPS, Intellectual Property Rights and Access to Medicines', *HIV/AIDS Antiretroviral Newsletter*, Issue No. 8. Online. Available at: www.who.int/3by5/en/Dec2002.pdf (accessed 20 May 2004).

World Health Organisation (2002) *25 Questions and Answers on Health and Human Rights*, Geneva: WHO.

Yamin, F. and Depledge, J. (2004) *The International Climate Change Regime – A Guide to Rules, Institutions and Procedures*, Cambridge: Cambridge University Press.

Yee, A. (1996) 'The Causal Effect of Ideas on Policies', *International Organisation*, Vol. 50, No. 1.

Yeo, C. (1975) 'Psychiatry, the Law and Dissent in the Soviet Union', *The Review – International Commission of Jurists*, Vol. 14, June, 34–41.

Young, O. (1990) 'Global Environmental Change and International Governance', *Millennium Journal*, Vol. 19, No. 3, 337–346.

Zehfuss, M. (2002) *Constructivism in International Relations – The Politics of Reality*, Cambridge: Cambridge University Press.

Articles

'Overview: the TRIPs Agreement', World Trade Organisation. Online. Available at: www.wto.org/english/tratop_e/trips_e/intel2_e.htm (accessed 31 January 2009).

'A War over Drugs and Patents – Johannesburg' (2001) *The Economist*, 8 March.

'Bush "Isolated in US" on Climate' (2005) *BBC News*, 9 December.

'Chilean Church Leaders Accuse Junta of Torture' (1974) *The Times*, 26 April.

'Congress Presses for Torture Ban' (2005) *BBC News*, 15 December.

'French Paper Seized in Algiers – Issue Containing Torture Report' (196) *The Times*, 6 January.

'Global Warming: New Scenarios from the Intergovernmental Panel on Climate Change' (2001) *Population and Development Review*, Vol. 27, No. 1, 203–208.

'Governments Share Interpretations on TRIPS and Public Health' (2001) WTO News, TRIPS Council, Wednesday 20 June. Online. Available at: www.wto.org/english/news_e/news01_e/trips_drugs_010620_e.htm (accessed 17 January 2009).

'House Supports Ban on Torture – Measure Would Limit Interrogation Tactics' (2005) *Washington Post*, 15 December.

'Human Rights in the World – Torture Continues' (1973) *The Review – International Commission of Jurists*, June, No. 10, 10–33.

'Jurists Condemn Torture in Uruguay' (1974) *The Times*, 17 June.

'Last Minute Climate Deals Reached' (2005) *BBC News*, 10 December.

'Law and the Prevention of Torture' (1973) *The Review – International Commission of Jurists*, Vol. 11, December, 23–27.

'Law Lords Rule against Use of Torture Evidence' (2005) *The Times*, 8 December.

'Lawyers against Torture' (1976) *The Review – International Commission of Jurists*, Vol. 16, June, 29–41.

'Lords Reject Torture Evidence Use' (2005) *BBC News*, 8 December.

'Modification of WTO Rules on Protection of Pharmaceuticals' (2003) *The American Journal of International Law*, Vol. 97, No. 4, October, 981–983.

'New Greenhouse Report Puts Down Dissenters' (1990) *Science*, Vol. 249, No. 4968, 481–482.

'Putin Clears Way for Kyoto Treaty' (2004) *BBC News*, 5 November.

'Report on Brazil Tortures' (1970) *The Times*, 23 July.

'The Right to Good Ideas' (2001) *The Economist*, 21 June.

'The Economics of Climate Change' (1988) *OECD Economic Outlook*, No. 63.

'Row over Passive Smoking Effect' (2005) *BBC News*, 16 May.

'Support from UK Churches Needed' (1984) *Amnesty*, October/November, 26.

'Torture and Philosophy – Editorial (1980) *Journal of Medical Ethics*, Vol. 6.

'Torture in Brazil' (1970) *The Times*, 28 May.

'Torture Still Used on Captured Rebels – Red Cross Report on Algeria Prison Camp' (1960) *The Times*, 5 January.

'UN Poised for New Climate Talks' (2005) *BBC News*, 9 December.

'US "Shifts" Position on Torture' (2005) *BBC News*, 7 December.

Websites

http://stweb.ait.ac.th/~tony/asep/index.php – Asian Society for Environmental Protection (ASEP).

www.accessmed-msf.org/prod/publications (accessed on 8 November 2004).

www.interenvironment.org/wd3intl/index.htm – World Director of Environmental Organisations: Part 3: Listings of International Organisations and Programs.

www.nobel.se/peace/laureates/1974/macbride-cv.html.

www.nobel.se/peace/laureates/1977/amnesty-history.html.

Index

For Product Safety Concerns and Information please contact our EU
representative GPSR@taylorandfrancis.com
Taylor & Francis Verlag GmbH, Kaufingerstraße 24, 80331 München, Germany